1. Books may be kept for three weeks and may
   be renewed once, except when otherwise noted.

2. Reference books, such as dictionaries and en-
   cyclopedias are to be used only in the Library.

3. A fine is charged for each day a book is not
   returned according to the above rule.

4. All injuries to books beyond reasonable wear
   and all losses shall be made good to the satisfaction of the Librarian.

5. Each borrower is held responsible for all books
   drawn on his card and for all fines accruing on
   the same.

DEMCO

Happiness

Happiness

The TM Program,
Psychiatry,
and
Enlightenment

Harold H. Bloomfield, M.D.
Robert B. Kory

Introduction
Maharishi Mahesh Yogi

Foreword
Bernard C. Glueck, M.D.

Dawn Press / Simon and Schuster
New York

First Printing 1976
ISBN 0-671-22269-4
Library of Congress Catalog Card Number 76-3754

Transcendental Meditation, TM®, Science of Creative Intelligence, SCI, and World Plan® are the service marks of the
World Plan Executive Council.

To our beloved parents
who launched us on the
road to happiness...and to
Maharishi Mahesh Yogi
who brought us to
the goal.

CONTENTS

ILLUSTRATIONS

ACKNOWLEDGMENTS

First and foremost, we are deeply indebted to Maharishi Mahesh Yogi for having brought the Transcendental Meditation program and the Science of Creative Intelligence into the world.

We are especially grateful to Jerry Jarvis for his support and encouragement as well as his editorial help. Also deserving of special mention is Dr. Bernard Glueck, for playing an intimate role in our professional development and for valuable editorial comments. We would like to thank Dr. Paul Levine, Dr. David Orme-Johnson, Dr. Demetri Kanellakos, Dr. David Doner, Dr. Bruce Wales, Allen Cobb, Nicholas Bedworth, and Al Rubottom for their helpful suggestions.

Paul Sutherland, our editor, significantly improved the flow of the manuscript. Frank Arundel transformed our seed ideas into the excellent illustrations throughout this book. We especially want to thank Jenny Sachs for an outstanding critical reading of the page proofs and for her warmth. We also thank David Bousfield for his cover design and Anabel Mintz for photography.

Liz Locati and Ann Sembower stand out for their typing, proofreading, and dedication to the project. Sharon Haggerty, Sandra Watkins, Connie Dawson, and Ken Weiner also have our thanks for their assistance.

Our deep gratitude to Peter McWilliams, our publisher, for his wonderful friendship and outstanding abilities in the editing and publication of this book. Our heartfelt thanks to William Fitelson for his friendship, wise counsel, and guidance.

Dr. Bloomfield thanks Dr. Clifford Ward and his wonderful wife Carol, and Dr. Nelson Leone for their inspiring professional association. Robert Kory wishes to thank his wife Robin for her love, patience, and understanding. Dr. Bloomfield also thanks the TM teachers of the San Diego World Plan Center for their skill and compassion with his patients.

This book is written in the first person singular because so much of it is based on Dr. Bloomfield's use of the TM program with his patients, but this should not imply that its writing has throughout been anything less than a collaboration of the highest order.

FOREWORD

I am sure people will tend to react in one of two ways to the title of this latest book from the authors of *TM: Discovering Inner Energy and Overcoming Stress.* Those who are seeking a magical answer to the solution of their personal problems will search avidly through the volume for a description of the special brand of magic that will give them peace and happiness. The serious professional who will be looking for further information about the impact of the TM program in his area of professional expertise may be tempted to ignore this book as too simplistic and euphoric. Both reactions would be erroneous and unfortunate pre-judgments of the contents of this volume. There is no magical solution, as Dr. Bloomfield proves, based on his extensive clinical experience utilizing the TM program as one of his therapeutic approaches. On the other hand, there is ample evidence, again from the clinical data, to reassure the skeptical professional that the TM program can be added to whatever else is going on therapeutically, usually with considerable benefit to the patient.

It is always refreshing to deal with discussions of behavioral disturbances and emotional problems from a positive point of view. The theme of this entire volume is that one can go beyond the treatment of symptoms of emotional distress, putting out the fire, and work to achieve a positive pattern of adaption. One of the distinguishing features of positive adaption is the ability to engage in activities that provide a pleasurable outcome, since a healthy self-concept involves seeing oneself as a *proven provider of pleasure.* Much of the discussion in this book deals with the factors that interfere with this capability, especially the emergency response patterns or dis-stress, and the ways of coping with these problems, among them the use of the TM program.

The concept of the "average middle-class neurotic," as described and defined in this book, is an excellent portrayal of many individuals who live their lives in a chronically anhedonic fashion. There is always enough of an emergency response pattern, even in the absence of real threats, to block their ability to relax and enjoy themselves. I would agree with Dr. Bloomfield that the usual prescriptions for this kind of "existential stomach ache," namely the wide range of minor tranquilizers and sedatives and the various forms of individual or group psychotherapeutic intervention, are minimally effective. The examples provided by Dr. Bloomfield from his own clinical experience document in a very convincing fashion his argument that, for many of these individuals, starting in the TM program is the key that unlocks the pleasure response mechanisms. Our own speculations about what happens in the central nervous system as a consequence of utilizing the TM technique certainly follow this same line of reasoning. We have hypothesized that the effect of the mantra may be directly upon the limbic system structures, starting with the dominant temporal lobe. If the mantra has a quieting impact on the excitatory feedback circuits in the limbic system, as is suggested by the psychophysiologic data, especially the brain wave changes, this could easily be perceived subjectively by the individual as a rapid drop in the general levels of tension and anxiety. This would then lead to the opening up of the pleasure response systems, providing for both the neurophysiologic experiencing and behavioral enjoyment of pleasure.

That this speculative framework may have validity is suggested repeatedly in this book by the various case reports. These case histories also provide an answer to the opposing points of view mentioned at the beginning of this foreword. They document the requirement for an adequate commitment and daily effort on the part of the patient if the pleasurable goals are to be achieved. They also emphasize the need for a sophisticated under-

standing of the TM program by the therapist if he is
going to utilize its potential with maximum effectiveness.

Perhaps the most important aspect of this book,
however, is the inescapable inference that the addition
of the TM program to whatever else is going on in an
individual's life is an enriching experience. For the
patient suffering from a variety of symptoms, the TM
technique not only helps to reduce these symptoms, but
goes beyond this useful outcome to open the door to a
more rewarding, fulfilling, and pleasurable existence.
For the individual who either has minimum impairment
of his day-to-day functioning, or in fact feels that he is
operating with a reasonable degree of effectiveness, it
seems clear that regular TM practice will enrich his life
experience and may also prove to be an effective means
for neutralizing daily stresses and preventing the
development of incapacitating symptoms. If this proves
to be the case on further long-term follow-up upon the
impact of the TM program, then we may indeed be
entering upon an era of increased personal happiness for
the individual and of increasing enlightenment for
mankind.

BERNARD C. GLUECK, M.D.

Hartford, Connecticut
February 9, 1976

INTRODUCTION
MAHARISHI MAHESH YOGI

Throughout recorded history, mankind has known life to be a struggle, because that has been the experience of almost everyone. About seventeen years ago, with the blessings of Guru Dev,* we came out to say, "Life is bliss; no person need suffer anymore" — people all over the world were surprised. How could we dare to say "Life is bliss" when everywhere people were suffering and struggling, when everywhere it was said "To err is human," as if man were born to make mistakes.

It was the confidence and experience given to us by Guru Dev to know that life is bliss. Life is full of boundaries outside, but it is unbounded deep within. Therefore, we advised people to turn the attention within, experience that unbounded wholeness of life, and bring the mind out fully saturated with it to start living unboundedness in the field of boundaries.

Hardly believing our words, people started the Transcendental Meditation program. Through this simple, natural technique they experienced that unboundedness and started enjoying a better life. And then, from individual to individual, the experience that life is bliss and no man need suffer anymore began to spread, year after year.

The TM movement has grown in this way throughout the world for the past seventeen years, but people concerned with society kept asking one question: "Your meditation is all right for the individual, but what about society? A person may practice the TM technique for fifteen minutes morning and evening — he may gain some relaxation, lose some stress, and thereby become a better man—but what about the whole society?"

In answer to this question, we had been saying simply that if individuals become better, society will become

*Swami Brahmananda Saraswati, Shankaracharya of Jyotir Math in the Himalayas—Maharishi's teacher.

better. We felt confident in saying this because the individual is the unit of society. But recently, a new finding arose from research on the sociological effects of the TM program, showing that the TM program can change the trends in society from confusion and suffering to harmony and happiness.

The sociologists found that when the number of people following the TM program in a city reaches one per cent of the population, the city's crime rate falls. This new evidence added to the experience of over one million people in the world that the TM program improves the quality of life, to the several hundred scientific experiments on the benefits of the TM program to the individual, as well as to the endorsements from legislators, governors, mayors, educators, doctors, lawyers, businessmen, and organizations gives us confidence to proclaim the dawn of the Age of Enlightment and the coming of a better world.

When people first hear that we are proclaiming the dawn of the Age of Enlightenment, it seems a shock, but a pleasant, gentle, delightful shock. We are certainly aware that we are living in a troubled world, but we have a formula — practical, natural, and scientifically validated — whereby we know that the world of suffering and troubles will soon become a world of ease, comfort, happiness, and fulfillment. To inaugurate the dawn of any day, we have to do it during the night time when it is still pitch dark. We don't inaugurate the dawn when we have already seen the light come up; we do so when the sun is still deep in the horizon. We all see the situation in the world today — all turmoil and confusion everywhere — but the window of science allows us to see a better world on the horizon and to proclaim the oncoming dawn.

When intelligent people hear that we see the dawn of the Age of Enlightenment, they naturally want to know what is the basis of our vision. Is the Age of Enlightenment just an idea of some good-willed people who want to inspire hope in a troubled world, or is it something real? If it is a reality, what is the proof that the dawn is here? What laws of nature have come into play to bring on this new age?

First, let us get a clear vision of the Age of Enlightenment. It will be marked by good health, good behavior, abundant love and happiness, and harmony everywhere. Crime, wars, and all negative behavior will have no ground to appear. There will be no obstructions on the path to material and spiritual progress; all the gates will be open. People will find the path of evolution and progress easy, because they will act in accordance with all the laws of nature and not make mistakes. The old proverb "To err is human" will become obsolete because people will not err. With the support of nature, people will act flawlessly and faultlessly for maximum achievement and evolution; as a result, they will not meet restrictions in the expansion of happiness.

The proof upholding our vision of an Age of Enlightenment is very profound. Our strength is scientific research. Such a large number of physiological experiments have been performed in all parts of the world to show that the TM program improves physiology, unfolds full mental potential, and leads to ideal behavior that we can be confident of a new age dawning. A very good mind, ideal social behavior, and a very healthy body are the characteristics of people in the Age of Enlightenment. Now the additional finding that only about one per cent of a population need take up the TM program to reduce the crime rate and change the trends of society is the signal of success. Through the window of science, the dawn of the Age of Enlightenment can be clearly seen.

The vision of this new age is very beautiful, very uplifting, and very concrete; it is not a dream. We have confidence in it because it is grounded in scientific data. This is not a time when someone comes out to announce from a mountain top that a new age is coming. Rather, this is a scientific age, and we have learned to say only what we can prove objectively. We do not ask the people to accept what we say on faith. Belief has no role in bringing on the Age of Enlightenment. Our inspiration is not emotional; our vision is not mystical.

We are very straightforward, natural, and down to earth in what we see and what we say; because our position is very clear, it should not be misunderstood. The experience of over one million people and several hundred scientific experiments have shown conclusively that the TM program enriches all aspects of life. On this basis, not on the basis of a mystical vision or a fanciful dream, we feel confident in proclaiming the dawn of the Age of Enlightenment.

Scientists from many branches of learning have explained the effects of the TM program in terms of the natural laws of their particular fields. Every branch of science is capable of verifying how increasing orderliness in the individual can provide a basis for society to be free from problems and to be always evolutionary. This systematic investigation into how the TM program unfolds full mental potential, increases orderly thinking, and thereby leads to orderly behavior and a society free from suffering allows us to rejoice in welcoming the Age of Enlightenment through the door of science.

New discoveries in physics illustrate the convergence of all the branches of learning toward an understanding of how the TM program frees life from weakness and suffering. Physics now recognizes a basic value of life that harmonizes everything, a state of wholeness of life where there is no impulse of activity; it is a state of least excitation, which is the direct experience when the mind transcends all activity by means of the TM technique. This state is the level of all possibilities, the field of perfect order from which all activity springs in accordance with all the laws of nature.

No aspect of any activity arising from the state of least excitation of consciousness violates any natural law, and therefore problems do not arise. The basis of problems is weakness and violation of natural law. That field of all possibilities does not allow any weakness; being perfect order, it does not allow violation of natural law. Therefore, there is no ground for problems in life if that field is lively in one's awareness. In this way, physics explains how the Science of Creative Intelligence renders life free from problems, free from weakness, and therefore free from suffering.

How can just a few orderly people, perhaps only one in one hundred moving around in society, produce that degree of orderliness necessary for an Age of Enlightenment to dawn? A few examples will illustrate. The volume of a light bulb is very small compared to the volume of the room that it illuminates. But when lit, one small bulb can save us from all the hazards of the room.

When the sun sets and the moon is yet to appear, it may be pitch dark outside, yet only a few light posts will keep the whole street lit up. In the same way, it takes just a few people becoming more orderly by practicing the TM technique for the whole of society itself to start becoming more orderly and for the social trends to change.

The statistics show that the crime rate falls when about one per cent of a city population follows the TM program. This decrease in crime rate means that the increased orderliness of just a few people practicing the TM technique is sufficient to influence the most intense stress and negative tendencies in society. If a few meditators can have such an effect, how much greater is their influence on the majority of people, who are not nearly as stressed as the criminals in society? This observation means that we do not have to be concerned with what ninety-nine per cent of the people do; they can, if they like, continue to move around in a very disorderly manner. Merely one per cent of the people practicing the TM technique for a few minutes morning and evening and behaving in a more orderly and intelligent way throughout the day is sufficient to bring on the Age of Enlightenment. The demand is so little and the rewards are so great. There are enough intelligent people in the world to begin the TM program in every country and bring about a phase transition in society from suffering and disharmony to happiness and all progress.

How does the TM technique increase orderliness in the individual? Experiments show that it creates a more orderly functioning of the brain. When the brain becomes more orderly, the mind becomes more orderly and behavior improves. With this orderly brain, a few people can change the trends of society from negative to positive. Without even knowing the mechanics of how the brain becomes more orderly or how one orderly mind influences a less orderly one, the TM meditator invariably produces a harmonious influence around himself.

What is the one per cent required to do? Twice a day for fifteen minutes they stop their activity, close their eyes, and fathom the unboundedness deep within the mind to realize that fullness of life, that wholeness of life, that level of enlightenment which is kindled deep within everyone's heart. Unfolding that experience is enough to make the whole day more orderly, to set one's thoughts, feelings, and actions in perfect accordance with all the laws of nature.

In the coming of the Age of Enlightenment, who will be responsible? The person who spends a few minutes morning and evening experiencing that state of least excitation, the field of all possibilities — unbounded awareness. He will be responsible for inspiring the course of history with happiness, peace, harmony, and unrestricted progress. These few individuals will propel time in the direction of enlightenment.

Time is in the hands of individuals; it has always been in the hands of individuals. When individuals become more orderly, time takes a direction of peace, happiness, and progress. If individuals become disorderly, then time takes a different direction. So the time has always been in the hands of each of us, and now these scientific experiments have demonstrated that one per cent of the city population participating in the TM program can change the course of time.

What we see in these scientific results is that the time is coming when war will have no ground to appear. The United Nations charter indicates that war is fought in the minds of men. Because the Science of Creative Intelligence makes the minds of men orderly, it eliminates the basis of war. This is a formula for permanent world peace. As time goes on, world peace will become more and more intensified; peace will continue to be strengthened year after year, generation after generation. This is the achievement of the individual TM meditators in the world today. We practice the TM technique morning and evening for our own peace of mind, for our own harmony inside, for removal of worries and anxieties, but look what we are doing to the world. We are contributing that irresistible influence of orderliness which will maintain world peace in stronger magnitudes with each new day and in all the generations to come. This is the universal effect of the individual action of the TM meditator.

The basis of this vision is science, and therefore the practicality of it is beyond doubt. The effects are so far-reaching that for thousands of years to come, peace, happiness, and progress will continue to grow in this snowballing process that has been set in motion. It will expand automatically because with all these validations by scientific research — good effects on the body, on the mind, on behavior — more and more people are going to participate in the TM program. And as more and more people practice the TM technique, a growing influence of orderliness in society will automatically generate that situation which will be characterized by enlightenment for every man everywhere.

The Science of Creative Intelligence holds such beautiful prospects. It is a new science, but it is a very fortunate, new-born science, which is going to enhance the dignity of the whole family of nations and the whole family of scientists. This new science is giving rise to a phase transition in society that we will soon be witnessing; we will see very vivid signs of something good starting to happen. Once the good starts, it won't stop after some degree but will continue to grow naturally by itself until the Age of Enlightenment shines in full glory. The phenomenon is entirely inspiring and so real. The drop in crime rate where one per cent of the people are in the TM program is just the beginning of the universal effect of individual TM practice.

In 1972 we inaugurated the World Plan to train teachers of the TM program and the Science of Creative Intelligence. This led to the Year of Action in 1973, which in turn resulted in the Year of Achievement in 1974. This World Plan met with unprecedented success; it was an achievement unmatched in history. Towards the end of 1974, the scientific data showed that crime rates fell in cities all over the world with one per cent of the population practicing the TM technique. This achievement allowed us to open 1975, the Year of Fulfillment, with the inauguration of the dawn of the Age of Enlightenment. Now in 1976 we see the sun of the Age of Enlightenment rising steadily, and it is clear that the whole world will soon be basking in the light of all positivity.

Growing fulfillment for mankind is inevitable because the TM program is so simple yet has such universal positive effects. It may be thought of as a kind of vaccine against suffering and stress. When Dr. Salk discovered the polio vaccine, in one stroke polio was gone. One single person invented something of great benefit, and people all over the world took it up. Had single individuals not taken the vaccine, polio would not have been eradicated.

Any good discovery or great invention will be adopted by the people because of its great benefit, and people naturally will put their minds on deriving the maximum from it. In this same way, people all over the world are adopting the TM program. Those who are concerned with health problems see how the TM program and the Science of Creative Intelligence can improve health. Those concerned with education take it for the betterment of education. People concerned with business, creativity, and productivity adopt this knowledge to improve their field. All people can benefit from something of universal value. Because the TM technique takes the awareness beyond boundaries, it enriches every aspect of life from this boundless infinite field. It is of universal value.

Once we are in the light of life — which is unbounded, eternal, indestructible, infinite — life will not be lived in suffering; life will not have to move through problems. Society does not have to continue living with problems. Nations do not have to continue living with problems. Here is the declaration of the possibility of the Age of Enlightenment, which can be the dawn of the bright sun of the Age of Enlightenment. It can be brought about in any country at any time — now. This is our joy to say: Any country, whatever be the condition today, whatever has been the story until yesterday — here is the possibility of rising to a highest state of harmony, happiness, and freedom from problems and suffering, at any time the people of the country demand or desire it.

It is very fortunate to find an experienced psychiatrist like Dr. Bloomfield coming out to proclaim that the TM program leads to fulfillment in the search for happiness. No desire is more fundamental to life than the desire for more happiness. Everything we do is in that direction. When this desire goes unfulfilled, it is the psychiatrists who are pressed from all sides and who must listen to people in misery saying, "Life is a struggle" or "Life is suffering." But with the Age of Enlightenment on the horizon, psychiatrists will have a very good time in the years to come. They will be able to enjoy our saying that no man need suffer anymore. The TM program will eliminate weakness in the people and prevent emotional illness before it has a chance to develop. This prevention is a great promise for the future of psychiatry and medicine.

It is a great joy that this book has been written. Now all the people will know it is possible to fulfill their deepest desires for happiness. In its clear expression of this profound and valuable knowledge this book will herald the rising sun of the Age of Enlightenment.

PREFACE

The morning after Maharishi Mahesh Yogi gave his first public lecture on the Transcendental Meditation (TM) program in the continental United States in February of 1959, a San Francisco reporter wrote: "Yogi Offers New Cure for Insomnia."

When Maharishi heard this news, he is said to have commented with a hearty laugh, "Here I bring a technique for people to wake up and they take to it because it helps them fall asleep."

Ever since that first lecture, interest in the TM program has grown steadily until it has reached tidal wave proportions. A decade ago, only a few thousand Americans practiced the TM technique. Today, that number is nearing one million, up one hundred per cent from a year ago. From twenty to thirty thousand people are learning the technique each month. Why?

Scientific research has proved beyond reasonable doubt that the TM program more than any other mental technique produces real, measurable, and practical benefits in improving mental functioning, health, and human relations. Over 300 separate scientific studies from all over the world, many reported in the most respected scientific journals, document the many benefits of the TM program. The graphs and charts summarizing all these studies make a very impressive display, a small part of which was presented in our book, *TM: Discovering Inner Energy and Overcoming Stress.** In this book we presented the TM program along the same lines that the San Francisco reporters took in writing about Maharishi's first lecture in America. Since that book became a bestseller, many similar introductory books on the TM program have appeared. Though valuable in their own right, all these books have not dealt directly with what Maharishi meant when he called TM "a technique for people to wake up." TM practitioners

*Co-authored with Michael Cain and Dennis Jaffee.

know that the TM program produces something more than any of the measured benefits taken individually. It helps them discover happiness as a baseline experience of living and awakens them to life's full glory. This book is not another general introduction to the TM program; it examines humanity's possibility for happiness and explains how the course of history may be changing with the discovery that happiness can be a baseline experience for almost everyone.

No desire is more basic than the desire for happiness; yet the common idea today is still that life is a struggle. Most people believe that achieving happiness is at best very difficult and that self-development demands enormous effort. We have written this book to challenge these ideas and help people learn how to unfold their full natural capacity for happiness, no matter what their circumstances may be. In providing a systematic means for almost anyone to discover that happiness is natural, the TM program is shaking the foundations of these old ideas about the mind, personality development, and the human capacity for happiness. Must living be filled with problems? Is life a struggle? Must happiness remain a fleeting experience? Or can living become an experience of steadily expanding happiness and overflowing joy? The TM program provides a new window for modern science to look into these perennial concerns.

This idea about the TM program helping people enjoy steadily expanding happiness in life may sound abstract, but only because few people can pinpoint what happiness is. Most people find it far easier to talk about their misery than their happiness, perhaps because misery seems so common and happiness so rare. Research is proving that the TM program has the potential to reverse this imbalance, for the most profound and far-reaching significance of the TM program lies in the way it helps people get in touch with their full potential for joy and happiness. Now almost anyone can discover in his or her own life that happiness need not remain a rare moment hoped for or remembered, but can become, in a simple and natural way, an everyday experience.

As a means of fostering the growth of happiness, the significance of the TM program is nowhere more evident than in the field of psychiatry. At the junction of science, philosophy, and the humanities, psychiatry consists of a broad range of knowlege that aims at helping people relieve their suffering and regain their natural capacity for pleasure and happiness. The psychiatrist faces a very pragmatic test of this knowledge with every patient who enters his office. The person seeking psychiatric help may be suffering from a variety of symptoms — anxiety, depression, insomnia, bodily aches and pains, to name a few — but underneath all these complaints, he is saying, "I'm unhappy, I'm hurting. Please help me regain or experience for the first time some happiness in my life." Psychiatry's ultimate goal, prevention of emotional disorder, lies in the expansion of happiness for one and all.

However, few psychiatrists are satisfied with what they have been able to achieve with their patients through drugs and psychotherapy alone. Because of its concern with finding testable and effective ways to relieve suffering and to help people reawaken their full capacity for happiness, psychiatry provides perhaps the best modern arena for examining the full significance of the TM program.

In this book, I will show how the TM program can be a significant adjunct to the treatment of severely disturbed individuals. I will also show how the TM program is a boon for the majority of people not severely disturbed but still seeking psychiatric help. With this group, who make up the majority of people seen in psychiatrists' offices and whom I call "average middle-class neurotics," psychotherapy has in general proved to be only minimally effective. *For this reason, the greatest contribution of the TM program to clinical psychiatry may be in*

helping millions of middle-class neurotics to begin solving their
problems and enjoy growing happiness in their lives with little or no
professional psychiatric help. Finally, I will discuss how the
TM program awakens the individual to the full glory of
life. I will explore how the TM program enhances
marriage, work, creativity, personality integration, and
ultimately unfolds the highest possibility for fulfillment
— enlightenment.

The main themes of this book follow very directly
from the four elements in the title: happiness, the TM
program, psychiatry, and enlightenment. My foremost
intent is to show that steadily growing happiness is
natural for the person who systematically unfolds his
full potential through the TM program. I hope this book
will contribute to making obsolete the common un-
derstandings that life is a struggle and true happiness a
rare reward or illusion. Drawing upon many case
histories to make this point, I also hope to show how the
discovery of the TM program constitutes a major
breakthrough in psychiatry. This breakthrough is of
such great significance that it could foreseeably mean,
for neurosis and stress-related illness, what the polio
vaccine has meant for polio. Drawing on the teaching of
Maharishi Mahesh Yogi, as well as current ideas in
Western psychiatry, I will present a psychophysiological
theory that attempts to explain the origin of distress,
and more importantly, the unique effectiveness of the
TM program in relieving that distress. Throughout this
discussion of the TM program and psychiatry, I will be
building toward an understanding of the ultimate
possibilities for human development and fulfillment in
the state known as enlightenment. I will show how the
TM program makes enlightenment, long regarded as the
privilege of geniuses and saints, a practical possibility for
almost anyone.

My intention in writing this book has been to paint a
broad view of the overwhelming significance of the TM
program for psychiatry and the primal search for

happiness. Toward this end, I have made extensive use of case histories* and little use of published research reports. If the reader is interested in a review of the scientific research on the TM program, I suggest he consult *TM: Discovering Inner Energy and Overcoming Stress* and *Scientific Research on the Transcendental Meditation Program: Collected Papers* (MIU Press, 1976). Neither of these books, however, are prerequisites for understanding this book. I do not intend that this report of case histories be seen as definitive proof of or a replacement for controlled investigations of the use of the TM program with psychiatric patients. My hope is that this preliminary survey will stimulate such research, which would require the collaboration of psychiatric professionals and TM instructors in carefully designed programs. I also wish to make clear from the outset that I have not tried to write a textbook for psychiatrists on how to use the TM program in their practices. Such guidelines need to be written, but the best way for a psychiatrist to begin using the TM program in his practice is to become as knowledgeable about it as he can through courses at local centers offering the TM program and to review the growing number of reports on its application in the psychiatric literature.

I hope readers will not be disappointed because they do not learn how to practice the TM technique from this book. If it were possible to teach the TM technique effectively by writing a book, Maharishi would have been the first to have done so. Why the TM technique cannot be learned from a book and how it compares with other meditation techniques is the subject of extensive discussion in chapter 3 of this volume. The many books that have outlined step-by-step recipes about how to practice one or another form of meditation *do not and cannot teach the Transcendental Meditation technique.*

Several other precautionary notes are necessary for people who may wish to begin the TM program for the

*Names have been changed to maintain confidentiality.

purposes of medical or psychiatric treatment. First of all, I will make the point throughout that *although the TM program has tremendous therapeutic value for many medical and psychiatric conditions, it is not basically a therapy.* What this means in practice is that TM instructors are not therapists. Though a growing number of medical professionals are becoming qualified TM teachers, the TM student should not expect medical or psychiatric advice from his instructor. A person with a serious emotional disturbance should not begin the TM program without first consulting his psychiatrist. Second, a person should not conclude from the case histories presented in this book that the TM program is a panacea for all psychiatric diagnoses. Though the TM program may prove to be all that is necessary for many patients whom I have called average middle-class neurotics, many of these patients benefit from some form of psychotherapy in addition to the TM program. This is because the TM program does not magically produce an instant cure nor does it lead to an immediate resolution of a lifetime's accumulation of problems.

The TM program alone is definitely not a sufficient treatment for severely disturbed or chronic patients. These individuals require appropriately designed pharmacological and psycho-therapeutic support in addition to the TM program. People taking medications prescribed by a physician or psychiatrist should not conclude that they can stop taking them as soon as they begin the TM program. It would be a serious mistake for a chronic schizophrenic to discontinue his medication as soon as he began the TM program. Similarly, the diabetic should not think that the TM program is a substitute for insulin, nor should the epileptic think that the TM program will replace his need for Dilantin. Though the TM program often leads to a reduced need for some types of medication, especially tranquilizers and sleeping pills, it should be reduced or discontinued *only under the guidance of a physician or psychiatrist.*

A final purpose of this book is to help alert people to what may be the dawn of a new age. On January 12, 1975, at an all-day ceremony attended by over one thousand teachers of the TM program, including the authors, and eminent scientists, including a Nobel Laureate, Maharishi inaugurated what he proclaimed to be the dawn of the Age of Enlightenment. Referring to the published research on the benefits of the TM program to individuals and society, he asserted that through the window of science can already be seen the dawn of a new age in which happiness, order, and peace will replace current suffering, confusion, and chaos. Many persons before Maharishi have announced the coming of golden ages that have yet to materialize, so skepticism is natural. However, for those scientists fully aware of the research on the TM program, as well as for many people practicing the technique around the world, Maharishi's assertion may seem optimistic but not unbelievable. Scientific research clearly indicates that the TM program enriches people's lives sufficiently to have significant social impact. One study already suggests that when as little as one per cent of a city's population practices the technique, the crime rate decreases. It has been hypothesized that the social effects of the TM program will become very apparent when one per cent of a country's population is practicing the technique. Will our nation's long-standing social problems such as crime, the mental health crisis, or economic travail, begin to give way to solutions when the number of TM practitioners nears the two million mark? If so, people aware of the dawning of a new age will be best able to enjoy the earliest signs of social change. The person who sleeps late may enjoy the sun at midday but misses the chance to enjoy the dawn.

HAPPINESS
The TM Program,
Psychiatry,
and
Enlightenment

The purpose of life is the expansion of happiness.

Maharishi Mahesh Yogi

1

Why Not Happiness?

Lack of happiness is a troubling though often unspoken concern for millions. While opportunities for "fun," "kicks," and enjoyment abound, it is all too obvious that most people have a far bigger share of problems, worries, anxieties, and hang-ups than they have of lasting happiness. Perhaps the best illustration of this lack of genuine happiness today lies in attitudes toward growing older. Children regard growing older as the blossoming of ever wider possibilities for joy and happiness. A five year-old will delight in the thought of becoming eight or ten; the young teenager will long for a sixteenth, eighteenth, or twenty-first birthday. Before most people are many years out of their teens, however, aging seems to lose this intimate association with the expansion of happiness. Rarely do adults say, "I can't wait till I'm thirty" or "I'm so much looking forward to my fortieth (or fiftieth) birthday." For most people, a subtle fear accompanies the transition from young adulthood to middle age. This fear begins as a vague feeling of missing out on life and often grows into a panicky "grab it while you can" attitude. This book is about how to be happy, how to live life to the fullest, no matter what your life circumstances happen to be.

Already enriching the lives of hundreds of thousands of people, the Transcendental Meditation (TM) technique is beginning to revolutionize the branch of

medicine most intimately concerned with happiness —
psychiatry — and may even be changing the course of
history. Two hundred years ago the founding fathers
recognized how intimately the pursuit of happiness is
interwoven with life and liberty in declaring all three to
be humanity's basic inalienable rights. How much
happiness a person can rightfully expect in his lifetime
has long been in dispute among philosophers, scientists,
and theologians. One point in this debate is clear: the
pursuit does not guarantee the experience of happiness.
The founder of psychoanalysis, Sigmund Freud, gave
expression to what has been perhaps the predominant
view of mankind's possiblity for happiness when he
wrote, "The intention that man should be happy is not
included in the plan of Creation."[1] This pessimistic view
echoes the centuries of suffering that fill the pages of
human history. Today, scientific research on the TM
program, as well as the experience of thousands upon
thousands of people practicing it, suggests that
humanity's possibility for happiness deserves re-
examination.

Is living essentially a struggle for survival? Is
happiness meant to be a rare reward? How much
happiness can an average person expect out of life? How
come some people seem to be naturally happy while
others are mostly miserable? Is it wrong to want to be
happy all the time? How thoroughly does science
understand happiness? Is there a secret to happiness?
How can a person increase his or her share of happiness?
Can increasing happiness in individuals affect the
destiny of communities, nations, or the world?
Historically, these questions have mostly been a matter
of philosophical speculation; however, scientific interest
in the TM program has broadened the base for their
investigation. Scientific research on the TM program is
providing systematic, verifiable answers to these age-
old questions. The principle discovery at the heart of this
research is that the expansion of happiness is easy and

natural for anyone who systematically unfolds his or her full potential through the TM program.

Our society supports and encourages the advertising concept that material rewards are the ultimate goal of life, but once a person finds that a nice home, two cars, and a vacation in Europe do not guarantee happiness, a quiet panic about the purpose of living begins to set in. The outpouring of psychological literature, from professional journals to *The Reader's Digest*, has exacerbated this panic by raising peoples' expectations about how fulfilling life can be. The latest bestseller on "how to cope" inevitably becomes the rage of cocktail party conversation because so many people are looking for ways to become happier. "Human activity is dominated by the search for happiness," said Nobel Prize laureate Albert Szent-Gyorgyi; but more and more frequently patients are telling me, "I'm unhappy, but I don't know why." A successful architect, an attractive high school girl, a young man about to graduate in engineering, and a middle-aged housewife — all relatively well-integrated psychologically — are among the people who have recently come to me as patients implicitly asking, "What does it take to be happy?"

Over the past decade, the phrase "mental health crisis" has attracted widespread attention from government and the media. What this phrase means is that psychiatrists, psychologists, and social workers are swamped with cases. This big increase in people seeking psychiatric help is not among psychotic patients, whose numbers have remained relatively constant, but rather among less disturbed people who feel they are facing increasing difficulty in leading satisfying lives. The social taboo against seeking psychiatric help has largely disappeared, and as a result, fewer and fewer people are willing to accept, in Thoreau's words, "lives of quiet desperation."

The difficulty which most people are having in leading truly fulfilling lives has been so well documented

through psychological research as to be almost discouraging. The late Abraham Maslow, one of the great
psychologists of this century, summed up the situation
when he wrote that so-called "normal" people live for
the most part "in a state of mild and chronic psychopathology and fearfulness, of stunting and crippling
immaturity."[2] Though a rapidly rising number of
"normal" people are seeking help of one sort or another
to increase their share of happiness, a much larger
percentage of them is miserable but almost willing to
accept the infrequency of their happiness. They either
avoid facing their lack of fulfillment by getting caught up
in a hectic daily routine, or recognize their lack of
happiness but say to themselves, "Well, I'm not as happy
as I would like to be, but who is?" Like many educated
but unhappy people, they take comfort in grim
philosophical or religious beliefs that life is basically and
inevitably a struggle, that unhappiness is a "natural part
of life."

On the contrary, a basic principle of the TM program
is that happiness *is* natural to living. Maharishi Mahesh
Yogi, the man who brought the TM program to light in
the world, makes this point emphatically when he
writes: "Man is born of bliss, of consciousness, of
creativity, of wisdom....It is only necessary to begin to
enjoy. But not finding it anywhere, obviously missing it
in day-to-day life, the majority begin to suffer. It is just a
little ignorance which makes man suffer, ignorance of
his own potentiality."[3] He adds that the person who
pursues the fleeting joys of life while not unfolding this
natural potential for abundant happiness is like a thirsty
man who concerns himself with dew drips and ignores a
huge lake.

Profound and lasting happiness is not a state to be
pursued, which suggests a panicky chase of some kind. It
results from a person unfolding his full measure of
energy, intelligence, and creativity along the path to
enlightenment. Nevertheless, the pursuit of happiness

is a pressing concern for spiraling numbers of people, many of whom are turning to psychiatry for help.

It has been estimated that 60 to 70 per cent of the people seeking help from mental health professionals are not seriously ill. They are among the vast number of people whom Maslow despairingly called "normal," affected with chronic but low-grade psychopathology. The symptoms which these people report as their primary complaints — tension, headaches, vague gastrointestinal discomforts, anxiety, mild depression, overweight, high blood pressure, insomnia, too many cigarettes, too much alcohol, marital, family, or business troubles, and just plain "I'm not happy" — are common to most people today at one time or another. However, I do not choose to call people suffering from mild chronic psychopathology "normal." Mararishi points out that, "Only living the full potential of life can be said to be normal."[4] Maslow agrees when he states that in the final analysis, normality "is the highest excellence of which we are capable. But this ideal is not an unattainable goal set out far ahead, rather it is actually within us."[5] In this light, I choose to reserve the word normal for discussion of the physiology and psychology of the enlightened person, because enlightenment is humanity's most healthy and natural state and can become the norm for all mankind. I like to use another term, *mild middle-class neurosis,* to describe the mental health of the average person today. This term is descriptive of the condition and it is easy for people to understand. It does not refer to people who have been miserable all their lives or who are currently miserable all the time; rather it refers to that vast group of non–mentally ill people who might occasionally wind up in a psychiatrist's office, or even more likely, the family doctor's office, with common mild symptoms of stress. Almost everyone knows what is meant when it is said, "We are all a little neurotic."

The term mild middle-class neurosis is necessary in discussing the TM program and new horizons of happiness for two reasons. First, psychophysiological research indicates that happiness is the natural state of the person free from stress. Few people today are free from some distress or emotional "hang-ups"; yet evidence suggests that such a state of freedom is a natural possibility. It has long been described as the state of enlightenment and is the end result of regular practice of the TM technique. The second important function of the term mild middle-class neurosis is to distinguish the psychopathology of everyday life from that of the severely disturbed neurotic or psychotic person. This distinction is critically important in order to understand how much the TM program alone can accomplish for different types of people and also when it must be supplemented by traditional methods of psychiatric treatment.

What does psychiatry have to offer the average middle-class neurotic? In one sense, too much; in another sense, very little. Psychiatry has come under fire both from outside and inside the profession. Well-known psychiatrist Roy Grinker, Sr. has voiced concern that psychiatry is "running madly in all directions." Today, if a person says "I'm seeing a psychiatrist," it is almost impossible to know what is actually going on. Is he in individual therapy or group therapy? Is he in analysis? If so, which of several brands? Is he receiving supportive psychotherapy, reality therapy, behavior therapy, family therapy, marital therapy, Primal therapy — or what? If he is in group therapy, is he in an orthodox group, a nude group, or a "feel" group? Is it a weekend marathon group, a confrontation group, or a "T-Group"?

Of all these therapies, what works? All have proven to be of some help to some people, but none alone or taken together have made a dent in the general malaise that troubles almost everyone today. Although psychiatry has made great strides over the last two decades in treating people who are truly mentally ill, an honest appraisal of its results shows it has failed to come up with much that has proven helpful to the millions of average middle-class neurotics. Maharishi echoed this sentiment when he wrote, "When we consider the immense possibilities in the field of psychology and review the achievements so far, we find them discouraging.... The inner discontent felt by the great majority of people who are neither neurotic nor psychotic certainly indicates the need of a technique for achieving inner happiness."[6]

Mild middle-class neurotics are rushing to psychotherapists in such large numbers that many psychiatrists have chosen to make less and less time available for treating severely distrubed patients. If psychiatry could help the average middle-class neurotic, then the time could be justified, but clinical experience and research have confirmed that a psychiatrist is no more help to most mild middle-class neurotics than is a wise and loving friend. A growing number of psychiatrists, including myself, believe that the time has come for our profession to admit that psychotherapy per se is not the answer to the pursuit of happiness. We are calling for a return to the medical model and a redefinition of what psychiatry can and cannot do.

What Psychiatry Can and Cannot Do

Many mild middle-class neurotics now knocking at psychiatrists' doors first tried to find help from friends, clergymen, books, drugs, and a host of self-improvement techniques. Because their symptoms were mild and their primary complaints were anxiety, vague aches and pains, or simple disenchantment with their lives, the search for help outside psychiatry was natural. After finally turning to psychotherapy, however, the vast majority soon become disappointed. While psychotherapy alone may provide hope, solace, and some abatement of symptoms, it rarely if ever opens any doors

to lasting happiness. Although psychiatry has made
tremendous progress in helping psychotics and severe
neurotics through pharmacological intervention, psychiatric methods alone have proven inadequate and
often unhelpful for the mild middle-class neurotic.

All too many psychiatrists and psychotherapists still
reinforce the idea that life by its very nature is a
struggle. Most mental health professionals explicitly or
implicitly continue to define the aim of therapy as
helping a person to cope, adjust, or "accept reality."
Underlying such a world view is a basic assumption,
glaringly evidenced in the writings of Sigmund Freud,
that life necessarily involves conflict, neurosis, and
suffering. Yet many progressive therapists have begun
to project greater possibilities for their patients than
merely "making a go of it." Expanding the patient's
capacity for intimacy, love, self-sufficiency, awareness,
and pleasure and opening the door to enduring
happiness are becoming important goals of many
current therapies. Psychiatry is in the process of
awakening to the deepest meaning of the words *psyche*
(spirit, soul, mind) and *iatros* (healing, making whole).

Phychiatry in general offers three principal means of
helping people. These are psychotherapy, psychopharmacology, and community psychiatry. All three of these
methods continue to be very helpful to many people, yet
all fall short of enabling a person to unfold his or her full
capacity for happiness. I do not say this critically but
simply to encourage people in the mental health field to
continue raising their vision of what it means for a
person to be fully healthy and truly normal. Enlightenment represents a pinnacle of human growth worthy of
investigation.

Psychotherapy is the most widely practiced yet least
well-defined of the three methods psychiatry offers to
help people. Almost any interaction between two people
in which one person enhances the emotional well-being
of the other may be called psychotherapy. Is friendship

psychotherapy? Technically, no; actually perhaps. From a technical standpoint, psychotherapy is defined as that relationship in which a person seeking help with an emotional or interpersonal problem receives the assistance of another person presumably trained in helping people with psychological difficulties. Clearly, the process of helping others with emotional and interpersonal problems is not solely the province of psychotherapists. Yet the art of psychotherapy is a skill that can be cultivated, and a considerable body of knowledge, theory, and experience has been collected to help people learn this skill. There is little doubt that some forms of psychotherapy are helpful to some people.

Yet a great debate rages both inside and outside the mental health professions about how effective psychotherapy really is. The continual upsurge of new therapies every few years is perhaps the best indication of the limitations of psychotherapy. The number of people complaining about how much time and money they spent and how little they got out of psychotherapy seems to be rising just as fast or faster than the number of people seeking psychotherapeutic help. A colleague recently told me a joke which illustrates this point almost too well.

Psychiatrist: Yes Mr. Hayes, I think I can help you. It will mean coming here three times a week for about a year at fifty dollars a visit....
Patient: That takes care of *your* future, doctor. Now how about mine?

Psychoanalysis and psychoanalytically-oriented psychotherapy have long aimed at helping people unravel the deep stresses, that underlie neurotic symptoms. Because most people carry so much excess emotional baggage around with them, the process of analytic psychotherapy is almost never complete. Most patients simply come to the point where they feel, "Well, I guess I've accomplished about as much as I can this way," and they stop therapy. Many patients quit when they feel, "I'm not going to get very far doing this." A review of the psychiatric literature reveals how limited psychoanalysis and analytically-oriented therapy have been in helping people. Psychologists Bergin and Garfield have even reported that analytic exploration of a person's past in psychotherapy can often be harmful.[7] On the other hand, there is increasing evidence to show that some forms of psychotherapy can help people get out of old behavior patterns that cause misery. Because of accumulated stress many people suffer a lag in their emotional maturity and interpersonal skill. Psychotherapy seems to be valuable for many people in helping them make up for this developmental lag by improving their interpersonal skills and increasing self-understanding. At the same time, it is becoming increasingly clear that psychotherapy alone will never meet the needs of the average middle-class neurotic. Psychotherapy does not succeed in dissolving the backlog of old stresses that inhibit a person's full capacity for happiness.

The second method that psychiatry offers to help people handle the stress cycle is psychopharmacology. The discovery of tranquilizers in the early 1950s came as a great advance in psychiatry. When used appropriately, these drugs can be highly effective in reducing the debilitating symptoms of severe psychiatric disturbances. The major phenothiazines have proven very valuable in the treatment of schizophrenia, the tricyclics and MAO-inhibitors for mobilizing those suffering from psychotic depression, and lithium carbonate for controlling manic-depressive illness. These drugs are not only valuable in treating the acute psychosis but in maintenance doses can aid in the recovery period and help prevent future psychotic breaks. Though these drugs are indispensable in the treatment of the truly mentally ill, the massive ingestion of mild tranquilizers, sleeping pills, mood elevators, aspirin, antihistamines, alcohol, and cigarettes by tens of millions of people is now regarded as a major health problem. The mild drugs have become the primary way in which the average middle-class neurotic deals with symptoms of distress. They provide some relief but do little to slow the stress cycle and the gradual deterioration in the quality of a person's life.

Americans consume approximately five billion doses of tranquilizers, five billion doses of barbiturates, and three billion doses of amphetamines prescribed each year. A recent National Prescription Audit showed that the mild tranquilizer Valium is the most frequently prescribed drug in America; it is more often prescribed than any leading antibiotic, prescription pain medication, or birth control pill. Number four on the list of the top ten prescribed medications is Librium, Valium's leading competitor. Clearly, mild middle-class neurosis is reaching epidemic proportions. These statistics define the magnitude of the problem without even including the statistics on the consumption of alcohol, cigarettes, and non-prescribed medications.

Most psychiatrists and physicians find themselves unwillingly colluding with this massive and growing dependency on pills. When a patient comes to the doctor's office and complains, "Doctor, I'm worried all the time. I'm tense. I get angry easily and I can't sleep at night," the doctor must do what he can to help. He cannot just say, "Oh, you're just a little nervous; it will be all right." In order to relieve the suffering human being who sits before him, the doctor feels almost bound by his Hippocratic oath to reach for his prescription pad and put the patient on Valium or Librium. Yet every physician knows that his prescription will not solve the patient's real problem, that the patient may develop a dependency on the drugs, and that something more is needed to help the patient relieve the cause of his distress.

The third approach which psychiatry has tried in

order to stem the tide of increasing distress is known as the community psychiatry movement. For the past decade or so, mental health professionals have sought to extend their expertise to social engineering. They have worked in school systems, businesses, and neighborhood mental health centers in an effort to prevent mental illness by developing healthier and more responsive institutions. This movement has failed to fulfill its promise of solving the mental health crisis. Although some schools and businesses have begun to change their anxiety-producing ways of operating, institutional changes have not really made much difference in the social stress cycle. It appears that institutional change does not guarantee individual change. Consequently, much of the funding for the community psychiatry movement has been to help severely disturbed patients, with therapeutic support from local mental health clinics, get out of the hospital and back into the community. This success once again illustrates the progress psychiatry has made in treating the truly mentally ill in contrast to its failure in helping the average middle-class neurotic.

In light of what psychiatry knows about the origin of middle-class neurosis and what little it has to offer the middle-class neurotic, the significance of the TM program is evident. A major advance in human well-being may be at hand. I am convinced that the TM program can substantially enrich the lives of millions upon millions of people. I have written this book to show how the TM program has actually helped hundreds of patients at the Institute of Psychophysiological Medicine discover that life need not be a struggle and happiness can be natural. Of course, a "true believer" attitude is always suspect. I acknowledge the need for scientific scrutiny. The clinical reports and scientific research documenting what the TM program has to offer must stand on their own.

In his book the *Structure of Scientific Revolutions*, Thomas

Kuhn has documented the great resistance that meets almost every major scientific discovery. Kuhn points out how major scientific advances require shedding old world views or paradigms, as he calls them. Old assumptions about man and his place in the universe must give way to the new. Copernicus risked execution when he insisted that the sun and not the earth occupied the center of the heavens. Freud nearly suffered banishment from his profession when he proposed the notions of the unconscious and infantile sexuality. The TM program may also be leading to a shift in paradigm. The long reigning assumption that life is a struggle may gradually give way to the discovery that happiness is easy and natural. In this process, resistance is inevitable. The TM program may be attacked as a sham or a fad. Equally likely is the appearance of hucksters and charlatans who promise an imitation TM program to be learned from a book or magazine "for only a few dollars." This book will hopefully contribute to the rapid recognition that through the TM program happiness can be a baseline experience of living for nearly everyone.

The New Technology of Happiness

In all its years of existence, psychiatry has not provided a means which people could use on their own to promote psychological integration and growth and therefore happiness. The TM program has. Coming on the horizon of psychiatry out of an ancient tradition rather than a modern medical laboratory or off a Viennese couch, the TM program is showing increasing promise of success in helping millions of people find the happiness which they seek. A growing number of people in the sciences have begun noting that the TM program may be the new technology of happiness.

To many people, the phrase "technology of happiness" has the frightful ring of *Brave New World* and *1984*.

Technology has become so closely linked with control, manipulation, and the destruction of the natural that it has become suspect in many people's minds. At the root of the word technology, however, is the word *technique*, which means a simple, skillful, artful way of doing something to facilitate achieving a goal. Five men may try together to move a boulder and fail; one person may come along with knowledge of a lever and move the boulder by himself. The lever is a technique. Almost everyone uses techniques to enrich his life and the lives of others. There are techniques of cooking, gardening, playing tennis, manufacturing, teaching, and perhaps for every conceivable human activity. In light of the enormous contribution of technology to the comfort and ease of living, it is ironic that a technique for happiness has so long been missing.

The pursuit of pleasure and happiness is a basic biological and psychological law governing human behavior. Freud called it the "pleasure principle" and later the "life instinct." This drive for the expansion of happiness compels people to strive for more affection, more wealth, more prestige, more comfort, more knowledge, and more satisfaction in every area of life. For many people, this drive for more leads to frustration because they fall short of their goals. For those who may achieve their goals, the stress and fatigue accumulated in their efforts often block the enjoyment of their success. These two conditions describe the plight of the average middle-class neurotic. Patients complain of frustration because they cannot be what they want or because they have achieved their goals but are not happy. The conclusion is inescapable: because they lack the proper technique, people make themselves unhappy in pursuing happiness.

TM is a technique, not a faith or a philosophy. It is a simple mental technique that unfolds each person's natural capacity for happiness. What laws of nature does the TM technique harness to help people in the pursuit of happiness? The impelling drive for the expansion of happiness itself. In making use of this natural drive almost anyone can unfold his full capacity for happiness and strengthen his ability to fulfill his desires without accumulating stress, strain, and tension.

How the TM technique accomplishes this is very simple. It enables a person to gain a unique state of restful alertness. In this state, the body rests more deeply than in sleep while the mind becomes inwardly stable, relaxed, and alert. The experience of this state is profoundly refreshing and enjoyable on two levels. Subjectively, the state of restful alertness is soothing. Objectively, the state produces a unique quality of *ease* and *order* in the functioning of the brain and body. The subjective and objective components of the experience make it highly rewarding and beneficial. Scientific research, which will be discussed in more detail later, indicates that this state is probably the most strengthening, enlivening, and rejuvenating experience a person can have.

Though the possibility of this experience has been recognized for thousands of years, it has long been thought difficult to achieve. The TM technique, usually practiced twice daily for 20 minutes each time, represents a revival of an ancient method for achieving this state in an easy and natural manner.

The TM technique has its origins in the ancient Vedic tradition of the Himalayas. This tradition is concerned with unfolding the full capacity of human life and speaks of the need for living a fully developed inner and outer life, which the Vedic tradition specifically defines as the state of enlightenment. Psychologists have for some time recognized that most people use only a small fraction, perhaps 5–15 per cent, of their mental, physical, and emotional potential. Enlightenment presumably represents a state of human development in which a person has gained access to his untapped reserves of energy, intelligence, and creativity.

What is the relation between enlightenment and the everyday pursuit of happiness? Through the pioneering work of Sigmund Freud, Western science has returned full circle from its almost exclusive interest in the study of nature to a recognition of how important a person's inner life is to his happiness and well-being. An archetypal myth at the root of almost every culture is that of the Fall: Mankind, at one time in harmony with creation, has somehow fallen out of tune with the laws of nature. This myth explains human unhappiness as the inevitable consequence of the Fall. A degree of truth to this myth may be seen every day in psychiatrists' offices. The people who come seeking help are nearly all suffering because they have broken natural laws. One person controls his emotions to the point where tension, frustration, and anger are produced — requiring more control. Another patient is meek and compliant with her spouse in order to make him happy; this in the long run has the opposite effect. Still a third tries to achieve a sense of security and success through the accumulation of material goods, but mounting bills and a financial tightrope produce insecurity instead. These patients will not be happy until the conflicts between their inner and outer lives are resolved.

The process of gaining happiness through the TM program may be understood as a reattunement to the natural. Not that everyone who practices the TM program goes back to nature in the sense of retreating to the woods, but the TM program promotes a spontaneous accord with nature whether in mid-town Manhattan or in the middle of a mountain meadow. This attunement is basic to the process of becoming enlightened.

Scientific investigation of the TM program is leading to the integration of ancient knowledge with modern science. This research has contributed to the birth of a new science of consciousness and human development called the Science of Creative Intelligence, founded by

Maharishi Mahesh Yogi. Nowhere is the impact of this science along with its practical aspect, the TM technique, becoming more dramatically felt than in psychiatry. Some people still think of TM as primarily a relaxation technique. How the TM program is beginning to transform psychiatry illustrates that the TM program offers much more than mere relaxation. In order to appreciate fully the significance of the TM program for the pursuit of happiness, the practice of psychiatry, and the growth to enlightenment, some understanding of what psychiatry already knows about the roots of human discontent is necessary. I have tried to avoid technical language throughout this book. However, the technical information about the physiology of human distress presented in the next two sections of this chapter are unavoidable.

Freud Revisited

Psychiatry gained a scientific foundation with the work of Sigmund Freud. Many of his theories are controversial, but his basic insights into the source of human emotional distress and unhappiness remain the cornerstone of psychiatry. What Freud discovered is that most people's conscious mental life, behavior, well-being, and happiness are largely determined by mental and physical processes of which they are unaware. He called these processes the unconscious mind and located their origin in the genetic, personal, and cultural histories of the patients. He noted that early childhood experiences are particularly important to a person's later happiness. Most people are familiar with this idea and have thought at one time or another about how their childhood rearing has affected their present behavior and outlook. In fact this idea is so common that most patients who come to a psychiatrist's office today still expect to dredge up all of their childhood miseries in the hope of finding the key to reducing their current emotional, mental, or physical distress.

From the first years that Freud gave birth to psychoanalysis, his followers began reformulating some of his basic ideas and developing their own approaches to psychotherapy. Dozens of new psychotherapies have arisen. The humanistic psychology movement disagrees radically with Freud's pessimistic estimate of humanity's hope for happiness. Yet, the common theme of nearly all the new psychotherapeutic approaches remains the need to free the mature adult or maturing adolescent from the tyranny of early traumatic and stressful experiences deeply imprinted in the psyche.

This agreement reflects Freud's profound insight into how emotional stresses and traumas affect the functioning of the mind and brain just as powerfully as a physical wound affects the body. When a person comes to his doctor's office complaining of a pain in the chest, the doctor begins by trying to find out what disease or injury might be causing the pain and disabling the patient. On this basis, the doctor prescribes appropriate treatment. Freud devoted his life to exploring why people suffer from emotional distress, behavioral problems, and unexplainable bodily aches and losses of function. He discovered that the emotional traumas and stresses which people suffer throughout their lives can be as mentally and physically crippling as any organic disease of the nervous system. Furthermore, he discovered that many of the stresses people suffer fail to dissolve naturally over time and continue to be troubling long after their initial occurrence. These findings are consistent with the general medical approach to disease. If a wound does not heal properly, it will continue to cause suffering or loss of function. Freud added the additional insight, however, that when these stresses remain tension-charged long enough, the mind automatically tries to put them out of the purview of consciousness, almost as the body forms an abscess around a splinter embedded in the skin.

How the accumulation of these stresses, which I like to call excess emotional baggage, undermines a person's well-being and happiness has been described in detail by the great men of psychiatry. Some of the most graphic descriptions come from the newer schools of psychotherapy. For example, the Transactional Analysists vividly describe how people get "hooked" by an emotionally laden memory when the right stimulus presents itself. If a person had some difficulty with a first grade teacher who embarrassed or shamed him, he might get "hooked" by similar feelings whenever he has a difficult interaction with a boss or other authority figure. It is not uncommon in some families for young girls to get frightful warnings from their mothers that "all men are just out to use you,they're up to no good." When such a girl grows up and marries, she may get "hooked" by these fearful messages during marital relations with her husband. These feelings can make relations with her spouse a painful burden and affect all of her activities.

The psychiatric term for the result of accumulating a backlog of stresses and pent-up emotional baggage is *neurosis*. For most people this remains mild but can become severely disabling. Freud argued that neurosis represents an emotional condition in which an individual is controlled by a need to satiate an early impulse that was never satisfied due to the presence of a painful or absence of a supportive childhood experience. I find that people can understand neurosis most easily when I describe it as a state of *dis-ease* and *dis-order* in the functioning of the mind and body. Old stresses and excess emotional baggage block the natural ease and order of feelings, thinking, and behavior. People suffer a variety of feelings of *dis-ease* (e.g., shame, depression, anxiety, tension, guilt, anger) and an equal variety of thought or behavior *dis-orders* (confusion, mistakes, impairment of concentration, lack of motivation). This *dis-ease* and *dis-order* shows up in a wide range of specific complaints, but the overall result is that most people miss out on experiencing their full capacity for happiness.

Many thousand years before Freud's insight into the cause of neurosis, the Vedic seers constructed an analogy to explain why people act in disharmony with nature and suffer. The Vedas point out that almost everyone has deeply rooted tight "knots" within his nervous system. These knots supposedly obstruct the natural functioning of the body, thereby limiting individual potential and causing suffering. When all of these knots are completely dissolved, enlightenment is said to result. The Vedas prescribe the regular experience of restful alertness, naturally achieved through the TM program, as the simplest and fastest means of dissolving all the knots of accumulated stress which a person might have. Maharishi sometimes uses this analogy to explain how the TM program improves the functioning of the nervous system. He notes that these knots refer to "any chemical or structural abnormality resulting from an overloading of the machinery of perception," and he calls these abnormalities stresses.

This picture of stresses as knots is remarkably consistent with recent psychological and physiological evidence concerning the origin of neurosis. In his early writings, Freud gave the impression that a person's emotional distress had its roots in one major traumatic event. It was thought that if the repressed feelings associated with that one big trauma could be uncovered and resolved through psychoanalysis, the patient would be cured. The 75–year history of psychotherapy has convinced most psychiatrists that the big trauma theory is inaccurate. Instead it appears that almost everyone accumulates a vast pool of mini-traumas, each of which gets laid down in the memory banks along with the emotional tension — shame, guilt, fear, pain, excitement, anxiety, and so on — which accompanied its initial occurrence.

Support for this idea comes from many quarters. The body-oriented therapists, Wilhelm Reich and later Alexander Lowen (the founder of Bioenergetics), have described in detail how people develop chronic muscular tension in responding to one mini-trauma after another. A person might hold his breath when frightened, tense his shoulders when angry, or choke back tears. When these experiences occur over and over again even in relatively mild forms, chronic tension — a lump in the throat, a tight chest, stiff shoulders — results. In his book *I'm OK — You're OK*, Thomas H. Harris describes lucidly how children gradually, not all of a sudden, accumulate NOT OK feelings about themselves. These accumulated mini-traumas finally coalesce into an inner feeling of fearfulness and poor self-regard. These NOT OK feelings lead people to play the games described by Eric Berne rather than interact in a natural, warm, and intimate way. One of the best descriptions of the accumulation of stresses comes from the founder of Primal Therapy, Arthur Janov, who writes, "Each time a child is not held when he needs to be; each time he is shushed, ridiculed, ignored or pushed beyond his limits, more weight will be added to his pool of hurts....Each addition to his pool makes the child more unreal and neurotic."[8] Fritz Perls, founder of Gestalt Therapy, discusses the effect of accumulating thousands of mini-traumas as creating a fantasy world that clouds a person's awareness. Maharishi uses a Vedic analogy to describe this situation. Their minds clouded by old stresses, most people are living in what might be compared to a dimly lit room. Lying on the floor might be a piece of rope; however, in their readiness for alarm and cloudiness of perception, most people would see a snake. Without even noticing it, almost everyone lives a little out of touch with what is really going on around him because every perception, thought, and action is colored by this backlog of old stresses.

The best neurological evidence for the accumulation of stresses and their impact on feelings, thinking, and behavior comes from Canadian neurosurgeon, Wilder Penfield. During certain kinds of neurosurgery, patients receive a local anaesthesia so they can remain awake to assist the surgeon on locating those areas of the brain which control specific bodily functions. Penfield conducted a series of experiments in which he directly stimulated the brains of a series of his patients with a minute electrical current. His findings were extraordinary. He discovered that he could elicit detailed memories of events which the patient had completely forgotten. The memory response was so complete that a 43 year-old woman could give details of her birthday when she was three years old. Such memory was particularly significant because the woman not only recalled the scene of the party, but re-experienced very fully on the operating table how she felt at the party.

Most people are familiar with how an unexpected stimulus can evoke a gripping recall of an earlier experience. A theme from a song often calls forth a forgotten place or person. A patient once reported to me how a gesture and simple turn of a phrase by one of his professors triggered an overwhelming sadness. He left the classroom perplexed. All day he remained troubled by a strong desire to cry. Toward evening, he finally recognized that his professor reminded him of his father who had died many years earlier. Only seven years old at the time of his father's death, my patient remembered trembling with grief yet being unable to cry at the funeral. The professor's few words and gestures were enough to evoke that unresolved grief. The great French author Marcel Proust immortalized the power of a taste to stimulate memory when he wrote: "....so in that moment all the flowers in our garden and in M. Swann's park, and the water-lilies on the Vivonne and the good

folk of the village and their little dwellings and the parish
church and the whole of Combray and of its surroundings, taking their proper shapes and growing solid,
sprang into being, town and gardens alike, from my cup
of tea."[9]

Two of the most significant elements of Penfield's
work have begun to unravel the mysteries of memory
and tell us that the brain evidently functions like a tape
recorder in the precision with which it registers
experience. First it records not a jumble of memories but
a library of discrete events each available for individual
recall. Second the feelings that occurred with each
event, whether pleasurable or painful, are recorded in
tact along with all other details of the memory. It is
interesting to note that the Vedas describe a portion of
the brain containing a vast storehouse of impressions,
many of which are laden with intense emotional charges
said to be the seeds of suffering. It may be that only
those events which command a particular degree of
conscious attention during the day are stored permanently in the memory banks. Though this question
remains unresolved, the compelling influence of these
emotionally laden stresses is clear: they affect
everything a person thinks, feels, and does, even though
the person is mostly unaware of this process.

Among the principal aims of many psychotherapies is
helping a person discharge the emotional tension
associated with old memories. This tension presumably
keeps the body and mind in a state of dis-ease and dis-
order while consuming vast amounts of energy that
could be better spent on enjoyable activity. When these
stresses dissolve, the weight of worries, anxieties,
depression, anger, headaches, and other bodily complaints gradually lifts, and a person's natural capacity for
happiness blossoms. A person experiences more and
more ease, order, and happiness spontaneously, and he
begins to get in touch with his full measure of energy

and intelligence. Psychotherapy has, however, remained very limited in its success at helping people heal these deep-rooted stresses and unload their excess emotional baggage. The TM program is a major scientific advance because it appears capable of accomplishing for the middle-class neurotic what psychotherapy cannot — the dissolving of old stresses and the natural unfolding of a full capacity for happiness. Before the mechanics of how the TM program heals the psyche can become clear, further knowledge of how stresses and excess emotional baggage affect behavior and the functioning of the body is necessary.

The Stress Cycle

Every time a chronically anxious person worries about a job he has to do or a place he has to go, he reinforces his general anxiety level. The unassertive person reinforces his inability to assert himself every time he succumbs to the excessive demands of his boss, friends, or family. When a patient suffering from self-doubt becomes afraid and fails to enjoy social life, his or her problems get worse. At the same time, if a person can do one job well or successfully assert himself once, or have a good time at a party, he can start a cycle that leads to a steady increase in psychological integration and rewarding behavior. Both healthy and unhealthy feelings and behavior are self-reinforcing. This is why people find it so hard to change themselves and why many of my patients will so often complain, "I can't believe it, I keep doing the same dumb things over and over again!" At the root of this process is a physiological and behavioral interplay which I believe can best be called the *stress cycle.* To enjoy life fully, a person must gain mastery over this cycle.

Stress is a somewhat ill-defined term. It means one thing to the general public, another thing to the mental health professional, something else to the engineer, and still something different to the physiologist. Medicine borrowed the word stress from physics and engineering, where stress means a force sufficient to distort or deform when applied to a system. From this point of view, when a person bends a paperclip, he applies stress to it. Most people think of stress in very much this way. A person will say "I am under a lot of stress" and mean he is feeling the pressure of a demanding situation. The physiologist thinks of stress quite differently. He is concerned with what goes on in the body when a person feels pressured. Consequently, he defines stress as the complex of bodily changes that occur when a person faces a demanding situation, whether physical, mental, or emotional. Another definition of stress, introduced by Maharishi Mahesh Yogi, I find most useful as a psychiatrist. Maharishi, as I have pointed out, defines stress as any chemical or structural abnormality that remains in the body after a person has experienced an overload of the system. When I use the term *stress* in this book, I am referring to these abnormalities — deep-rooted tensions and impressions laid down in the memory banks, "knots" in the nervous system — which result whenever a person experiences a physical, mental, perceptual, or emotional overload. To make my use of the word stress clear, I will use the term *stressful situation* when I am talking about the environmental pressures which most people think of as stress. And I will use the term *stress response* when referring to the physiological changes which immediately take place during a stressful situation. These three related but distinct elements — stresses, stressful situations, and the stress response — are the principle components of the stress cycle. Almost everyone knows what a stressful situation is, and I have outlined in some detail how stresses get laid down in the body and brain. What remains to be defined before the stress cycle can be understood is the stress response.

The Canadian endocrinologist Hans Selye gained worldwide recognition for his first paper on the stress response in 1935. Since that time, Selye's discovery has emerged as one of the great medical advances of the twentieth century. Selye tells a funny story about what prompted him to begin looking for the stress response. When still a medical student, he sat in a large amphitheater listening to a professor outline the specific signs and symptoms which permit doctors to diagnose diseases. The professor took medical histories and examined patients with pneumonia, diabetes, cancer, and heart failure. All the professor spoke about was the differences between the patients, their distinguishing signs and symptoms. Selye recounts that he could not help but ask himself why nothing was said about the similarities between the patients. "After all," he has said, "all the patients looked sick!" This simple observation led Selye to discover the common set of physiological changes that occur whenever a person is under any kind of pressure. He called these changes, technically, the General Adaptation Syndrome, or more simply, the stress response.

Not just a response of one organ or one part of the body, the stress response involves a whole constellation of physiological changes. In the case of the patients whom Selye was so keenly observing as a medical student, they showed the common signs — fatigue, general discomfort, weakness, and a sick appearance — of their bodies trying to fight disease. Selye has demonstrated that the body will show the same characteristic set of changes in response to a loud noise, a sudden temperature drop, a viral infection, intense pleasure, extended worry, or a critical memo from one's boss. In short, the stress response is an invariable result of any demanding situation, be it physical or mental, pleasurable or painful. (See diagram 1.)

The stress response unfolds in three stages. The first is the stage of alarm. When a person meets a stressful situation, a very important midbrain structure known as the hypothalamus receives a message to begin

Diagram 1
THE STRESS RESPONSE

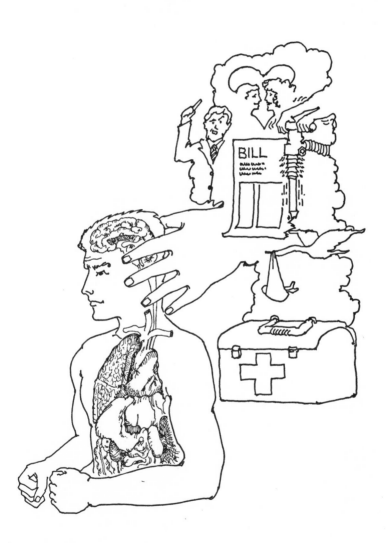

mobilizing the stress response. The hypothalamus is the seat of our emotions and basic drives such as hunger, thirst, and sex. Once the hypothalamus gets the demand message, it signals the pituitary gland, the master gland in the body. The pituitary gland then sends hormonal messages to the adrenal glands, sitting atop the kidneys. Immediately the adrenals secrete adrenaline to mobilize the system. Depending upon the intensity of the stress response, a person may feel tingling in the hands or butterflies in the stomach as blood rushes to the brain and muscles; he may notice his heart racing and his breath rate speeding up; he may feel some excitement, pleasure, anxiety, fear, or anger. Drs. Schachter and Singer have shown that the emotional component of the stress response also depends on how a person interprets his situation. Watching a thrilling football game and fighting rush hour traffic may produce the same intensity of stress response, but the football game results in pleasure and excitement while the traffic causes anger and frustration. The alarm stage of the stress response is closely related to the emergency response, called "fight or flight," and identified by Dr. Walter B. Cannon in 1941 as the body's natural reaction to impending danger. Selye's work showed that the alarm stage encompasses more than "fight or flight" because non-threatening pleasurable as well as threatening painful situations can elicit the same physiological changes.

Dr. Thomas H. Holmes, psychiatrist at the University of Washington Medical School, has explored in depth the stress-producing impact of various common events in people's lives. He has found that a pleasurable event such as marriage can produce more stress than the obviously painful situation of being fired from work. Similarly, his interviews with hundreds of people revealed that retirement is experienced as more stressful than the death of a close friend or a major change in financial status. Of course, a potentially stressful event will have a different impact on different individuals. One person may find the stress response produced by troubles with the boss a nightmare while another person may undergo a much more stressful situation such as personal injury, but will remain emotionally stable, optimistic, and happy. How much stress is actually incurred does not just depend on life events but also on the health of the individual's nervous system.

Critical to understanding how the stress response affects behavior and happiness is Selye's distinction between good stress and bad stress. Selye calls a beneficial stress response *eustress* and a debilitating stress response, *distress*. The alarm reaction in mild and occasionally intense forms is an important component of excitingly pleasurable experiences. It adds to our *joie de vivre* as long as it does not become excessive. Furthermore, an intense alarm response may be life-saving when rapid mobilization of energy is necessary (e.g., an unexpected automobile rapidly approaching as you cross the street or a fire in your home). Both mild and occasional intense alarm responses may be called *eustress* as long as they have an overall life-supporting effect. On the other hand, chronic or inappropriate alarm reactions seriously disrupt the healthy functioning of the body and mind. A prolonged alarm response leads automatically to the second stage of the stress response, in which the body begins consuming all its vital resources to fight the stressful situation. This stage of resistance eventually gives way to the third stage, which Selye calls exhaustion. When chronic distress builds up, fatigue becomes a paramount feature, bringing many people in to see their family doctor or a psychiatrist. It has been estimated that 70–80 per cent of patients seen by family doctors are suffering from stress-related symptoms. The symptoms of this chronic distress include anxiety, tension, depression, irritability, worry, high blood pressure, insomnia, headache, constipation, confusion, fatigue, difficulty in solving problems — all the symptoms of mild middle-class neurosis.

I find Selye's distinction between good stress and bad stress insightful but in some ways confusing. Creative Intelligence (CI) is a broader concept than Selye's *eustress*. Maharishi defines *creativity* as the cause of change present everywhere at all times and *intelligence* as the basic quality of existence exemplified in the purpose and order of change. Therefore, *creative intelligence* means the single and branching flow of orderly and purposeful energy observable in all phenomena. The origin, range, development, and application of creative intelligence may be studied everywhere in nature. This study constitutes the Science of Creative Intelligence. In this book, I will be discussing the growth and development of creative intelligence in human physiology, psychology, and behavior. Diagram 2 contrasts the effects of distress and creative intelligence.

Everyone faces pressures throughout his life. What determines whether a person will enjoy CI or suffer distress in meeting these pressures? The key to happiness lies largely in the answer to this question. Creative intelligence is healthy, dynamic, and fulfilling; distress indicates some malfunction, some abnormality, some violation of a law of nature. The difference between CI and distress is primarily a matter of degree. Whenever the stress response becomes chronic or excessively severe, what started out as CI soon becomes distress. What this means very practically is that the person who meets pressures quickly and effectively enjoys CI, and the person who gets caught up in problems suffers distress. Many people believe that getting caught up in problems, and consequently distress, is inevitable. This belief is what lies behind the old idea that life is a struggle and suffering is unavoidable. History records thousands of years of problems and distress, but more and more psychiatrists and psychologists today are calling for a re-examination of human potential. Studies by Maslow show that the most dynamic, creative, and fully healthy people in society enjoy substantially greater happiness than the average individual. These self-actualizing individuals tend not to get caught up in problems and do not show the symptoms of distress. Though only a very small number of people today are currently self-actualizers, the joy, happiness, and success of these few indicates that problems and distress are not an unavoidable part of living.

Diagram 2

CREATIVE INTELLIGENCE VS. DISTRESS

energy-relaxation-pleasure	anxiety-tension-depression
health-vigor-vitality	illness-discomfort-lethargy
heightened alertness	irritability-fatigue
flexible-stable-progressive	rigid-labile-stagnant
broad comprehension-mental acuity	narrow vision-poor concentration
love-harmony-peace	anger-discord-turmoil

Maharishi has identified five fundamentals of progress which I find useful in sketching the basic characteristics necessary for a person to meet pressures with creative intelligence rather than distress. These characteristics are adaptability, stability, integration, purification, and growth. It's important to note that superhuman characteristics are not included in this list. A person does not have to be a genius, exceptionally strong, or in some other way a highly unusual person in order to learn to meet all problems with ease and enjoy a full capacity for happiness. These five fundamentals of progress are the natural characteristics of anyone whose nervous system is functioning in an easy and orderly way, free from the burden of old emotional wounds and deep-rooted stresses. Based on the fundamentals of progress, diagram 3 illustrates the growth continuum along which everyone falls and everyone moves.

Few people are at the extreme of enlightenment and full psychological health or at the extreme of severe psychosis and total psychological collapse. Most people are somewhere in the middle. What is highly significant for understanding how to master the stress cycle is that massive scientific evidence shows that the TM program enhances the fundamentals of progress throughout the whole fabric of a person's life. Where a person is on this growth continuum depends largely on how many deep-rooted stresses he has obstructing the normal functioning of his nervous system. How these stresses constrict natural adaptability, stability, integration, purification, and growth is intimately connected with the stress response itself.

The stress response is wholly automatic. It is mediated by the sympathetic (energy-expending) branch of the autonomic nervous system. When the hypothalamus receives a demand signal, the stress response begins. The hypothalamus does not carefully examine the demand signal to determine whether it is real or imaginary, whether you are actually facing a mugger,

Diagram 3

THE GROWTH CONTINUUM

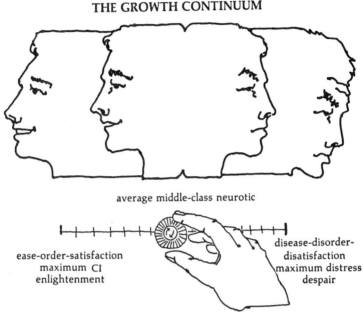

average middle-class neurotic

ease-order-satisfaction   disease-disorder-
maximum CI   disatisfaction
enlightenment   maximum distress
                                           despair

whether you are remembering a mugger, or whether
you are thinking you might get mugged. All three cases
can trigger the stress response with equal intensity.
Penfield showed how completely the brain records not
only past events but also the emotional charge connected with those events. These stresses work in the
brain like a whole battery of cortical triggers that fire
one after another and keep a person in a constant state of
emergency alert. For most people, this state of distress
remains mild and they remain average middle-class
neurotics. If the distress becomes severe, serious
symptoms may develop. Whether mild or severe,
chronic distress saps vital resources and contributes to
biochemical imbalances. This physiological dis-ease and
dis-order undermines physiological and psychological
adaptability and stability. A person becomes short on
staying power as well as on ability to flow with a

changing situation. Tension and fatigue inevitably result in inflexibility. Emotional dis-ease fosters psychological disintegration. Anxiety, worry, and tension fuel self-doubt and depression. The body's natural ability to purify itself is disturbed; susceptibility to infection increases; gastrointestinal problems may appear; and reliance on cigarettes, alcohol, and tranquilizers further undermines health. All these factors together impinge on a person's natural capacity to grow.

This pattern of distress triggered by old stresses bothers every patient who comes to my office. He is invariably worried, whether about his health, his job, his family, his future, or almost anything. What becomes clear with most patients is that the worry is far out of proportion to his or her actual situation. The patient may recognize this fact, but the worry persists. Why? The backlog of stresses and excess emotional baggage keeps triggering the alarm response. The patient suffers distress but does not really know why. Not knowing why can produce even more anxiety, so the patient finds something to worry about, something concrete to explain or account for the distress that he experiences. The purpose of tranquilizers is to dampen the distress and thereby help the person see his situation more realistically. Though tranquilizers are helpful in reducing distress, they do not dissolve the deep-rooted stresses which tend to keep a person in a state of distress. They do not help a person really master the stress cycle.

Now that the basic components of the stress cycle have been defined, the cycle itself may be better understood. Diagram 4 illustrates the stress cycle. When pressure becomes great enough on a person with an average backlog of old stresses, he can hardly help getting into a state of mild or moderate distress. In this state, his emotions are unstable and his mind lacks clarity. The likelihood of mistakes and maladaptive behavior is great, and these inevitably lead to failure and frustration. Each failure and each frustration reinforces the backlog of stresses, lowers self-esteem, and leaves the person more susceptible to distress in the future. Each time the person gets into a pressure-filled situation, he may remember what he did wrong last time and try to change, but his physiology responds automatically; he slips into the state of distress, and mistakes occur despite his best intentions.

The stress cycle is at the root of the unhappiness troubling nearly every patient who comes to see me. Mr. R, a 36 year-old assistant vice-president in a large firm, was feeling the pressures of work and his own drive to become a vice-president. Not quite satisfied with his own performance, he began putting in longer hours and pushing himself to his limits. Soon he began to show signs of distress—headaches at the end of the day, irritability, and insomnia. Tension grew in his marriage. Worry and guilt became a burden. Eventually his work began to suffer; so he put in still longer hours. When he finally made a poor presentation before the company executive committee, his confidence suffered a severe blow. He tried to make up for his mistakes by pushing still harder but finally wound up consulting me for help.

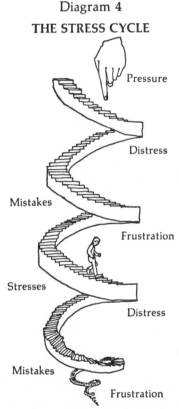

Diagram 4

THE STRESS CYCLE

Pressure

Distress

Mistakes

Frustration

Stresses

Distress

Mistakes

Frustration

Sally was a 23 year-old woman with a chief complaint of low response in her marital relations. She was quite attractive, but some very deep stresses kept her feeling tense. She desperately desired to have satisfying relations but the pressures of her own self-doubt kept her in distress. She tried to relax but remained tense. The more she tried, the more tense she became, and the more her self-esteem suffered.

Mr. J was 47 years old when he came to see me complaining of years and years of insomnia. His case was classic. He worked as a dispatcher in a large trucking firm. During the day, he would become so tense that even though he often came home exhausted, he frequently had difficulty falling asleep. When he woke up tired the next day, his work became a nightmare for him. His fatigue contributed to mistakes, which reinforced his tension, so that at night sleep would again be impossible. He reported periods like this lasting for weeks at a time.

Ron and June had been married for several years and both wanted more than anything else to make a happy home for themselves and their two young children. Ron was holding down two jobs to pay for the new house they had recently bought. June spent the day making curtains and decorating in addition to taking care of the children. Ron began to come home tense and get angry with June for no good reason; each time he would relieve some of his tension but his behavior toward his wife soon aroused feelings of guilt. June became frightened and withdrew whenever Ron got angry. She resented his inability to appreciate how hard she worked to make the house beautiful. When June would withdraw, Ron would keep his guilt and tension bottled up inside until he would have another angry outburst. The marriage became progressively more miserable.

None of these people had severe psychological problems; all were mild middle-class neurotics suffering from symptoms and problems that trouble millions. They remained caught up in unhappiness until they finally learned how to transform the stress cycle into the growth cycle.

Diagram 5 illustrates the growth cycle. The key to the growth cycle is the ability to meet pressures with CI. If a person sustains a high degree of ease and orderliness in the functioning of his mind and body, pressure will automatically trigger CI and increase energy, mental clarity, and concentration. This increase in ability helps a person turn obstacles into opportunities, problems into achievements. Success in the face of pressure naturally generates fulfillment, happiness, and heightened self-esteem. This growth experience strengthens a person's ability to meet pressure with CI.

Diagram 5

THE GROWTH CYCLE

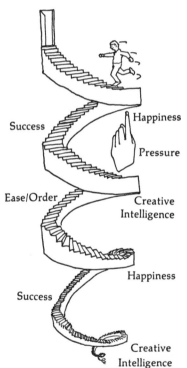

Two factors determine whether a person gets caught up in the stress cycle or the growth cycle: how much pressure a person meets and where that person stands on the growth continuum. The average middle-class neurotic shifts back and forth from the stress cycle to the growth cycle. When pressures are minor, a person enjoys the growth cycle. If the pressures build sufficiently, he slips into the grind of the stress cycle. Because a dynamic life inevitably involves pressures of all kinds and intensities — work, family, personal goals, financial problems — a person cannot master the stress cycle by expecting environmental pressures to accommodate his abilities. The key to happiness lies in increasing personal adaptability, stability, integration, purification, and growth. Psychotherapy helps toward this end, but psychotherapy alone is slow and costly. The TM program is an exciting advance in psychiatry and holds promise for helping millions because it is a means whereby almost anyone can, on his own, begin naturally moving on the growth continuum toward enlightenment.

How We Differ

What determines how many stresses a person accumulates growing up and where he stands on the growth continuum? The answer to this question is as yet unclear. Some people have had the good fortune of an upbringing where they were subjected to the fewest possible traumatic experiences. Guilt, shame, fear, and anger were not important tools which their parents used to control behavior, and the parents were relatively sensitive to their children's needs for love, affection, support, and guidance. Perplexing though it may seem, this happy childhood does not guarantee that a person will not have accumulated a backlog of stresses upon reaching adulthood. On the other hand, some people may have had much less ideal home environments as children but were fortunate to be endowed with emotional and intellectual strength. Despite the turmoil they suffered, they managed to grow up relatively free from stresses to display their natural brilliance. Scientific knowledge of why and how people accumulate stresses is still very limited.

Unfortunately, it is almost discouragingly clear that most people feel varying degrees of unhappiness which they would like to change. Many people would like to improve their marriages. Parents cannot help but feel frustrated when, despite all they do, they cannot establish a ground for communication with their teenage sons and daughters. Literally tens of millions of people want to find relief from anxiety or depression. An equally large number of people are troubled by bodily aches and pains, insomnia, high blood pressure, or other physical symptoms of tension. Shame and guilt are troubling feelings which plague still untold numbers of people. Some people would like to learn how to stand up for themselves, others would like to improve their personalities and learn how to form warmer and more intimate friendships, while still other people would simply like to reach the performance level they are capable of but somehow fail to achieve.

What I and most other psychiatrists find frustrating is that people may want to change but do nothing about the stress cycle until they become truly miserable. Many people will have some minor feelings of tension and disease but will ignore these feelings as long as everything is going reasonably well in their lives. Then a person will suddenly meet a string of failures and problems and within days or weeks get into a state of troublesome distress. Prior to that time, the person was undoubtedly acting in ways that were reinforcing his old stresses. He may have felt mildly uncomfortable at times as he slipped into distress but was blind to his becoming progressively more and more troubled.

When people begin to suffer distress, their perceptions and attitudes change profoundly. For years, patients have been telling me, "Doctor, when I'm not under pressure, everything goes great, but then I get under stress and I start feeling lousy about myself and my whole life. Everything seems to fall apart." Psychologist Charles Tart of the University of California has summarized recent research which helps explain this phenomenon. What a person knows and how he perceives his world are dependent on the underlying status of his mental functioning, better known as his state of consciousness. Almost everyone has experienced this fact. When you wake up well-rested and fresh, you perceive yourself and the world very differently than you do after a poor night's sleep. Alcohol and other mind-altering drugs can markedly change perception and knowledge. The basis of a change in consciousness is a change in how the brain and nervous system function. Distress causes such a profound change in body functioning that the state of distress may be understood as a generalized state of consciousness with its own laws of perception and knowledge. The Vedas anticipated this relationship of consciousness to perception and knowledge over 5,000 years ago with the statement, as brought to light by Maharishi, "Knowledge is structured in consciousness."

What I find hopeful in these investigations of how perception and knowledge depend upon consciousness is that happiness, optimism, and well-being seem to be natural to the state of consciousness free from distress. A patient may come to me complaining that everything is awful, he is no good, he can't live with his spouse anymore, he hates his job, his health is bad, and on and on. If the person is not severely disturbed, it soon becomes apparent that the stress cycle is at the root of many of his negative feelings. In such cases, I almost always prescribe the TM program. Within just weeks or months, as the TM program increases ease and order in the functioning of the person's mind and body, he emerges from the stress cycle and starts describing the world much differently. He still may face problems but he will begin talking about how he has started to enjoy himself, how worries have lessened, how he has rediscovered his love for his wife, how he can put up with his job for the time being until he figures out how to improve his situation. In all the cases I have seen, it is very apparent that just as unhappiness is the natural experience of dis-ease and dis-order, happiness is the natural experience of ease and order.

Particularly important to understanding how distress leads to maladaptive behavior, is a fact closely related to the principle that knowledge is structured in consciousness. This principle is: what a person learns in one state of consciousness may not be available as knowledge in another. Kathy, a 33 year-old housewife married to an airline pilot, is a good example. In my office, Kathy can recognize that she is attractive, a good wife, creative, and capable, but that a backlog of childhood stresses causes her to have low self-esteem and a tendency to become mildly depressed. She leaves my office feeling positive and optimistic. When she goes home, howevever, she may learn that her husband will be flying for five days straight and not be home. Kathy knows rationally that this is part of her husband's job, but she almost inevitably gets hooked by old feelings of rejection and gets all wound up in a state of distress. When Kathy gets back into distress, she starts to put herself down, feels guilty about snapping at her husband, and loses interest in her gardening and art work, thereby further lowering her self-esteem. She comes back to see me a week later, depressed and saying, "I'm no good. You're just telling me I'm attractive and capable to make me feel better." Then we start all over again.

The amount of pressure necessary for people to forget all the good things about themselves varies from person to person. A harsh look is enough to send some of my more neurotic patients into a tizzy of distress. A few people can go through even extremely severe financial or emotional crises and still keep their balance, self-esteem, and happiness. Most people are somewhere in between.

People react to distress in different ways. Depending on a person's genetic or constitutional make-up, he may develop psychosomatic or emotional symptoms, or even both. Chronic distress, with its vague symptoms, leads most people to their family doctor, who has little difficulty identifying "a case of nerves." With the doctor's imperative "you've got to learn to relax" and a prescription for Valium, the person leaves the doctor's office with some hope that things will get better. For some people, the particularly pressure-filled period passes and things do get better, but for most, distress intensifies and major symptoms may develop.

The development of symptoms is a very insidious process. A person with his body frequently in a state of alarm due to cortical triggers may not notice any changes in his life at first. He may simply feel a bit more "nervous" or "tense" than usual. If this state of hyperarousal and dis-ease continues or increases, the first symptom to show up will probably be disturbed sleeping. Few people consider disturbed sleep a serious symptom because half of all Americans suffer from difficulty falling asleep, sleeping through the night, or awakening too early in the morning. Disturbed sleep may not be a symptom in most people's minds, but the sale of prescribed and over-the-counter sleeping pills (many billions are consumed annually) is a very good index of how much people want and need to get a good night's sleep. Inability to get rest stokes the coals of the stress cycle. When a person begins to feel more tired than usual and starts exhibiting lowered resistance to disease, i.e., frequent colds, cough, or sore throat, he is well into the stress cycle. Irritability and even temper tantrums are not unusual signs of a person slipping into chronic distress. Heartburn, constipation, and acne in adolescents are other frequent indices of increasing distress.

This process begins with a general and vague deterioration in a person's feelings of happiness and well-being and can culminate in serious emotional or psychosomatic symptoms. The number one killer in the United States is heart disease; 53 per cent of all deaths (over 1,000,000) were caused by heart disease in 1975. One quarter of these deaths were among young men in the midst of dynamic careers. The chances are now one in five that a man under 60 will have a heart attack. An important component of almost all coronary disease is high blood pressure or hypertension. One out of every three adult males in the United States has high blood pressure and 99 per cent of these cases involve essential hypertension (high blood pressure without a specific physiological cause such as kidney disease). Chronic distress seems to be among the best ways of explaining essential hypertension. Twenty-five to thirty per cent of the people seeing general practitioners are suffering from anxiety neurosis, inappropriate alarm responses that can mimic the symptoms of many serious organic diseases. Because anxiety neurosis can cause gastro-intestinal, cardiovascular, respiratory, or dermatological symptoms, it has been called the "great pretender." But make no mistake about it, these patients are not pretending; they are genuinely suffering. One out of ten males will develop peptic ulcer disease and another one out of ten people will need psychiatric treatment sometime in his or her life. Hundreds of thousands of people suffer from allergies, bronchial asthma, rheumatoid arthritis, ulcerative colitis, and tension headaches. All of these health problems have been closely linked to chronic distress.

For several years now, there has been a growing sentiment that social problems are getting out of control. The crime rate continues to rise. High unemployment seems to be a problem that will linger for years. The planet appears to be moving headlong toward exhaustion of many basic resources with substitutes or solutions still far off. More and more marriages are ending in divorce; more and more children are growing up with only one parent. Criticism of the educational system began years ago and shows no signs of letting up. Americans are spending more on health, yet their collective health seems to be worsening. The average life expectancy, which had risen steadily for decades, has not changed for the last ten years. Suicide rates have skyrocketed, especially among younger people. All these trends and statistics can be used to paint a very grim picture of the future. Whether the world situation is as grave as some doomsday prophets (many of whom are leading men of science) would have us believe, remains to be seen. One good explanation for the increasing feeling that things have gotten out of control is the stress cycle.

When individuals get caught up in a cycle of pressure leading to distress, which in turn results in maladaptive behaviors, frustration, more stress, and more pressure, social consequences are inevitable. The stress cycle at the root of so much individual unhappiness may have an analogue on the social level. Diagram 6 illustrates what I believe may constitute the social stress cycle. Stressed individuals respond to pressure with distress. When many individuals suffer distress, the social tone becomes one of confusion and chaos. People see problems everywhere. Many of these problems are genuine and require creative solutions. But an equal number are created by the distress that people are feeling and would disappear if the level of collective distress could be lowered. When distress continues unabated, it inevitably results in disorganization, which

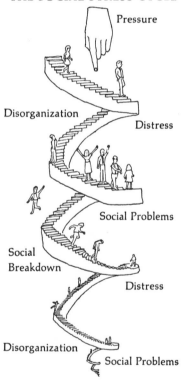

Diagram 6

THE SOCIAL STRESS CYCLE

Pressure

Disorganization

Distress

Social Problems

Social Breakdown

Distress

Disorganization

Social Problems

reinforces social problems. This increase in social problems cannot but make people feel more pressured and more tense, thereby fueling the cycle of distress, mistakes, and problems. This cycle could easily account for the widespread feeling that things are out of control.

Can reducing distress improve society? A sometimes spoken but most often unspoken goal of psychiatry has been to try to do so. Many great men in psychiatry have echoed the imperative, "Get Freud off the couch and to the masses!" Despite all the new therapies that have come and gone over the past decades, the social stress cycle has continued to escalate. However, a dramatic change may be at hand. The TM program is a unique, easy, and highly effective way for almost anyone to begin reducing distress and discovering that happiness is natural. Never before has it been possible to conceive realistically of such a technique becoming available to the whole population. The implications of widespread practice of the TM program are staggering.

2

TM and the Mind

For the past several years, the TM program has been sweeping the country. Over one million people have learned the technique to date. Is the TM movement another fad? Is the TM technique attracting so much attention just because it is something new that can break up the humdrum routine in people's lives? The answer to both questions is an emphatic No! In the dual role of practicing psychiatrist and trained TM instructor, I have had an opportunity to gain in-depth insight into how the TM program heals the psyche. What this program accomplishes in promoting psychological and physiological integration at the deepest levels of the mind makes clear that it is neither a fad nor just a simple relaxation exercise. How the TM program dissolves accumulated stresses and the backlog of emotional baggage must be grasped before the full significance of the TM program for human happiness and the practice of psychiatry can be understood.

Psychiatry has long held that uncovering and dissolving the tension associated with old repressed memories and deep-rooted stresses almost inevitably involves slow and often painful hard work. A favorite phrase of many psychotherapists is, "You've got to work it through," meaning the patient must grapple emotionally and intellectually with each stress that psychotherapy uncovers until it finally dissolves.

Because almost everyone has thousands of mini-stresses to deal with, not just a few major ones, the traditional psychotherapeutic approach to dissolving stress involves much emotional turmoil and seems to go on without end. As noted earlier, however, the TM program indicates that a shortcut is possible. The Vedic metaphor comparing stresses to knots in the nervous system will help explain how.

Imagine the whole fabric of the nervous system cluttered with knots. What keeps each knot tightly bound is tension. If the tension on all the knots could be reduced at the same time, even slightly, then the knots would have an opportunity to unwind. During the practice of the TM technique, a person gains a state of physical rest deeper than sleep, while the brain and nervous system begin functioning in a way more integrated and orderly than usual. This state of unique physiological ease and order literally bathes all of a person's stresses in very deep relaxation, thereby exposing them to the full intensity of the body's regenerative and purifying mechanisms. Dipping the body and mind in this exceptionally deep rest twice a day for a few minutes permits the whole backlog of stresses to begin dissolving naturally and automatically. The principle is simple; the results are profound.

This process may be compared to the way in which the body heals a physical wound such as a cut finger. Healing a cut requires nothing more of a person than covering the wound and allowing the finger to rest. It's not necessary for the person to think, "Ah, I've been cut! White corpuscles must hurry to the site of the wound. Fibrinogen must be laid down immediately to help clotting. Red blood cells have to bring up more oxygen." Similarly, it appears that through the TM program a person can promote natural healing of even the deepest stresses in the mind without struggling to recall and resolve past miseries. Equally important, the person need not even be aware of which stresses are dissolving during or after the healing process takes place. This entirely physiological approach to healing the psyche softens the psychological impact of dissolving deep-rooted stresses.

These concepts are new to psychiatry. Before they can be explored further, a review of what the practice of the TM program actually involves is necessary.

The TM Program

Many people still associate the TM program with archaic images of meditation. They believe that the TM technique must be difficult because they have always heard that meditation is very hard and requires considerable discipline. Or they believe that the TM program may be good but takes a long time to produce results because meditation is supposed to produce results only after many years of practice. Sometimes people fear they cannot learn the TM technique because they believe it must require the ability to assume difficult postures or have access to an absolutely quiet room. Often people express concern that the TM program may demand a change in belief or lifestyle because they have always associated meditation exclusively with religion. In fact, the TM technique is easy, works immediately, requires no special postures, and does not involve a change in religion, belief, or lifestyle. It requires no monastic surroundings; people often practice the TM technique riding in cars, airplanes, commuter trains, and subways.

The technique of TM represents a revival in the understanding of how simple and effective meditation can be. The TM technique is a natural procedure for allowing the mind to gain a state of maximum strength and clarity while the body settles into deep rest. The physiological changes which accompany this state of restful alertness account for the wide range of immediate and cumulative benefits of the TM program.

Though the TM technique is enjoyable to do, people do not practice it for the experience of meditation but rather for the benefits in daily life. For maximum results, a person practices the TM technique for about 20 minutes in the morning and again in the early evening before dinner. What distinguishes the TM technique from all other meditation techniques is its ease, effectiveness, and the systematic way it is taught, which explains, in part, why it cannot be learned from a book. In the words of psychiatrist Frazier of the Harvard University School of Medicine, "It works!"

Because the TM technique is a soothing and enjoyable *experience*, it defies precise description. Describing the TM technique is as difficult as describing the taste of a new flavor of ice cream; you can attempt to describe the flavor, but, in the end, it must be tasted. If a picture is worth ten thousand words, then one experience must be worth ten thousand pictures. Nevertheless, what happens during the TM technique may be described as diving from the active surface of the mind to its quiet depths.[1] Presumably, a thought begins as an imperceptible impulse at the depth of the mind and grows in clarity as it rises to the mind's conscious thinking level. The experience of having a name on "the tip of the tongue," as opposed to remembering the name clearly, illustrates how the mind may entertain thoughts at varying levels of clarity and distinctness. The fact that the same word may be spoken, thought, whispered, or faintly remembered also illustrates that the thinking process proceeds in stages. The technique of TM involves allowing the mind to experience consciously earlier and earlier stages in the development of a thought until the mind transcends the thinking process and gains the source of thought.

What is the source of thought? An analogy will help. A person watching a movie in a darkened theatre might believe that the images on the screen had a life of their own. If the images gradually faded until they disappeared but the movie projector light remained on, the person in the theatre would see the white screen. At that point, he would recognize that the images required the white screen to come alive. Thoughts and perceptions are similar to movie images in that they depend on consciousness, the screen of the mind, to become real. A person must be conscious in order to think. If a person were able to take a thought and let it systematically and gradually fade while he remained awake, he would eventually experience the field of consciousness in a pure state. This field of pure consciousness, simple inner wakefulness without thought or perception, is what is meant by the term *source of thought*. Another term which Maharishi uses to describe the source of thought is "the state of least excitation of consciousness." When a thought rises in the mind, it excites a person's consciousness just as a wave excites the surface of the ocean. When a person experiences consciousness without a thought or perception, he experiences the least excited state of consciousness, comparable to the calm depths of the ocean without waves. The physiological effects of the TM technique are a natural result of the mind settling down to its least excited state.

The Transcedental Meditation technique is a unique means of going beyond (transcending) the thinking process (meditation). If you allow your mind to take its own course, you may note that thinking is an effortless process. The mind automatically and incessantly generates thoughts. Because thinking involves no effort, the natural thinking process provides no resistance to the mind going beyond thinking. When some people fear they will never be able to practice the TM technique and say, "If the TM technique means quieting the mind, I can't do it because my mind won't stop thinking," I tell them this worry is unnecessary because the TM technique makes use of the mind's natural tendency to transcend thinking.

When learning to dive, a person simply masters the art

of taking the correct angle and then lets go. Once a diving student takes the correct angle, he may continue without concern because gravity will do the rest. He does not even have to believe in gravity. During instruction in the TM technique, a person learns to give the mind a gentle inward turn and then allow it to follow its own natural tendency to seek increasing happiness. The source of thought provides the mind with the experience of concentrated happiness. The mind flows toward the source of thought during TM practice just like a person walking toward a dim light in a dark room. With each step toward the light, its intensity increases. Similarly, the mind finds increasing happiness on its way toward the source of thought. The mind moves as comfortably during the practice of the TM technique as it shifts from reading a book to listening to music when a favorite song comes on the radio. The TM technique is so simple that it may be considered effortless.

Sometimes people think that the TM technique must involve simply diving to the source of thought and remaining at this most quiet level of the mind for the entire 20-minute meditation period. In fact, a typical session involves several dives. The mind may settle down to the source of thought only to rise again to active thinking a few moments later. Once a person notices he is again on the surface level of the mind, he simply takes another dive, easily and comfortably. The TM technique does not produce a trance state. On the contrary, the technique is a dynamic process which heightens awareness. To facilitate the process of diving during practice of the TM technique, a person must use a suitable thought as a vehicle for the mind's descent to the source of thought. The thought-vehicles used during practice of the TM technique are called *mantras.*

Thought has two basic qualities: sound and meaning. Recent linguistic research suggests that sound is more basic to thinking than meaning. While some sounds, such as the screech of chalk on a blackboard, may have disturbing effects on the mind and body, other sounds, such as the gentle flow of a brook, may have soothing effects. The word *mantra* is a Sanskrit term derived from the verbal root *man*, which means "to think," and the suffix *tra*, which indicates instrumentality. So the word *mantra* means "an instrument of thought" or a "mental device." Mantras are chosen for their sound quality and life-supporting effects. One of the principle effects of a mantra is to soothe mind and body. Because people are different, the same mantra will not be equally life-supporting for every individual. Consequently, the proper mantra for each person must be carefully chosen by a qualified TM instructor. The selection process is based on a tradition that extends back to the oldest records of human experience, the Vedas.

Maharishi has designed a seven step course, standard throughout the world, for learning the TM technique. The course begins with two introductory lectures. The first explains the general benefits of the TM program and the second gives an overview of how the technique works. The third step is a personal interview with a TM instructor. If a person decides to learn the technique after hearing the lectures, he must complete a one-page application form which becomes the basis of the interview. The next step in learning is personal instruction. At this time, the instructor gives the person a suitable mantra and shows him or her how to use it properly. From this fourth step on, as the new meditator begins practicing the TM technique on his own for 15 or 20 minutes morning and evening, he also begins enjoying the benefits of the program. The fifth, sixth, and seventh steps of the course are on the three days following the day of personal instruction. These steps consist of group and individual meetings with a TM instructor for all the people enrolled in a particular course. These meetings, which like the introductory lectures and personal instruction take from one and one-half to two hours, are essential for gaining a thorough understanding of how to practice the TM technique properly and what effects to expect over time. Once a person completes this seven-step course, he is capable of enjoying *all* the benefits of the TM technique on his own. To make certain that a person gets the most of practicing the technique, however, a well-structured follow-up program is available through the thousands of TM centers around the world (in the U.S. alone, there are over 400 centers). The term *TM program* includes the twice daily practice of the TM technique and all of the TM follow-up educational services. One of the most important elements of this follow-up program is a procedure for verifying a person's practice of the technique and helping anyone having difficulty with it. This procedure is known as "checking" and takes about 20 minutes. Checking ensures absolutely effortless practice of the TM technique. It is available on an individual or group basis by appointment at all TM centers. A second element in this follow-up program is the advanced lecture. Attendance of at least one advanced lecture 10–14 days after completing the seven-step course has become almost an eighth basic step in learning the TM technique. This advanced lecture allows people to gain further intellectual understanding of the technique and ask questions which inevitably arise during the first two weeks of practicing the technique. All TM centers offer advanced lectures regularly for meditators to ask whatever questions they may have and to expand their knowledge about the TM program and its effects. Additional optional elements of the follow-up program are the basic courses in the Science of Creative Intelligence (SCI) and residence courses. The SCI courses consist of videotapes of Maharishi and structured discussion; residence courses are two- or three-day "in residence" programs that enrich a person's experience and understanding of the TM technique.

How important is the follow-up program? Regular

"checking" must be considered essential for anyone wishing to get the maximum benefit from his daily meditations. Maharishi recommends checking at least once a month for the first year of the TM program and thereafter as needed. I have found repeatedly that those people who become irregular in their daily meditations have failed to go for monthly checking. The TM technique is simple but extremely subtle. Some people practice the technique incorrectly by making an unconscious effort to resist thoughts, direct the mantra, or otherwise control the mind. Regular "checking" assures correct and effortless practice of the technique. Advanced lectures can also be important. Because the TM program promotes growth, people inevitably have questions about their experiences both in and outside of meditation. For example, a person might notice that for several weeks his meditations are more filled with thoughts than usual or he might find himself needing more or less sleep for a period of time. If questions about these experiences go unanswered, they can cause concern. Advanced lectures provide a forum for these concerns to be resolved and for a person to learn more about how the TM program unfolds the state of enlightenment. Unlimited checking and advanced lectures are available through all TM centers absolutely free of charge to anyone who has completed the seven step course.*

---

*There are three basic requirements for taking the TM course. First, a person must have enough time to complete the basic course. Second, there is the course fee. The cost for the seven-step course is $125 for adults, $65 for college students, and $55 for high school students. Married couples may take the course for $200. Finally, a person must abstain from non-prescribed drugs (specifically marijuana, amphetamines, LSD, etc.) for 15 days prior to personal instruction to assure a clear mind for learning. Alcohol, cigarettes, and prescribed medications are not included in this prohibition.

People sometimes ask what practicing the TM technique feels like. The experience varies but is generally soothing and refreshing. During a typical 20-minute session, thoughts may come and go, but they will not obstruct the meditation process. Though a person may occasionally have moments of "blank awareness," "inner wakefulness," or "being aware inside with nothing going on," the TM technique involves no effort to achieve inner quietness or push thoughts out of the mind. Sometimes, a person may notice noises in his environment, while at other times he may be oblivious to noise. In either case, he is capable of responding to a question or handling an emergency. At the deepest point in the practice of the TM technique, the mind gains the source of thought, called the state of least excitation of consciousness. Any effort to achieve this state, however, obstructs the process. Because it offers the mind maximum strength and happiness, this state draws the mind toward increasingly refined and quiet mental activity. It is not a goal to be sought after during practice of the TM technique. Sometimes a person may experience this state of pure consciousness clearly, while at other times he may only approach it. Nevertheless, each TM session produces benefits due to the physiological changes that accompany the process of diving toward pure consciousness. The degree to which a person experiences the least excited state of consciousness will depend on the physiological conditions of the body.

Through the regular practice of the TM technique twice daily, the experience of pure consciousness grows both during and after the meditation period. This quality of heightened awareness and well-being seems to be the subjective component of increasing physiological ease and order. Maharishi points out that the mind becomes capable of assuming its most powerful and expanded state of least excitation more clearly as old stresses dissolve. In fact, the entire process of becoming enlightened through the TM program may be explained in terms of unfolding a person's natural ability to make use of his physical, mental, and emotional potential from the state of least excitation of consciousness.

What scientific evidence exists to back up these ideas? A review of a few crucial scientific studies of what happens to the body and brain during the TM technique will be very helpful in understanding how the TM program promotes psychological growth. (These next sections are the last in this book involving technical scientific material.)

Scientific Research I: Increased Ease

Scientific research on the short- and long-term effects of the TM program indicates beyond any reasonable doubt that the program is unique and probably essential to maximum human well-being. The first volume of basic scientific research and applied studies on the TM program fills 700 pages. Further basic research and applied studies are under way throughout the world in over 100 universities, hospitals, and research centers in 20 countries. Current data suggest that the TM program may be so fundamental to human health and development that it may improve every aspect of a person's life. Three principal changes that take place during the practice of the TM technique provide a basis for understanding how the program can effect comprehensive improvement in individual well-being. These changes are a sharp decrease in metabolic rate, improved balance in the autonomic nervous system, and increased orderliness in the electrical activity of the brain.

Scientific research on the TM program got off the ground in 1970 when physiologist Dr. Robert Keith Wallace published in *Science* the first major study of what happens in the body during 20 minutes spent practicing the TM technique. He had 36 people of different ages, sexes, and lengths of time practicing the TM technique meditate in his laboratory while hooked up to the latest scientific instruments for measuring basic bodily functions. His findings startled the world's scientific community. In each of his subjects, Wallace noted dramatic changes during the practice. The most startling was that a person gains a unique state of rest that is in many ways measurably deeper than the rest gained during the deepest point of sleep. The principal measure of a person's level of activity or rest is how much oxygen he is consuming over a specified time period. When a person runs up a flight of stairs, he consumes more oxygen than when he sits quietly. When a person sleeps, he consumes less oxygen than when watching television. After five or six hours of a good night's sleep, oxygen consumption drops 8–10 per cent lower than during wakefulness. Wallace noted that within the first few minutes of practice of the TM technique, oxygen consumption drops precipitously by an average of 16–18 per cent from the level when a person is sitting comfortably with eyes closed. By comparing this change in oxygen consumption with that which takes place during sleep, the significance of Wallace's finding becomes apparent. In a matter of minutes, the TM technique produces a level of rest much deeper than in sleep. In disbelief, several researchers (at the University of Colorado Medical Center and the University of Alberta) repeated Wallace's oxygen consumption study. To their amazement, they found a decrease in oxygen consumption during the practice of the TM technique equal to or greater than that reported by Wallace.

Wallace noted several other changes which indicate that the TM technique produces a unique and very deep state of physical rest. Galvanic skin response (GSR), used, for example, in the lie detector test, is a good indicator of a person's overally anxiety or relaxation. An increase in GSR signals relaxation, while a decrease accompanies anxiety and tension. This test is so sensitive that it can pick up the mild anxiety associated with telling a lie about even the most trivial matter. Over several hours of sound sleep, skin resistance increases, on the average, 50–100 per cent over the level when one is sitting comfortably with eyes closed. Wallace found that during 20 minutes of the TM technique, skin resistance increases 100–200 per cent. Again, numerous investigators have replicated Wallace's research and reported similar findings. Wallace also found that the concentration of blood lactate, a chemical in the blood associated with stress, drops three times faster during TM practice than during sleep. Furthermore, the amount of lactate in the blood remains very low even *after* the practice of the TM technique.

Wallace's initial findings account in large measure for many of the benefits of the TM program for improving mental and physical health. These findings indicate that practicing the TM technique produces a state of physiological ease exactly opposite to the stress response. This state accounts for the sharp reduction in anxiety levels and decrease in stress-related symptoms such as tension headaches, fatigue, and insomnia among TM practitioners. Wallace's findings also support the idea that the TM technique bathes old stresses in rest sufficiently deep to dissolve them gradually. By reducing the immediate symptoms of distress and gradually dissolving old stresses, the TM program halts the stress cycle and promotes the growth cycle. These findings help explain how psychologists could report that the TM program, as shown by dozens of scientific investigations, improves self-regard, increases intelligence, improves capacity for intimate contact, decreases depression, decreases hostility, improves ability to handle aggression, and increases spontaneity. Presumably, decreased anxiety and increased psychological well-being explain the decreased use of alcohol, cigarettes, tranquilizers, sleeping pills, and

other non-prescription drugs among people practicing
the TM technique.

In the July/August 1973 issue of *Psychosomatic Medicine*,
research psychologist David Orme-Johnson published a
landmark study on how the TM program effects
autonomic stability and resistance to stress. Using eight
experimental subjects who had practiced the TM
technique for an average of 15 months and a non-
meditating control group, he exposed them to a sudden
loud noise while he monitored their GSRs. When
person is subjected to a stressor such as a sudden loud
noise, his GSR will usually decrease sharply for a few
seconds and then return to normal. Repeated exposure
to the same stressor will eventually lead to habituation
and no further response. Rapid habituation to a stressor
generally indicates autonomic stability and ability to
withstand stressful situations. Orme-Johnson found
that TM practitioners habituated to the same stressor
more than twice as rapidly as the non-meditators.

In a second study, he measured spontaneous GSR,
or measurable fluctuations in skin resistance, which
occur independently of any apparent external stimulus.
The number of spontaneous changes appearing in a
person's GSR amplitude over a ten-minute period is a
good index of a person's baseline anxiety or relaxation
level and his emotional stability. Generally, the more
spontaneous GSRs a person shows, the more anxious
and emotionally unstable he is. Orme-Johnson reported
that a group of non-meditators showed an average of 34
spontaneous GSRs per ten-minute rest period—an
average amount for normal adults and college students.
On the other hand, the meditators showed an average of
11 spontaneous GSRs in the same time period. Furthermore, several of the non-meditators with the highest
levels of spontaneous GSRs showed an average of only
15 spontaneous GSRs several weeks after they began the
TM program.

Psychologists have shown that a low level of spontaneous GSRs is well correlated with a high resistance to stressful situations, psychosomatic disease, and behavioral instability. It also indicates general efficiency in the activity of the nervous system and extra energy available for perception, thought, and purposeful activity. The ease that the TM technique brings to the autonomic nervous system continues after meditation, even during activity, and apparently fosters a mature style of functioning of the nervous system and a stable, expressive personality. Since Orme-Johnson published his initial findings, a deluge of studies has substantiated the benefits which result from the increasing autonomic stability through the TM program. Physicians have reported that the TM program aids in reducing high blood pressure, lowers heart and respiratory rates, improves asthmatic conditions, and fosters increased resistence to disease. Longitudinal studies of the effects of the TM program so far have spanned a maximum of 16 months after subjects started the program. These studies have shown that, within this time period, significant decreases in anxiety, depression, neuroticism, and drug use result from the TM program. Also, a significant increase in intelligence, creativity, stability, organization of memory, academic performance among students, athletic performance and cardiovascular efficiency among athletes, self-actualization, field independence, and perceptual-motor performance were found to result from the TM program. All of these benefits result in part from increased autonomic stability and better balance between the energy-restoring and energy-expending branches of the autonomic nervous system.

What this can mean for millions of people seeking relief from troublesome but common symptoms of distress is well illustrated by the experience of a 43 year-old woman who came to me complaining, "I'm becoming a nervous wreck." Shirley reported great difficulty falling asleep and felt chronically fatigued, depressed, and irritable. Angry outbursts were becoming more common, and she would have anxiety attacks for "no good reason." A very independent woman, Shirley did not want to take tranquilizers, and she did not want to continue seeing a psychiatrist on a long-term basis. When told that the TM technique was something that might help her and that she could practice without depending on pills or a therapist, she expressed interest. She began the TM program, and I continued to see her once a week for the next three weeks and once a month for a few months thereafter in supportive half-hour long visits. After the first month of twice daily TM practice, Shirley showed a steady reduction in her symptomatology. The fatigue and insomnia began to disappear within the first six weeks, the angry outbursts and depression after two months.

Because the autonomic nervous system controls 99 per cent of all the activity in the body, everything a person does depends on its balanced functioning. This system may be considered the "roots" of the human tree of life, and through the TM program, a person waters the roots of his own life. By increasing autonomic stability, he or she not only relieves specific troublesome symptoms but also enlivens the whole personality. Six months after Shirley's last visit, I met her at the San Diego TM center. "My life has made a complete turn-around; there's so much more joy in it," she said.

Scientific Research II: Increased Order

Research on how the TM technique affects the brain offers further insight into the significance of this unique technique. In the late 1920s, researchers discovered that the brain gives rise to faint electrical impulses called brain waves. Electroencephalography is a technique of recording this electrical activity using electrodes attached to the skull and a highly sensitive voltmeter called an electroencephalograph (EEG). EEG research has helped delineate physiological differences between the states of waking, sleeping, and dreaming. Sleep generally seems to be correlated with slow wave activity in the range of 3–5 cycles per second (cps), known as delta waves. Theta waves of 4–7 cps occur during sleep, as well as during drowsiness, but have also been associated with serene pleasure and creativity. Alpha waves of 8–13 cps often become predominant during relaxation with eyes closed. This pattern usually disappears when the eyes are open but can occur even then if the person is in a state of extreme relaxation. Normal waking consciousness apparently requires brain wave activity between 13 and 30 cps, usually indicative of concentration and active thinking.

During the normal waking state of sitting comfortably with eyes closed, brain wave activity measured at different points on the scalp shows random, mixed, inconsistent brain waves with no general relationship to

Diagram 7
DISORDERLY BRAIN WAVES

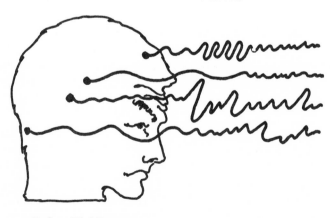

Before TM Practice

one another. The brain waves are of different frequencies and out of phase; they would be comparable to noise. Diagram 7 schematically illustrates this finding.

Recent research on EEG changes during TM practice has shown that it produces a unique style of functioning of the brain. In late 1972, neurophysiologist J. P. Banquet found in his studies at the Massachusetts General Hospital that during the practice of the TM

Diagram 8

ORDERLY BRAIN WAVES

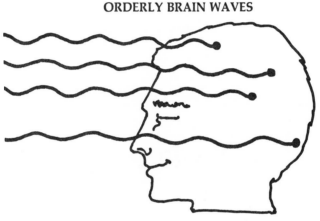

From TM Practice

technique, the EEG shows a marked uniformity of frequency and amplitude of brain wave activity from all areas of the scalp. The electrical activity of the brain tends to become more synchronous, appearing by analogy more like music than noise, as illustrated by diagram 8.

Banquet's data also distinguished the TM technique from the experience of drowsiness or sleep. Drowsiness is characterized by alertness alternating with light sleep, whereas brain waves during the TM technique show theta waves, indicative of the deepest physical rest, simultaneously and continuously with alpha waves, indicative of expanded alertness. Comparison of the known brain waves of waking, dreaming, and sleeping with the patterns that characterize the phases of TM meditation suggest that the TM technique gives rise to a fourth major state of consciousness—restful alertness.

Banquet found that after the first minutes of the TM technique, alpha waves spread synchronously from the back to the front of the brain and between the two brain hemispheres, as is illustrated in diagram 9. His data also suggest that synchrony occurs between the limbic system and the cortex. These initial findings have been

Diagram 9

INTEGRATION OF BRAIN FUNCTION

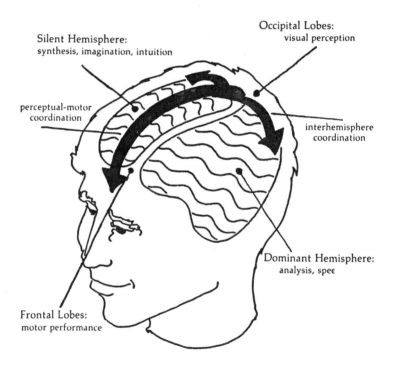

confirmed and further elaborated upon by several other researchers studying the TM technique around the world.

Dr. Paul Levine and his co-researchers at the neurophysiology laboratory of Maharishi European Research University in Switzerland have recently discovered a unique EEG "signature" of the physiological state reached during the TM technique. With the aid of a new signal processing method, the coherence spectral array, they found that the TM technique increases orderliness of brain functioning not only as reflected by hypersynchrony, but also, and even more importantly, as seen by increased coherence. The mathematical quantity called "coherence" provides a measure of the constancy of the relationship between the phases of the EEG at a specified frequency when measured at two spatially separated parts of the scalp. As such, it is a very sensitive indicator of the degree of long-range order in cortical activity as mirrored in the EEG. For all laboratory subjects the onset of sleep shows a marked decrease in alpha and theta wave coherence with loss of awareness. In contrast, 28 subjects, spanning a range of experience with the TM technique from a few days to 15 years, produced a very high incidence of strong coherence. These changes were unique to the TM meditators, particularly in the alpha and theta banks, relative to simple eyes-closed control periods. These findings indicate that the TM technique produces a unique long-range ordering of brain physiology.

I like an analogy that Dr. Levine uses to explain the value of brain wave coherence. When an army goes on parade, all of the soldiers in all of the specialized units fall into line to march as one harmonious unit. To an outsider, all the soldiers marching perfectly in step may seem like they are wasting time. In actuality, some of the harmony achieved from going on parade twice daily sticks with the soldiers when they return to their specialized units in the field, thereby increasing the entire army's efficiency and teamwork. In a similar way, the coherence of brain functioning achieved during TM practice carries over afterwards to improve neurophysiological integration, and as a result, all of the functions of the mind become more harmonious.

The significance of increasing brain wave synchrony and coherence during the TM technique becomes clearer when considered in light of what different parts of the brain do. For example, the front of the brain (frontal lobes) controls motor performance, while the back of the brain (occipital lobes) controls perception (see diagram 9). Increased integration between the front and back of the brain tends to improve perceptual-motor coordination. Laboratory studies have shown that the TM program improves reaction time and ability to perform complex perceptual-motor tasks. Quarterback Joe Namath, all-star shortstop Larry Bowa, and slugger Willie Stargell—all TMers—test the impact of the TM technique on perceptual-motor performance every time they compete.

Most people feel that since the body is symmetrical, one half is identical in fuction to the other. Brain research over the last 20 years has demonstrated, however, that the two halves of the brain control some very different mental processes. In general, the dominant hemisphere (the left in a right-handed person) specializes in analytic, rational, verbal, and temporal thinking. The silent hemisphere (the right in a right-handed person) controls imaginative, intuitive, synthetic, and spatial mental functions (see diagram 9). In the normal waking state, these two halves of the brain have apparently little opportunity to increase their ability to work together. Most people are predominantly intuitive or analytical, imaginative or rational, temporal or spatial, artistic or intellectual in their orientation to any tasks at hand, but great achievements often depend on an integration of both sides of the personality. The sculptor must intuit his creation, but then hammer his chisel with precision; the executive must make certain that his product is attractive as well as useful; the scientist must listen to the insights of his imagination in solving difficult problems. Research shows that the TM technique apparently provides a means of increasing communication between the two brain hemispheres. This finding may account for the improved intelligence, learning ability, creativity, and problem-solving ability found amoung TM practitioners.

One-sided personality development can render people incapable of enjoying themselves even though they may be successful in their fields. For example, the harried businessman may have become so competitive that he has lost his ability to appreciate the joys of life, including his family. Or the delicate poet may become so lost in his imagination that he becomes incapable of directing his life. These kinds of personality problems cannot be efficiently and effectively handled by psychotherapy alone. Psychotherapy can only help the person to unlearn bad habits and learn new and necessary interpersonal skills. For the average middle-class neurotic, however, the TM program appears to be the most effective way to maximize psychological integration and allow the full potential of the personality to blossom through natural integration of brain functioning.

The conflict between emotions and reason is as old as man and fundamental to much of the suffering that psychiatry tries to alleviate. Through harsh insensitivity or blind subservience, people become slaves to their feelings and end up suffering. The man of cold intellect may feel that he is master of his own destiny, but his actions are just as much determined by his failure to use the intelligence of the heart as are the actions of the woman whose every thought is colored by a depressive cast. By gradually dissolving old excess emotional baggage, the TM program fosters integration between the heart and mind. By increasing communication between the individual mind and heart, and then from person to person, before mistakes are made, the TM technique may help people avoid much interpersonal suffering.

Scientific research clearly confirms that the TM technique produces a unique state of deep rest, ease, and order in the functioning of the body and brain. What evidence indicates that just by experiencing this state of restful alertness, deep-rooted stresses dissolve?

How the TM Technique Heals the Psyche

Because most meditation techniques involve harsh control of the mind, some mental health professionals do not look favorably on meditation in general as a means of healing the psyche. Ignorance about the difference between the TM technique and other methods leads them to condemn all meditation techniques as repressive and potentially harmful. For example, in his book *Primal Scream* Arthur Janov quotes from several descriptions of meditation methods absolutely antithetical to that of the TM technique, yet calls all the techniques Transcendental Meditation. He then argues that meditation results in a "complete suppression of self" and "giving oneself over to a fantasy of one's own creation." Janov's criticism of repressive meditation techniques may have some validity, but had he done his homework more thoroughly he would have discovered that the TM technique is an easy and non-repressive procedure. During TM meditation, one has a cordial attitude towards thoughts and recognizes that they are a very good and necessary part of the technique, and one does not push thoughts out of the mind (this is suppression) or try to make the mind blank.

How the TM technique dissolves deep stresses may be understood by first examining the healing power of sleep. Twenty-five years ago, two University of Chicago researchers, Drs. Eugene Aserinsky and Nathaniel

Kleitman began to investigate what physiological changes take place during sleep. They measured bodily changes during sleep in much the same way that, 15 years later, Wallace measured changes during the TM technique. Prior to Aserinsky and Kleitman's ground-breaking research, most physiologists believed that during sleep the body settled into a very deep state of rest, remained at that level for a few hours, and slowly returned to the activity necessary for waking consciousness. Aserinsky and Kleitman showed that sleep is not that simple; it is cyclical. During an average night's sleep, most people will have three or four approximately 90-minute cycles in which the body gains very deep rest, but then returns to activity almost sufficient to wake up. They found that a peculiar event occurs at just that point in the cycle when it appears the sleeper is going to awaken. The eyes start to dart back and forth beneath the closed eyelids, making what are called rapid eye movements (REM). When Aserinsky and Kleitman wakened their subjects during these REM periods, the subjects consistently reported dreaming.

This research provides considerable insight into the restorative processes of sleep. When a person gains the deep rest of sleep, natural healing processes automatically become active throughout the body. Organs are repaired, tissues are revitalized, short- to long-term memory conversion takes place, and some of the deep stresses locked in the nervous system may be normalized. Rest activates this repair work, but the repair work itself causes the body to become active. When this repair work reaches a pitch of activity almost sufficient to waken a sleeper, the physical activity in the body and nervous system triggers a corresponding activity in the mind called dreaming. Dreams are the sign that stresses are dissolving and healing is taking place at the deepest levels of the mind.

The TM technique heals old emotional wounds and the backlog of accumulated stresses in a similar manner.

By allowing the body to gain rest much deeper than sleep, the TM technique permits daily stresses and strains to dissolve quickly while the oldest and most hardened stresses begin to heal. Just as dreams are the mental artifacts of stress release during sleep, thoughts, images, and feelings are the mental artifacts of stress release during the TM technique. The ease and order generated by the TM technique is apparently so profound that it allows even deeply repressed stresses— pent-up hostility, fears and frustration, guilt, anger, shame, and self-depreciation—to dissolve naturally and gradually. What I find most interesting psychiatrically about this process is that these very deep stresses usually dissolve without causing unsettling thoughts or feelings during or after the meditation period. The ease and order occurring during each TM session apparently cushion the meditator's thoughts and feelings from the disturbing impact of stresses dissolving. Most often the thoughts and images that appear during a TM session bear no obvious relation to the underlying stresses being released. People will typically not even notice that deep stresses are healing. Yet, changes in behavior and emotional make-up resulting from the TM program indicate that each TM session must be systematically dissolving very deep stresses.

The thoughts that accompany healing of old stresses during the TM technique are generally not troublesome for several reasons. First, relaxation reciprocally inhibits anxiety. Deep stresses dissolve during practice of the TM technique only when a person is enjoying very profound relaxation and inner stability. Consequently, memories or images that might enter the mind do not usually cause undue anxiety or alarm. The thoughts come and go without gripping the mind, even though the same thoughts might trigger anxiety outside of the meditation period. Second, if a particularly troublesome thought does linger during a session of the TM technique, the meditator simply allows his mind to

locate automatically the physical sensations in the body
that accompany the troublesome thought. As the
process of stress release completes itself, the
troublesome thoughts vanish. The third reason
thoughts and images are very rarely troublesome during
TM practice is that the meditator *refrains from analyzing any
thoughts or images which might appear.* Because thoughts are
the artifacts of an underlying physiological process of
stress release, the thoughts disappear as soon as the
physiological process completes itself. This process
completes itself most rapidly when the TM practitioner
takes an indifferent attitude toward whatever comes up
during the TM session. Analysis of thoughts during a
TM session only raises the metabolic rate and inhibits
the natural process of stress-dissolving.

People sometimes want to analyze thoughts or images
during the TM technique because they feel that such
analysis will be helpful. This belief arises from the
archaic notion that emotional conflict has its basis in the
mind and can be resolved solely on the level of feeling or
understanding. Nearly all current psychiatric research
supports Freud's original thesis that psychological
processes are grounded in bodily processes. This fact
suggests strongly that, as mentioned earlier, analysis of
thoughts, feelings, or images during the TM technique
is obstructive and contrary to its correct practice.
Analyzing thoughts raises the metabolic rate and
thereby inhibits natural healing processes. Once a
person begins to intentionally analyze thoughts during
the TM technique, he has effectively ceased practicing
the TM technique and begun sitting with his eyes closed
wasting time.

Can helpful insight be gained after a TM session
through analysis of thoughts or feelings which might
have come up? Most people find that even immediately
following a TM session, they cannot remember the
thoughts and feelings which might have appeared. In
general, no specific relationship can be discerned

between thoughts which appear and stresses which have been released, because the TM technique exposes all the old stresses to healing rest at the same time. Rarely does one stress dissolve all at once; instead a complex of stresses dissolves gradually with each additional meditation. This gradual healing of all the old stresses simultaneously accounts for the balanced psychological growth that accompanies TM practice. If, on some rare occasion, a person finds himself troubled by a hostile or depressing thought that continues to grip the mind after a TM session, a qualified TM instructor can take the person through a simple procedure designed to resolve such difficulties. If the person is in psychotherapy, the topic of the distressing thoughts may come up in the next therapy session, where understanding and support from the therapist can also be helpful.

If it does not make sense to analyze thoughts during TM practice, what happens to the old idea of analyzing dreams? Experience with the TM program lends support to current arguments that the technique of dream analysis may be intellectually interesting but not a very helpful therapy. If emotional stresses are physiologically rooted, analysis of the mental artifacts of physiological repair processes adds little to the repair processes themselves. Just as people forget about the thoughts or images which appear during practice of the TM technique, most people forget about their dreams. Though Freud, Jung, and other great psychiatrists have used dream analysis to learn much about how the mind creates and uses symbols, little evidence exists to suggest that dream analysis is an efficient means of allowing the mind to heal itself.

Freud argued that dream analysis was useful because it helped get behind the mind's tendency to repress and forget about old emotional wounds and unsatisfied needs. Though this theory appears valid, the question arises as to what is the best approach to freeing the mind and body from the need to repress and the process of repression. Talking about images that appear during dreams may gradually help a person relax his fears associated with those images and thereby permit natural healing, but this process is slow, difficult, costly, and often results in prolonged emotional distress as the defenses relax. By gently dipping all the old stresses in very deep rest, the TM technique appears to offer a shortcut to dream analysis. Just because the TM technique permits the healing process to go on "underground" in the natural workings of the body, it should not be argued that the TM technique is repressive. On the contrary, the TM technique appears to be the most thorough and powerful means available for dissolving the backlog of stresses and freeing the psyche from repression. The effects of the TM program simply demonstrate that talking about old stresses is, for the most part, unnecessary to healing them, just as a person need not talk about a cut finger in order for it to heal.

If talking about old stresses is no longer necessary, what happens to psychotherapy? I am excited about what the TM program can add to psychotherapy for two reasons. One, it promises to do for the average middle-class neurotic what psychotherapy cannot—open the door to expanding happiness. Two, for more seriously disturbed individuals, TM practice as an adjunct to psychotherapy accelerates progress in resolving specific emotional problems and enhances general psychological growth. Since I have been prescribing the TM program for my patients who need psychotherapy, they have been improving faster than I had ever seen before, sometimes two or three times the usual rate. The interface between the TM program and psychotherapy is one of the most exciting areas of investigation in psychiatry today and will be explored in more detail in chapter 7.

The Growth of Happiness

In discussing how the TM program dissolves old stresses, it is important not to lose sight of how this process stimulates growth. Stresses and distress block the flow of creative intelligence by keeping a person caught up in the stress cycle. When these old stresses dissolve, the stress cycle gives way naturally to the growth cycle. A person's desires for warmer relations with others, better performance at work, more money, or any other desire for more enjoyment start to lead to fulfillment rather than frustration. A graphic analogy makes clear how healing contributes to the growth cycle. If a person breaks his hand, he usually has to have it immobilized in a cast. During the mending period, he may want to play tennis, paint, write, or do any number of things which require the full use of his hand. Yet all these desires go unfulfilled. If the person uses the hand before it has mended properly, he may damage himself permanently and frustrate his desires for mobility still further. Once the hand mends, however, creative intelligence can flow freely through it. He can fulfill his desires easily whether they be to hold a child, hammer a nail, or play the piano.

Stresses act like a dam on the flow of creative intelligence. The words *uptight, hung-up, inhibited,* or *blocked* are common expressions which reflect quite accurately how stresses limit growth. When a person feels inhibited in some way, that inhibition affects his whole personality, not just that area in which he is particularly stressed. For example, if a person has a fear of public speaking, not only does he have difficulty before audiences but in some ways his whole capacity to share knowledge with others suffers. The person who has difficulty making friends misses out on unfolding his or her natural capacity for developing interpersonal skills and enjoying a blossoming of personality. If a person fears failure, he will not take the risks involved in starting new projects and will block his capacity for developing and implementing innovative ideas. Once the backlog of old stresses begins to dissolve, the dam on the flow of creative intelligence begins to melt. A person who was uptight in relating to other people will find himself spending more time with others and enjoying it. The unassertive person starts asserting himself. The inhibited person begins enjoying his life more. Because the stress cycle leads to low self-esteem, many people will doubt their potential to grow. "It can't be that easy," my patients will sometimes say when I explain how the TM program will unfold the natural flow of creative intelligence in their lives by dissolving old stresses. The average middle-class neurotic is convinced that growth must be a struggle. Experience with the TM program inevitably changes that conviction.

On a physiological level, the healing of old stresses opens a natural flow of energy. Among the first benefits people report from the TM program is, "I've got more energy than I used to have!" Stresses waste energy in two ways. First, they require a significant amount of energy to remain locked in the memory banks but out of conscious awareness. Repression consumes energy. Second, stresses contribute to the stress cycle in which energy is often wasted through disorganized thinking, alarm reactions, and unproductive actions. By triggering the stress response inappropriately, stresses drain energy in the same way that a physical illness does. The person caught up in the stress cycle expends large amounts of energy because he never gives his body a chance to recharge. His distress works like a constant drain on his "battery" (actually his autonomic nervous system), even while he is sleeping. On the other hand, the person who gets onto the growth cycle expends tremendous amounts of energy but never runs out because he is making use of his natural physiological recharging capacity. The TM program directly restores energy by providing deep rest and gradually increases available energy by dissolving old stresses.

I have described the growth cycle in terms of dissolving old stresses, but people practicing the TM technique do not generally experience their growth in those terms. On the contrary, my patients will become much less preoccupied with their stresses and problems, and much more involved with positive changes in their feelings and behavior within weeks after learning the technique. For example, one patient had complained for months about her "worries." Six weeks after I finally convinced her to begin the TM program, she came in one day and spent the whole session telling me about how much she was enjoying her new social activities at church and the gardening club. Another patient was miserable at home. All he could talk about were his problems with his wife and children; he saw no solution to his troubles other than divorce. Not long after he began the TM program, this same patient began to tell me how he felt that he was now ready to start working toward a better marriage. Other patients will come in and have nothing to talk about but their insomnia, their indigestion, their aches and pains. These symptoms may remain for a while even after a patient begins the TM program, but it is remarkable how quickly these symptoms cease to be the patient's overriding concerns. Once a patient begins the TM program, therapy sessions naturally become more filled with laughter and plans rather than fear and problems. When a patient and I begin spending whole sessions just laughing and enjoying one another's company, it becomes clear that therapy is no longer necessary. The person is well into the growth cycle and the expansion of happiness.

3

TM and Other Techniques Compared

What is the difference between the TM technique and other methods of meditation? Why can't the TM technique be learned from a book? Can a person get the same benefits from Dr. Benson's relaxation technique as from the TM program?

Is mantra selection really important or will any word do, as some authors suggest?

Is the TM technique a form of prayer?

Is it a form of self-hypnosis?

Can't a person get the same benefits from prayer as from the TM program?

How does the TM program compare with biofeedback?

How does it compare with deep muscular relaxation exercises?

What is the difference between the TM program and the new self-development programs such as EST, Arica, or Silva Mind Control?

In deciding whether to prescribe the TM program for my patients, I sought answers to these questions. My early personal experience with the TM technique, along with the scientific research, convinced me that the TM program was safe and deserved to be tried with my patients. But a medical scientist cannot help asking whether another technique might not produce the same effects more quickly, more economically, or more effectively for certain types of people. Almost every physician knows that one diet is not right for everyone; one medication is not right for everyone suffering from the same symptoms; one psychotherapy is not effective for all. People are different.

Maharishi Mahesh Yogi makes the bold claim that, despite individual differences, the TM technique can benefit almost anyone because it permits the experience of restful alertness. Considerable scientific evidence supports the assertion that experiencing restful alertness is inherently beneficial. In addition, Maharishi asserts that the TM technique is the simplest and most effective way to gain the state of restful alertness and that this technique can only be learned from a qualified instructor. These assertions have invited considerable controversy. Perhaps the best place to begin comparing the TM program to other techniques is to explore why the TM program can only be learned properly from a qualified instructor.

The Need for a Teacher

Many books have been written which give recipes for a variety of meditation techniques. None of these techniques have produced scientifically verifiable results comparable to those of the TM program. Were it possible to teach the TM technique properly by way of a book, Maharishi would be the first to do so. His sole interest for the last 20 years has been to share the TM technique with all who might want to learn it. A monk who owns nothing but a few personal belongings, Maharishi certainly has no proprietary interest in insisting that the TM technique be taught through personal instruction by a qualified teacher. Were it possible to write a book that would teach people the TM technique, and were Maharishi interested in money, what easier way to make money than by simply writing a book that outlined step-by-step how to practice the TM technique? However, exactly how to practice the TM technique cannot be learned from a book or a friend who has taken the initial TM course; personal, private instruction from a qualified instructor is necessary for several critical reasons.

Each person learns the TM technique at his or her own pace. Instruction in the technique is entirely experience-based, meaning that each succeeding step of instruction is tailored to each step of the person's experience in learning. Initial experiences during the first stages of learning the TM technique vary widely from person to person; therefore, instruction must vary widely from person to person. When a person takes the initial TM course, he learns the TM technique, but he does not learn how to show others the proper way to handle all experiences that arise when first learning the technique. Consequently, the initial TM course no more qualifies a person to teach the technique than a few psychotherapy sessions qualify a person as a psychotherapist.

Though all the possible experiences and appropriate steps in learning the TM technique could be outlined, instructions in written form would be useless to a person wishing to learn the technique, for as I sometimes like to point out, the first instruction would be "Close the eyes," making it hard to read the rest of the instructions. One of the most important elements in practicing the TM technique correctly is an innocent, non-analytical attitude. If a person set out to learn the TM technique from a book, he would be obliged to analyze carefully each step of his experience in order to identify the proper next step. However, this very need to process information, to analyze what happens during the initial steps of the practice, would block the person from correctly experiencing even the first stages of the TM technique and render all further instruction useless. When a qualified instructor takes responsibility for determing what to do next during each step of instruction, this problem disappears. The person learning the TM technique from a qualified teacher can sit back and simply enjoy his experience. He just answers the teacher's questions and follows the teacher's instructions, which lead step-by-step to the state of least excitation of consciousness.

Even if a person did manage to grope his way through some written set of instructions, a further critical problem would arise. How can a person be sure he is correctly practicing the TM technique? The teaching of the TM technique involves more than the communication of objective knowledge; it requires the verification of a subjective experience. If a person has never had a particular experience before, no amount of written instruction can verify whether or not the person is having the experience correctly. For example, the expert tennis player may recognize the written description of a good forehand, but the novice player obviously cannot. Having read about how to hit a tennis ball properly, the novice may go out on the court and hit some balls for the first time. But no matter how many tennis books he may have on the court with him, he cannot be certain that his timing, form, balance, backswing, follow-through, wrist position, and shoulder motion add up to the best possible forehand stroke. If the need for verifying correct practice is important for a novice tennis player, it is essential for a new practitioner of the TM technique. Learning the TM technique involves delicate and subtle experiences. A qualified teacher is absolutely critical for verifying the correct practice of the TM technique.

The desire for a book that explains step-by-step how to practice the TM technique emerges out of the same desire that fuels the massive sales of all the do-it-yourself therapy books. Though a book may provide information, increase self-understanding, or broaden perspective, it cannot usually transmit the kind of subjective experience necessary for profound psychological growth. Only a total experience triggers the physiological changes that genuinely foster growth.

None of the protein or vitamins in a glass of milk can ever get into a person's body through talking about milk. For milk to be useful, a person must drink it.

People also want a do-it-yourself TM book in hopes of saving money. Before learning the TM technique, people sometimes feel the cost of a course in the TM program is high. I have found that after a few weeks practicing the technique, few people continue to feel this way. By comparison with the price of psychotherapy, which often costs thousands of dollars, the TM technique is very inexpensive. For the average middle-class neurotic, who will get far more out of the TM technique than he will out of any form of psychotherapy, the TM technique is an absolute bargain.

On Choosing Mantras

For a tradition to remain intact for thousands of years it must have sound knowledge behind it. The procedure for choosing mantras, which Maharishi has passed on to his instructors, has its roots in earliest recorded history. Through careful insight and observation, ancient seers determined which sounds are most life-supporting for different types of people. To some people this may sound mystical; to others it may be intriguing. In either case, the mantra represents a very powerful input to the central nervous system. A person will think his mantra to himself many thousands of times in his life and in doing so will trigger a whole constellation of changes. To disregard the need for a mantra which will produce only life-supporting effects is foolish and possibly dangerous.

How does the mantra work? Maharishi explains that resonance is the key. The physics principle of resonance refers to the phenomenon whereby one vibrating object starts another object vibrating without direct contact. If I strike a tuning fork, I can start a similar tuning fork vibrating just by bringing the second near the first. When two violins are placed near each other and the E string of the first violin is plucked, the E string of the second will also vibrate, another example of resonance. According to Maharishi, mantras resonate with the baseline biorhythms of the central nervous system. A proper mantra will cause soothing and life-supporting effects. An improperly selected mantra will cause disturbing and possibly damaging effects, which may appear immediately or may not appear for several years of using an improper mantra daily.

Several researchers have explored systematically the importance of the mantra to the TM program. At the conclusion of a three-year study comparing the TM technique, biofeedback, and other meditation-relaxation techniques, Dr. Bernard Glueck of the Institute of Living in Hartford, Connecticut, wrote, "Maharishi insists that the mantra is a critical element in TM. On the basis of our research, we are inclined to agree."[1]

Diagram 10

VALUE OF A PROPERLY SELECTED MANTRA

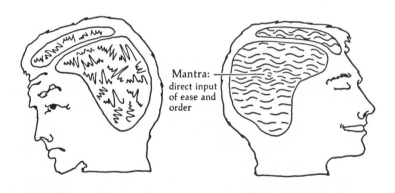

Mantra:
direct input
of ease and
order

Before TM Practice   TM Practice

Dr. Glueck offers what appears to be a sound neurological theory to explain why mantras must be carefully selected, which I would like to expand upon.[2] The mantra probably enters the central nervous system via the brain's speech area, located in the temporal lobe where memories are stored, and seems to represent a direct input of ease and order which reaches the innermost parts of the brain, as illustrated in diagram 10. By means of the direct fiber tracks linking the temporal lobe and the limbic system (the seat of the emotions), the mantra's resonant frequency apparently dampens limbic activity and unlocks the repression barrier which blocks communication between the two brain hemispheres. Because the mantra's soothing effects sustain quiet in the limbic system while it weakens the repression barrier, deep-rooted stresses stored in the memory banks have an opportunity to dissolve without causing overwhelming emotional upheaval. The repression barrier is also thought to fall for brief periods during dreaming, but soon rises again as dream imagery stirs limbic activity. As every reader has probably experienced, emotional turmoil of dreaming can be intense. By sustaining quiescence in the limbic system, the mantra permits the repression barrier to remain relaxed for long periods of time, allowing stresses to dissolve naturally and comfortably. The increased coherence of the EEG during the TM technique probably indicates sustained inter-hemispheric communication, which the mantra fosters. I sometimes compare the mantra to a key which, when inserted and used properly, permits the central nervous system to enter the state of maximum ease and order. The impact of mantras on the functioning of the brain is undoubtedly very profound. In this light, the importance of a suitable mantra should not be underestimated.

When a person learns the TM technique, he agrees to keep his mantra to himself. Some people believe that TM instructors ask for this agreement just to keep a corner on the mantra market. When I hear this objection raised, I always laugh. First, there are very good reasons for a person keeping his mantra to himself, and second, working as a TM instructor is no way to get rich.

Perhaps the most important reason for a person keeping his mantra to himself is to preserve its maximum intimacy and potency. Once having learned the TM technique, a person never speaks his mantra aloud to himself, even when alone. In general, thinking takes the body from lesser to greater activity. Sitting quietly reading, a person might begin to think about ice cream until that thought may eventually generate enough activity for the person to get up and eat some. Nearly all everyday thinking increases mental and physical activity. During practice of the TM technique, however, the thinking process takes the body from greater to lesser physical activity. The mantra is especially designed to promote this process silently. If it is spoken aloud, the mantra takes the mind and body from the lesser activity of silence to the greater activity of speech. Habitually using it in such an improper manner outside of TM meditation weakens its effect when used properly during practice of the technique. It is as if, when one is instructed in the TM technique and given a mantra, a seed is planted. If a person keeps pulling the seed out of the ground, he interrupts the process of growth. When the seed is left in the soil and watered as directed, growth can take place in an automatic, natural way.

Another important reason for a person keeping his mantra to himself is to avoid confusing others. People are only human; if they think they can get something "for free" and "try it," they will. I have seen cases where one person gives his mantra to a friend presumably to help his friend save the TM course fee. The result is analogous to a person, who knows nothing about piano, sitting down at a Steinway and haphazardly banging away at the keys without any professional instruction. The real tragedy in random use of TM mantras occurs when a person receives one from a friend, gets no results from using it, and concludes that the TM program does not work. Maharishi and his teachers place great emphasis on the "purity of the teaching" because the TM technique is so subtle that its full value can easily be missed. When people respect their agreement to keep their mantras private, they help maintain this purity.

The TM Technique, Concentration, and Contemplation

Most meditation techniques other than the TM technique fall into two categories: concentration and contemplation. Concentration techniques, nearly endless in variety, are all those which involve effort to focus the mind on a particular thought, sensation, image, part of the body, or other object of experience. Typical concentration techniques require that a person count his breaths, stare at a candle flame, maintain an image of light in the mind's eye or a sweet taste in the mouth, hold a particular thought in the mind, or try to make the mind blank. Concentration techniques waste energy in controlling and focusing mental acitivity, thereby increasing stress and strain, whereas the TM technique requires no effort either to control, direct, or focus the mind. A distinguishing mark of concentration techniques is the requirement to push random thoughts out of the mind and hold the mind on the object of concentration whenever the mind tends to wander. When learning the TM technique, a person discovers that a wandering mind and random thoughts are natural, and controlling the mind in such an unnatural manner is incorrect TM practice.

Most techniques currently practiced in India are of the concentration type. Because concentrative techniques can produce a detached and unrealistic attitude toward life, Maharishi comments that many concentration techniques tend to dull the mind and inhibit the natural process of evolution. Though concentration techniques often hold enlightenment as their ultimate goal, most teachers of such techniques warn that their techniques require many years of disciplined practice to produce any progress toward full human development.

Many of the great teachers in India are acknowledging that the TM technique represents a revival in understanding of the most effective meditation technique. In response to the question why India is in such a mess if the TM technique produces such strength in people, Maharishi answers, "They don't practice the TM technique in India. They may have been talking about the goal, but doing nothing practical and effective to get there."

Contemplative techniques comprise the second principle category of meditation methods other than the TM technique. When most Westerners describe what they believe meditation to be, they describe the contemplative process. Contemplation involves thinking about an important idea or question, (i.e., God, love, Who am I?) in a free and unconstrained manner. Distinctly different from problem solving, contemplation is usually practiced by philosophers and monks. While contemplation may broaden intellectual horizons or make a nice mood, apparently it does not foster the physiological changes which occur during TM practice. If the TM technique may be compared to diving to the mind's quiet depths, contemplation involves exploring the mind's active surface level. Contemplation does not seem to hold any of the dangers of concentrative techniques, but does achieve ends wholly different from those resulting from the TM technique. The effects of contemplation remain confined to intellectual understanding or a pleasant feeling, while the TM technique promotes comprehensive and balanced growth of the whole individual.

These distinctions between the TM technique and concentrative and contemplative techniques may seem on the surface like nit-picking, but in fact these distinctions are crucial. If a person starts contemplating or concentrating when he sits to practice the TM technique, he is practicing it improperly and will not experience its benefits. He may even get a headache or otherwise feel uncomfortable. The TM technique is uncontrived. It simply permits a person to make use of the mind's natural tendency to gain the state of restful alertness. Because the TM technique simply unfolds an innate capability of the mind and body, it works from the first moments of instruction. In their studies, Glueck and Levine found that often the same changes which occur after months of practice also occur the first time a person practices the TM technique. The immediate results of the TM technique stand in sharp contrast to the promises of results after decades practicing some concentrative and contemplative techniques.

The Japanese neuropsychiatrists Kasamatsu and Hirai studied brain wave changes in Zen monks with varying degrees of experience with Zen meditation. The researchers found four distinct changes in brain wave patterns among the monks during the meditation period. These changes were: (1) the appearance of 10–12 cps alpha waves, (2) an increase in the alpha amplitude, (3) a decrease in the alpha frequency to predominantly 8–10 cps brain waves, (4) and the appearance of 4–7 cps rhythmical theta waves. Further research demonstrated that the more years a subject has spent in Zen training, the more likely are pronounced brain wave changes during meditation. The monks practicing their meditation for less than five years tended to show only the first category of brain wave changes. On the other hand, monks practicing their meditation for over 20 years consistently showed the third and fourth phases of these brain wave changes. In addition, the Zen master's evaluation of each monk's spiritual progress closely paralleled the degree to which each monk showed the advanced stages of these brain wave changes during his meditations. The more spiritually advanced the monk, the more likely were third- and fourth-stage brain wave changes to appear. This study is significant because *research has shown that people practicing the TM technique often show stage three and four brain wave changes within just a few weeks after beginning the* TM *program.*

This EEG research points out very clearly that Zen meditation, which involves forms of concentration, may produce profound effects only after many years of disciplined practice. Few other meditation techniques have been studied thoroughly, but all the evidence to date clearly indicates that the TM technique produces far greater effects much more quickly than any other meditation technique. Moreover, TM is not of the "most superficial" meditations or a "simpleton's form of discipline," as some have unwittingly described it. What distinguishes TM from other techniques is that it involves no effort, contrivance, or intention to accomplish anything. It works naturally by making use of the mind's tendency to seek a least excited state automatically. Other techniques may only begin to work when a person gets so tired of trying to concentrate that he gives up. At this point, the mind's tendency to settle down can take over and the person can slip into the state of restful alertness. Because the TM technique makes use of the mind's natural tendency from the beginning, it involves no wasted effort and produces effects immediately.

I am fond of one of Maharishi's analogies to illustrate the difference between TM and other meditation techniques. If a person in New York wants to go to Los Angeles, he can choose many ways of getting there. He could walk, get on a Greyhound, hop a train, fly in a prop plane, or take a jet. All these means would get a person to Los Angeles, eventually. All meditation techniques aim at producing restful alertness and unfolding enlightenment. Many techniques may eventually work, but the TM program is the jet!

Interest in the TM technique among scientists all over the world has prompted some researchers such as Boston cardiologist Herbert Benson to try to come up with a laboratory analogue of the TM technique. Benson published some of the first research on the effects of the TM technique, so a comparison of the TM technique and Benson's relaxation technique is particularly interesting.

The Benson Relaxation Technique

Benson began research on the TM technique in 1969, when he noticed that TM practitioners consistently have blood pressures in the low normal range. He foresaw the TM program as potentially useful for the 24 million people suffering from high blood pressure. In collaboration with Dr. Wallace, Dr. Benson published one of the landmark studies on the TM technique, "The Physiological Effects of Meditation," in the February 1972 issue of *Scientific American*. What Dr. Benson gradually recognized was that everyone has the natural capacity to gain the state of restful alertness and that the TM technique simply permits a person to make use of that natural ability.

Apparently intrigued by the universality of the TM technique, Dr. Benson set out to see whether he could come up with a different technique for producing the same effects. He did some reading on meditation and relaxation techniques and finally developed a method which he claims combines various elements from such diverse practices as Zen and Yoga meditation, Western prayer methods, and secular relaxation exercise. His method involves four components: a mental device that "should be a constant stimulus" with "fixed gazing at an object also suitable," a passive attitude, decreased muscle tonus, and a quiet environment. He suggests specifically that a person sit comfortably in a quiet room, close the eyes, relax his muscles, and repeat the word "one" with each exhalation of breath.

The difference between the TM technique and Benson's technique should be clear from the outset. Typical of many concentration techniques that involve noticing the breath or counting the breath over and over again, the Benson technique prescribes repeating a sound with each breath. Because the Benson technique demands concentration, a quiet environment would be necessary, unlike the TM technique, which could be practiced while sitting in Times Square. In order to get started with the Benson technique, a person must try to relax his muscles. Because the TM technique is wholly natural, no "priming the pump" of relaxation is necessary. Within the first minutes of practicing the TM technique, most people notice their muscles relaxing automatically. These differences in method distinguish the TM technique from Benson's concentration technique, but do the two techniques produce the same effects?

The answer is simply no. Scientific research does show clearly that the TM technique and the Benson technique do not produce the same effects. Furthermore, Benson's written statement that all meditation techniques produce the same effects is surprising, especially from a scientist, because no research exists on all meditation techniques.

A major difference between the TM technique and Benson's concerns the level of rest elicited by the two techniques. During the TM technique, oxygen consumption drops by an average of 17 per cent (16–18 per cent), as shown in three separate studies. Benson reports an average reduction of 11.5 per cent (10–13 per cent) during his procedure, a drop comparable with measurements made upon other concentrative techniques. Akishige found an average 10 per cent drop in oxygen consumption among novice Zen meditators.

Dhanaraj reported a 10.3 per cent drop in oxygen consumption during the yoga posture, *shavasan,* performed lying down with eyes closed. Oxygen consumption drops by an average of 11.5 per cent during sleep. These data indicate that Benson's and other concentration techniques can elicit a drop in oxygen consumption roughly equal to that of sleep. The TM technique, on the other hand, produces a drop in oxygen consumption much greater than that occurring during sleep and, what is more important, in combination with other significant changes.

Brain wave studies also distinguish the TM technique from Benson's concentration technique. As part of his three-year study of the TM technique at the Institute of Living, research psychiatrist Dr. Bernard Glueck conducted sophisticated EEG studies on meditators practicing the TM technique as well as on people practicing other meditation techniques. At the conclusion of his study, he noted that several meditation techniques, including some subjects trained to do the Benson technique, produce some physiological changes similar to those which occur during the TM technique. He reports, however, that they are less consistent than the changes accompanying the TM technique, and that the brain wave changes are not comparable with those produced by TM meditation. Synchrony and coherence of brain wave activity, along with a large increase in low-frequency brain waves, distinguish that state of awareness produced by the TM technique. According to Dr. Glueck, other techniques rarely show any synchrony of brain wave activity, and "the density of the alpha waves produced with other techniques is considerably less that that seen with the TM technique." Dr. Glueck reported, in the July/August 1975 issue of *Comprehensive Psychiatry,* "As observed in our laboratory, TM would seem to produce a maximum effect more rapidly than any of the other techniques."[3]

Psychologist Richard Lewis at the Lawrence County Mental Health Clinic in New Castle, Pennsylvania, recently completed physiological and behavioral research comparing the TM technique and Benson's technique. The Pennsylvania Governor's Justice Committee funded the study. Thirteen volunteer outpatients learned the Benson technique while an equal number began the TM program. Lewis measured the galvanic skin response (GSR) of all subjects three weeks after they began their respective techniques. Over a seven-day period, he recorded the GSR of each subject's daily meditation sessions and then averaged these readings for each subject. GSR, as already noted, decreases with anxiety or stress and increases in proportion to the degree of relaxation. The mean rise in skin resistance for each Benson subject was only 25 K. (Kilohms), while each TM subject showed a mean rise of 138 K. The low changes of GSR among the Benson subjects is typical of measurements reported in scientific literature for people who are instructed to relax with eyes closed. In contrast, the much greater increase in GSR during the TM technique indicates a profound reduction in anxiety and a state of very deep relaxation.

Other objective indices and the subjective reports of the participants further highlight significant differences between these two techniques. Only one subject in the Benson group was able to reduce his need for psychotropic medication, while in the TM group, all ten of the subjects who had been on prescriptions ceased their use of tranquilizers. As reported by the subjects and their families, control over impulsive behavior, especially outbursts of anger and abuse of drugs, improved in the TM group but not in the Benson group. Finally, and most importantly, after six weeks the Benson group was extremely bored with the practice and all had discontinued it. In contrast, 12 of the 13 subjects practicing the TM technique still were meditating regularly after eight months.

Two dropouts from the Benson technique went on to take up the TM program. One subject demonstrated a rise in GSR from 18 K. with the Benson technique to 139 K. with the TM technique, while the other showed a similarly dramatic increase from 19 K. to 141 K. Subjectively they reported such comments as, "The Benson technique is a bore....The TM technique is much deeper....The TM program makes quite a difference."

In addition, the volunteers practicing the TM technique showed significant decreases in psychopathology, as measure by a standard psychological test. Twelve of the TM subjects had blood pressure higher than normal prior to beginning the program. After six weeks, all of these subjects showed a drop in blood pressure into the normal range. Researcher Lewis concluded "The results indicate that the TM program appears to be much more effective as a treatment procedure than the Benson relaxation response. Certainly more research is needed to substantiate our finding, but the preliminary results are certainly impressive."

From a medical standpoint, I have become deeply concerned about people practicing untested meditation techniques dreamed up in laboratories. Scientific research has shown that sounds have specific vibrational effects which can enhance or damage the growth of various forms of life, from plants to human beings. Dr. Luthe, the founder of autogenic training, persistently warned against the indiscriminate use of untried phrases in meditation-type exercises, which he noted in some cases produced unwanted side effects, including dizziness, dissociation, nausea, and severe anxiety attacks. With the Benson laboratory technique, there is the possibility that it may, in the long run, prove harmful to some people. Medicine simply does not know the long-term effects upon the nervous system of using any sound indiscriminately or other untried phrases as part of a laboratory meditation technique. Unlike Benson's technique, however, the TM program utilizes time-tested sounds, or mantras, whose effects are completely known for the individual; this is the value of tradition. I have confidence in the safety of the TM technique because medicne has had a chance to observe the effects of a person practicing it for many years.

My experience, and that of Dr. Glueck, has been identical to that of psychologist Lewis. After one month or less, people doing the Benson technique frequently become disenchanted and discontinue the practice. If they mistakenly think that the TM program and the Benson technique are the same, they may not go on to take the TM program. This would be a great loss, for they would be losing out on something potentially valuable to their lives. Research reports indicate the superiority of the TM program, and although scientific research alone seems unable to express fully the holistic effect of the TM program and its power to transform the individual's life, this transformation, as experienced personally by each meditator, will always be the ultimate validation of the TM technique. It is important, therefore, that the general public becomes aware of the great value in taking the TM course and follow-up program and recognizes that there is no effective substitute for this experience.

In his recent book, *Powers of the Mind*, Adam Smith made a very interesting comment that applies to the Benson technique. He informally polled ten people to see whether they would choose the TM program or a technique developed at Harvard Medical School. All ten chose the TM technique. Their comment was, "What does the Harvard Medical School know about meditation?" What indeed.

Alpha Wave Biofeedback

Several years ago, another laboratory meditation-type procedure known as "alpha wave biofeedback" received a good deal of media attention. Initially thought to be the key to "electronic enlightenment," alpha biofeedback became popular in the early 1970s but has begun to disappear from the scientific literature as researchers have discovered its limitations. Biofeedback is a procedure through which the activity of an involuntary bodily function is monitored and reported to a trainee. Alpha biofeedback utilizes an EEG to measure the brain's production of alpha waves. With an additional device connected to the EEG machine, a person can vary the loudness of a tone by increasing or decreasing the amount of alpha waves he produces. The amplitude of the tone gives the person information, "feedback," about the amount of alpha waves that he may be producing at any particular moment. By using this device, researchers tried to teach people to control their production of alpha waves, because some research has correlated alpha waves with relaxation and feelings of well-being. Presumably, people were supposed to learn to maintain those mental states which enabled them to produce more alpha waves. The researchers hoped that after ten sessions with a feedback machine a person would have learned to produce the alpha state on demand and would no longer need the machine in order to induce relaxation.

Despite initially promising results, alpha researchers ran into four critical snags. The first snag explains why public interest in alpha biofeedback has also dissipated. The researchers discovered that production of alpha waves does not always lead to relaxation. In fact, a person can be highly tense and still show significant production of alpha waves per se. Second, research has demonstrated that many people have little success with increasing their alpha waves using feedback equipment. Some subjects show no more alpha waves after 20 hours of training than they do after five minutes of training. Third, alpha subjects experience great difficulty in transferring their training to environments outside the laboratory. They literally become locked to the EEG feedback machine. Fourth, synchrony of brain waves across the whole brain, rather than the simple production of low frequency waves from just a few points on the skull, appears to be the major EEG correlate of the transcendental state. Alpha biofeedback does not result in significant synchrony of brain waves. In short, alpha wave biofeedback increases neither ease nor order in the functioning of the nervous system.

Though alpha wave biofeedback fell short of its initial promise, other feedback techniques, aimed not at supplanting meditation but at helping relieve specific symptoms, are proving useful. For example, a biofeedback technique which teaches a person to raise hand temperature is helping in the treatment of migraine headaches. Biofeedback techniques are also being used for the treatment of chronically tense muscles and Reynaud's disease, a neurovascular disorder that causes poor blood circulation to the fingers. Preliminary attempts to reduce high blood pressure through biofeedback technology, on the other hand, have proved very disappointing in clinical trials. These clinical uses of biofeedback are much more conservative in their goals than were the initial claims for alpha wave biofeedback.

The alpha wave biofeedback craze appears to have been a case in which the popular press publicized a discovery before all the data were in. Amidst claims of "electronic enlightenment" many electronic firms began mass marketing cheap "alpha wave machines." These machines were generally quite ineffective and even contributed to such harmful side effects as clinical nystagmus (involuntary rapid movements of the eyeball). A good alpha wave machine costs several hundred dollars, which makes it rather impractical for biofeedback subjects trained in a laboratory setting to purchase a machine for home use. Besides, research on the TM technique indicates that, when properly tuned, nature's "alpha wave machine" is far superior.

There is a powerful lesson to be learned from the superiority of the TM technique to alpha wave biofeedback. If it were suddenly announced in the newspapers that a machine had been developed in the laboratories of UCLA, Harvard, or MIT which could produce a new state of consciousness — a state of restful alertness involving dramatic changes in oxygen consumption, blood lactate, GSR, and EEG, and producing cumulative benefits to health, family life, job performance, and general well-being—very few people would raise skeptical eyebrows. There would be headlines and a tremendous rush to buy these new machines, even if they each cost hundreds of dollars. Why? Because most people today have become indiscriminate consumers of technology in their search for more achievement and pleasure. But, in the whirl of spiraling technology, many people have lost much of their respect for the natural, for the tremendous potential which nature has designed into the human biomachinery and which lies waiting to be tapped. It comes as a shock to some people, consciously or as an unconscious resistance, that the TM technique can produce so many beneficial and profound changes on every level of physiology, psychology, and sociology. The revival of the TM technique is the revival of nature's supreme wisdom for relieving the straining gears of mankind's stressed biomachinery.

In general, people lack confidence in their innate capability to promote their own psychological growth. They tend to look for help outside themselves, to the psychiatrist, to some machine, or to the newest do-it-yourself therapy book. In fact, the human body is already equipped to heal itself and unfold its full capacity for happiness. The TM technique enables a person to take advantage of this natural capability and maximize psychological growth without the need for therapists, do-it-yourself psychotherapy books, or expensive electronic gadgetry. The TM technique permits nature to do its own retuning and rewiring of the human biomachinery. It does not take many months of the TM program for many patients to begin recognizing that nature spent millions of years evolving the human mind for much more than struggle and fleeting happiness. The TM technique permits nature to unfold all the potential lying dormant in its greatest evolutionary achievement. In getting back in tune with nature through the TM program, a person can regain appreciation of nature's larger design for the expansion of happiness. The concept of enlightenment loses its connotation as the "electronic high" of the space age and becomes a natural goal for anyone wishing to enjoy the full glory of living.

The TM Technique and Prayer

When I discuss the TM program in terms of getting back in tune with the larger design of nature, people often ask about the relation between the TM program and religion. How do the benefits of the TM program compare with those of religion? Is TM a form of prayer?

The TM technique is not a religion. It is a simple mental procedure for gaining a state of deep rest coupled with heightened alertness. TM instructors confine themselves to teaching this technique, and in their professional work offer no codes about how people should behave toward other people or how they should behave in relation to any God.

The TM technique is not a form of prayer. Communication is the essential goal of prayer, and, for it to be meaningful, a person must have some purpose or intention in communication. In whatever way a person prays, he addresses himself to someone or something. He hopes that he will be heard and receive a response, or he simply takes joy in giving thanks. The correct practice of the TM technique involves no such address or supplication. The TM technique is competely not-intentional; a person practicing it does not try to accomplish anything. Any sense of intellectual intention during the TM technique gets in the way of the correct practice of the technique.

When both prayer and the TM technique are properly understood, it can be seen that there is no conflict between them. Because the TM technique produces physiological changes that strengthen the whole individual, it may strengthen a person's ability to pray and lead a religious life of his own choosing. People of all faiths—priests, rabbis, ministers—and even atheists have endorsed the TM program publicly for its contribution to human well-being. Donald Craig Drummon, Presbyterian Minister, writes to his fellow sisters and brothers in Christ:

> In the past seven years of practicing Transcendental Meditation I have found nothing in the daily practice of this very simple and natural technique that detracts from the Gospel, from faith and obedience to our Lord Jesus Christ. Rather, my own experience has been one of deepening faith, an opening of the heart to His grace, to the love of God, and the power of the Holy Spirit for life. This easily learned and practiced system of meditation involves no commitment to Maharishi Mahesh Yogi, the one who has made this meditation available to the world, nor to the movement that gives instruction in the technique. Neither is there any change in faith, life-style, or diet.

Rabbi Raphael Levine, Rabbi Emeritus of Temple De Hirsh Sinai in Seattle, Washington, writes that the TM technique "has nothing to do with religion except as the easiest technique I have yet discovered for making religion become more alive, more meaningful, by helping people to live the way their religion teaches them to live—on the level of love and self-giving... achieving this miracle for us not by the disciplines of self-denial, but by the joy and happiness of self-enlargement, the enlargement of our state of consciousness; and the miracle is that it works!"

In several monasteries, the TM technique has proven so helpful to the practice of worship that nearly all the monks practice the technique. At my teacher training course, a Jesuit priest became a qualified instructor in the TM program. Father Placide Gaboury of the University of Sudbury, Ontario, writes: "I am a jesuit priest teaching philosophy and religion at the University of Sudbury in Canada — a jesuit-run institution. I am also a teacher of the Transcendental Meditation technique, which is to my knowledge the most useful, effortless and thoroughly efficient technique now available for developing the individual's full mental and physical potential." He went on to say:

> But I am not the only priest practicing TM. At the University of Sudbury there are eight jesuits including the President and Registrar and one Episopalian minister and one secular priest practicing the technique which they find extremely useful in freeing the nervous system of its stresses and strains and thereby clearing the mind and broadening one's awareness of life. There are also three parish priests now meditating in the Sudbury region. In Montreal and Quebec City, we have quite a few jesuits meditating, and our Father Provincial not only encourages the technique, but is very interested in seeing as many jesuits as possible practice this technique. . . .

The TM technique no more replaces prayer than does any natural part of a person's daily routine that strengthens his life.

When I first began prescribing the TM program, I wondered whether it might be objectionable to several of the devout athiests whom I was treating. I did meet some resistance when I first suggested it to one of my highly anti-religious patients. I overcame his objections by explaining that the TM program involves no beliefs, is not a form of prayer, and works physiologically. My patient, who had been suffering from anxiety attacks, got almost immediate benefit from the technique. Several months later, he told me a bit sheepishly,"I sure was foolish thinking you were going to make me into a Hindu. This technique involves about as much religion as brushing your teeth." Religion is such a personal matter and the TM technique is so universal that athiests seem to find the TM program as simple and useful as devout believers.

What about the physiological effects of the TM technique and prayer? How do they compare? No evidence exists to suggest that prayer, in some ways a quiet form of speech, produces the same physiological changes as does the TM technique. The natural and complete reduction of mental activity during TM meditation seems to be the key to its effectiveness in triggering a state of deep rest coupled with heightened awareness. The mind-set of prayer, in some ways related to contemplative meditation techniques, would presumably sustain a degree of mental activity which would not permit the state of restful alertness to unfold fully. The physiological benefits of TM meditation do not serve to replace but rather enhance the benefits of prayer.

Hypnosis, Relaxation, and Catnapping

Just as some people confuse the TM program with religion, an equally large number seems to believe that the TM technique is a form of hypnosis, just a relaxation exercise, or something similar to a catnap. The evidence that can clarify this confusion deserves consideration. The confusion about the TM technique and hypnosis arises from the belief that the TM technique produces a trance state in which a person loses touch with the world and surrenders his judgement. Scientific research and clinical hypnotherapists have verified that the TM technique is neither related to hypnotic induction nor produces a state even vaguely similar to a hypnotic trance.

Numerous differences distinguish the state of a person practicing the TM technique from that of a person in hypnosis. During the TM technique, a person is not subject to the power of suggestion, as he is during hypnosis. During hypnosis mind-body coordination may be diminished (e.g., a person can eat an onion but taste an orange), while substantial evidence indicates that the TM program increases mind-body coordination. Studies show that during TM practice oxygen consumption drops 16–18 per cent and brain waves become highly synchronous; research shows no such consistent changes during hypnosis. Hypnosis involves belief in the powers of the hypnotherapist, while even a total skeptic can benefit from the TM technique. In short, the TM technique is completely unlike hypnosis both in terms of the effects and the actual mental practice.

The TM technique and hypnosis also differ markedly in their purposes. When a psychiatrist uses hypnosis, it is generally aimed at relieving a particular symptom or changing a maladaptive behavior pattern. Sometimes, self-hypnosis may be used to help people stop smoking, control their weight, or reduce a fear of dental work. When a psychiatrist prescribes the TM technique, it is not as a specific treatment for a specific symptom, but as a means to promote the patient's overall well-being. Because it depends upon suggestion, hypnosis requires repeated reinforcement to sustain symptom relief. Some hypnotherapists, such as Dr. Margaretta K. Bowers, a New York City psychiatrist, have begun prescribing the TM program for their patients in hopes that it will reduce the need for repeated hypnosis to control a particularly painful symptom by gradually healing the emotional wound at the root of that symptom.

The TM technique is also more than a relaxation exercise. A person cannot expect the same benefits from catnapping, taking 10 minutes to lie down on the floor, just getting a good night's sleep, or going to a health spa. Beginning in 1908, Dr. Edmund Jacobson, author of *You Must Relax*, began developing a method of progressive muscular relaxation. Jacobson's techniques are perhaps the best-known and most widely used relaxation exercises. His original techniques, as well as the more widely used abbreviated versions employed by behavior therapists in their relaxation training, essentially involve systematically tensing and relaxing each muscle group in the body. In his study at the Institute of Living, Dr. Glueck compared the effects of the TM technique and progressive muscular relaxation on psychiatric patients. He found that over a three-month test period the patients who learned the TM technique showed very significant improvements, while the group that learned Jacobson's technique demonstrated very little improvement and had a dropout rate close to 70 per cent. Most of them asked to stop by the fourth week because they were bored and, having seen considerably greater progress and enthusiasm in their fellow patients who were meditating, wanted to switch to the TM program.

Jacobson's technique takes longer to learn than the TM technique, and some patients have difficulty achieving even a minimal state of relaxation. The relaxation achieved using Jacobson's progressive relaxation depends on peripheral stimuli from the musculature, which may act on the brain to relax control processes, but reach the brain as very weak third- or fourth-order effects. The TM technique starts in the brain, where it engages the central nervous system directly to reduce mental activity. Relaxation is achieved centrally and then extended to the peripheral musculature. Instead of resting one muscle group at a time, the whole organism relaxes spontaneously.

Physiological evidence clearly distinguishes the effects of the TM technique from relaxation exercises and catnapping. Neurophysiologist J. P. Banquet demonstrated that the brain wave changes during TM meditation are different from those occurring during relaxation, drowsiness, catnapping, and deep sleep. Biochemical research adds further evidence to Banquet's work. Wallace showed that blood lactate drops three times faster during the TM technique than during relaxation or sleep. This precipitous drop in blood lactate is another indication that the TM technique produces a deeper level of rest more rapidly than sleep or ordinary relaxation. In an article recently published in the *Proceedings of the Endocrine Society,* Dr. Ron Jevning and his co-workers compared measurements of plasma cortisol, the body's major stress hormone, during the TM technique, simple relaxation, and sleep. Cortisol levels stayed the same during simple relaxation and showed no specific relationship during the stages of sleep. During the TM technique, however, cortisol levels showed a significant decrease. Jevning also found that long-term TM practitioners showed much lower plasma cortisol levels during normal daily activity than the average person, a finding which suggests that meditators tend to be more stress-free than the average person. Another dramatic difference discovered by the Jevning group between the TM technique and sleep was reflected in measures of plasma prolactin. Plasma prolactin remains stable during the TM technique and rises after the period spent practicing the technique. The opposite is true of sleep; plasma prolactin rises during sleep and decreases after awakening. This is another apparent sign of the unique bodily quiescence achieved through TM meditation.

Upon hearing that the TM technique produces rest deeper than sleep, some people wonder if it will replace sleep. It will not. However, it does often relieve the need that some people have for catnapping. Most people look forward to having 20 minutes twice daily to do the TM technique because it is pleasurable, restful, and enlivening. I find that taking time for my TM sessions adds so much to the rest of my day that it actually saves time. It is not uncommon for people to note that the TM program keeps them from getting tired in the evenings. Instead of falling asleep in front of a TV at 9 P.M., people find themselves wide awake for the late show, or work, or whatever they might like to do in the evenings.

EST, Arica, and Silva Mind Control

The TM program is not the only self-development program to receive attention lately. Others include Erhard Seminar Training (EST), Arica, and Silva Mind Control. How does the TM program compare with these other self-development programs? For the average individual, trying to distinguish between the various programs can be quite confusing, for they all promise benefits which sound very much alike. What I use as a criterion for whether or not I can, as a physician, recommend a program, is scientific research. Over 300 scientific studies, many published in the most prestigious scientific journals, have defined how the TM technique works and what benefits a person can expect from the TM program. When I refer a patient to the local TM center, I am confident that my patient will learn a specific technique that produces well-defined positive changes in the functioning of his mind and body. I am also confident that the TM technique will not cause any negative effects even after many years of daily practice. Though Erhard Seminar Training (EST), and Silva Mind Control have been around for several years, the scientific literature shows a conspicuous absence of any studies validating the benefit these programs claim to produce. Consequently, I cannot in good faith recommend these programs to my patients.

Does this absence of research mean that these programs produce no effects? No, but it does raise some question about what a person will get out of any of the unresearched programs. For example, EST has become somewhat popular lately with its promise of helping people escape self-limiting belief systems. Two weekends of EST training may be exhilarating but are not sufficient for lasting growth. I think more and more people are coming to recognize that real growth is natural, systematic, and takes time.

The TM program has my respect for not promising overnight transformation based on sudden insights, but instead pointing out the need for measurable change in how the body and brain function in order for real growth to occur. The EST program seems to be heavily oriented toward a person growing on the basis of purely psychological changes, i.e., "geting it."[4] Yet this approach to personality change from psychoanalysis onwards has not held up under scientific scrutiny. Research has just not shown insight therapies to be particularly valuable in promoting long-term growth. Psychologist Daniel Fillmer, chairman of the Hawaiian Board of Practicing Psychologists, believes that the real benefit in EST may be in helping a person regain a sense of community. This may or may not be true. The fact remains that comprehensive psychological growth requires equally comprehensive physiological integration on the order of what the TM program fosters.

Arica is another program which has recently received some attention. Founded about five years ago by the Bolivian Oscar Ichazo, Arica training involves a for-day intensive course in residence (cost $750–$800) at which a person learns an extensive smorgasbord of "psychocalisthenics." One such exercise involves two people sitting face to face across from one another and staring into each others left eyeball. In the exercise called the "Desert," the trainee spends two days completely isolated in a room. These mental and physical exercises undoubtedly produce some effects, but what kind? Answers to this question must await scientific research, if any on the Arica program is under way. By comparison with the TM program, Arica training is elaborate and expensive. What the complexity of the Arica program can add to the benefits of experiencing the state of restful alertness twice a day through the TM program remains to be seen.

Research clearly indicates that the state of restful alertness promotes comprehensive growth and that the

TM technique allows a person to gain this state easily, simply, and naturally. Great scientific discoveries are simple, not complex; the principle of vaccination is a good example. Just by making use of the body's natural ability to develop resistance to disease, medicine has conquered diseases that killed and crippled millions. Similarly, the simplicity of the TM technique is one of its principle strengths. A brief period spent practicing the TM technique morning and evening is sufficient for almost anyone to experience its wide range of benefits.

Yet another self-development program to receive some attention lately is Silva Mind Control, founded nine years ago by the Texan Jose Silva. What distinguishes this program from others is its emphasis on mental feats such as transmitting psychic cures and the like. The training sessions, which like EST requires four entire days, involve considerable suggestion. For example, training involves frequent repetition of such phrases as, "My increasing mental faculties are for serving humanity better....I will never allow myself to develop diabetes, glaucoma, diseases of the heart or circulatory system, or the disease known as cancer." This appears to be nothing more than a form of self-hypnosis. Granted, modern science has much to learn about the powers of the mind, and some excellent research on parapsychology is under way in several laboratories around the world, but in all the scientific publications I have read on this subject, Silva Mind Control never appears.

The Silva people offer an intricate theory which attempts to explain how to increase mental capacity by producing certain kinds of brain waves; yet no published research exists to corroborate this claim. Furthermore, no existing research correlates alpha or theta waves (which Silvans claim their techniques enable people to control) with psychic abilities. I am surprised that with their scientific jargon, the Silva people make no mention of brain wave coherence, which has recently been shown to be far more important to the meditative state than any one frequency of brain waves appearing at any one point on the scalp.

The reasoned approach to human development inherent in the TM program contrasts sharply with the Silva program. The TM program uses scientific research, not scientific jargon, to help people understand how it works and what they can expect. The TM program makes no claims of psychic muscle-building, but does offer comprehensive individual growth. A person impressed by promises of psychic feats, such as those claimed by Silvans, is like the patient who is very caught up in the stress cycle with all the symptoms of anxiety, headaches, and poor job performance, but gets all excited about sex therapy. Far more important than having one positive relationship, although it is reinforcing, is the balanced growth that would enable all relationships to blossom along with every other aspect of the personality. Scientific research indicates beyond any doubt that the TM program promotes balanced growth. Maharishi has pointed out that if psychic abilities are inherent faculties of the human mind, these abilities may be expected to unfold naturally as a person practices the TM program for a period of years. Parapsychological research on long-term TM practitioners may be in order. This sensible, scientific approach, characteristic of the entire TM program, keeps the whole area of psychic abilities in perspective. In this way, Maharishi emphasizes genuine and measurable growth rather than flights of fantasy.

I have two additional concerns about some of these new self-development programs. First, nearly all of them have been conjured up recently by individuals who try to draw on a variety of ancient and modern methods of human development; a unifying tradition to assure the safety and correct use of these various techniques is conspicuously absent. When a technique has been time tested, it deserves some degree of confidence even without modern research evidence. I have no confidence in a technique that has neither tradition nor the support of scientific research. A person who gets involved in such a program should note that the long-term effects are unknown. Getting involved in some of these other programs may be a bit like getting on a train with an unclear destination. My second concern also relates to the importance of tradition. The TM program leads to a specific result from long-term practice—enlightenment. Maharishi discusses this state as a person living a fully developed inner life and a fully developed outer life. The basic qualities of the enlightened person are definable and open to scientific research. Some investigations are already under way with the study of enlightenment physiologically, psychologically and sociologically.

The TM Program: Westernized Hinduism?

When I discuss the value of tradition standing behind the TM program, questions about the tradition inevitably arise. Where does the TM program come from? Is the TM program just a Westernized form of Hinduism? People generally believe that the TM program is Westernized Hinduism for three reasons: (1) Maharishi is a Hindu monk, (2) the TM instructor performs a brief ceremony before teaching, and (3) other yogis have come to the U.S. to teach meditation techniques with all the trappings of Hinduism. Each of these issues deserves consideration.

Great contributions to the world are often made by people of profound religious convictions. Does Maharishi's religious affiliation make all his contributions to the world a part of Hinduism? No more so than the contributions made by other religious persons. Gregor Mendel, the father of genetics, was an Augustinian priest, but genetics is not thought to be Catholic.

Albert Einstein was a Jew, but the theory of relativity is not Jewish.

The TM technique has its origin in the Vedic tradition, which antedates all modern religions including Hinduism. For thousands of years, the TM technique has been largely preserved by a few monks. Maharishi's teacher, the great Indian sage Swami Brahmananda Saraswati, revived the ancient Vedic understanding that gaining the least excited state of consciousness is so natural and beneficial that a technique to do so should be available to all. Maharishi brought the TM technique out into the world and founded the Science of Creative Intelligence to make the whole phenomenon of growth to enlightenment accessible to modern science.

What about the ceremony? Prior to teaching a person how to practice the TM technique, the TM instructor performs a three-minute non-religious ceremony of gratitude to the great teachers who have preserved the TM technique in its integrity throughout history. The ceremony is performed in Sanskrit and the person about to learn the technique may witness it but does not participate. As an expression of good will, the person learning the TM technique brings half a dozen fresh flowers, two sweet fruits, and a new white handkerchief to be used by the teacher in performing the ceremony. No one need fear that the ceremony is a surreptitious conversion or a mystical rite; it is not.

Is the ceremony an essential part of instruction in the TM program? Does it serve an important purpose? These same questions might be asked about the Hippocratic oath, which medical students recite before becoming physicians. This oath begins, "I swear by Apollo the Physician and Aesculapius, and Health, and All-Heal, and all the gods and goddesses, that, according to my ability and judgment, I will keep this oath...." and goes on to outline the highest ideals and ethical principles of medical practice. Some hardened cynics might argue that the Hippocratic oath means nothing.

However, this oath to uphold the age-old traditions of medicine draws the physician's heart and mind to the most noble spirit of his profession. If physicians would recite with sincerity this three-minute oath before office hours each day, the practice of medicine would undoubtedly improve.

By performing a three-minute ceremony of gratitude to the tradition of great teachers from which the TM program comes, the TM instructor improves his ability to teach. The brief ceremony reminds him of his responsiblity to teach as he was taught, and he collects his mind for the work at hand. This ceremony of gratitude enlivens the teacher's mind and heart with the ideals of this age-old tradition of knowledge and undoubtedly contributes to each teacher's dedication and success. For the person watching the ceremony, it serves as a reminder that the TM technique comes from an ancient tradition and was not dreamed up in a laboratory at Harvard. Most people find the ceremony beautiful and delightful. Those people who do not like ceremonies are comforted by the fact that it is very brief and they in no way participate in it.

Some people still confuse the TM program with groups teaching meditation techniques loaded with Hindu trappings. There is the Divine Light group, which worships a boy guru. There is the Hare Krishna group whose members wear orange robes and chant on street corners. There is a Swami group that teaches yoga classes. And there are many lesser known groups and gurus. None of these groups teach the TM technique, and the TM organization has no affiliation with any of them. None of the techniques taught by these groups have been studied scientifically. I think that the differences between the TM organization and these other groups are so obvious that people are confusing them less and less as the TM program becomes more and more well known.

However, a new source of confusion has begun to appear. Imitation TM.

The TM Technique or Brand X

It has become clear over the past several years that the TM program represents the standard of excellence to which all other self-development programs aspire. Consequently, the TM program has become the prime target for imitators. TV personality Merv Griffin once commented to Maharishi that imitators are a "flattering sign of success." This may be true, but the general public should know how to distinguish the imitators from the real thing.

The TM program is taught only under the auspices of the World Plan Executive Council and its associated educational service divisions such as the International Meditation Society. This non-profit education organization is responsible for the activity of the thousands of qualified TM instructors teaching through centers for TM instruction all over the world. I have recently seen ads which promise bargain TM instruction by mail order or other means. "Save the $125 course fee; learn TM at home or in one evening for only $5.95" some ads will say. I have also seen some groups advertising what they call the "original" Transcendental Meditation technique for just a few dollars or even for free. Some of these imitators may be well meaning; others may be out to make a fast dollar. In either case, the old sayings "Buyer beware!" and "You get what you pay for" should be kept in mind. When I talk about the TM program unfolding a person's full capacity for happiness, I am referring only to the technique taught by qualified TM instructors who teach the standard course that Maharishi has designed.

The steady and rapid expansion of interest in the TM program has begun raising questions in some people's minds about the financial aspects of the TM organization. Adam Smith called the TM program the Mc-Donald's or Howard Johnson's of the meditation business. I have yet to meet a member of the TM organization who is out to corner the meditation market. From a very practical viewpoint, the TM organization offers a unique meditation technique which works. Its cost is minimal, the benefits great, and the teaching procedure standardized. In this light, the phenomenal increase in the number of TM practitioners each year is not surprising. Yet, it has also become clear to me that no one works for the TM organization to get rich.

All course fees are sent to the national organization, which then returns half to the local centers to cover salaries and operating expenses. A full-time teacher makes about seven or eight thousand dollars a year. The other half is used to support administrative overhead, advanced teacher training, expansion, videotaping, and printing material. Teachers attend in-residence advanced training courses for two six-week periods each year to ensure maximum skill in teaching and professional development. The TM movement recently purchased Parson's College in Fairfield, Iowa, and established the main campus of Maharishi International University. To maintain tax-exempt status, the TM organization undergoes a meticulous audit every year. When I spoke to one of the trustees (non-salaried as are most leaders of the TM movement) of the TM organization in the U.S., he mentioned that the organization already involved many millions of dollars. He added, however, that billions would be necessary for the TM program to be enjoyed by all.

To some people, the prospect of billions of dollars spent on making the TM program available to tens of millions of people sounds frightening. To a physician familiar with what widespread practice of the TM program can mean for the nation's health, it sounds hopeful. Last year, Americans spent over 115 billion dollars on health care, and many statistics show that the national health level did not improve. If even one billion dollars were spent to make the TM program available to 10 per cent of the people whom I have called average middle-class neurotics, I would anticipate savings of billions of dollars in health bills alone.

Maharishi has designed a World Plan and an organization to make the TM program universally available. Like all great men, he has his detractors. People are especially skeptical of any man who seems motivated only by the good of the world. Yet, it does not take much contact with Maharishi to recognize that here is in fact a man who has the good of the whole world at heart in everything he does. His intent is simple: sharing. He has the joy of living the full glory of life. He shares that joy by offering the world a simple program which can unfold any person's full capacity for happiness.

4

The Psychophysiology of Happiness

Snoopy:	(Bouncing gleefully past Charlie Brown and Lucy, who watch chagrined)
Lucy:	Look at that crazy dog!
Charlie Brown:	I sure wish I could be that happy all the time.
Lucy:	Not me. It's too hard to feel sorry for yourself when you're happy.

What has Schulz captured in this cartoon that lets most people get a glimpse of themselves and laugh? Charlie Brown represents everyone ready to admit how much happier he would like to be. Lucy is everyone else who finds reasons, sensible or not, for not chasing after what "realistic" people know to be "unrealistic." And Snoopy bounces around gleefully telling us that full and lasting happiness is natural, at least for a crazy dog.

Philosophers, clergy, and politicians have passed the questions of individual and social happiness back and forth to one another like a football for thousands of years. One group says wealth is the key to happiness, while another says that happiness lies in a simple life with few comforts. Does love assure happiness as some people believe? Fulfillment of duty to family, country, or God has been called the path to happiness as have the return to nature, to sensual pleasures, and to simply "being yourself." Though ideas about where to find happiness have been many, happiness has remained elusive for most people. In the last several decades, society has passed the "happiness football" to psychiatry and said "Here, catch! You're a doctor, see what you can do with it." Psychiatry has not done too well with the happiness football either. People still expect a poker face or frown more readily than a smile, and the happy person is still thought to be a bit unrealistic or at least deserving of suspicion. Within the past decade, however, a new branch of science has come to the aid of psychiatry in trying to solve the mystery of happiness for all. This new science is called psychophysiology.

What's that? *Psycho* refers to the mind, *physiology* to the functioning of the body. Psychophysiology is the study of how mental and physical states depend upon and influence one another. Perhaps the best known psychophysiological discovery is that when a person tells a lie, his skin will show a decreased resistance to the flow of a minute electrical current. Thus, the lie detector test. In 1970, psychophysiologist Elmer Greene of the Menninger Clinic in Kansas summarized the basic postulate of psychophysiological research when he wrote: "Every change in the physiological state is accompanied by an appropriate change in the mental-emotional state, conscious or unconscious is accompanied by an appropriate change in the physiological state."[2]

Maharishi anticipated this idea in 1966 by pointing out that "any state of consciousness is the expression of a corresponding state of the nervous system."[3] Happiness is a mental-emotional state. Therefore, it must have roots in how the body and brain function. Here lies the key to unlocking the mystery of happiness.

Baseline Happiness

Psychophysiologists have begun studying happiness and the closely related experiences of pleasure and excitement. Current research indicates that emotions are monitored in that portion of the brain called the limbic system (already mentioned in conjunction with the stress response). During the course of a single day, the limbic system has millions of momentary fluctuations in pleasure-pain, as well as extended experiences of enjoyment or distress. Memory, apparently stored throughout large regions of the cortex, records this on-going stream of a person's positive (life-supporting) and negative (life-damaging) experiences. The sum of this storehouse of impressions, distinct from moment-to-moment fluctuations in emotional experience, seems to be the basis of a person's degree of happiness.

When an average middle-class neurotic tells me that he's not happy, he does not mean he never experiences any pleasure, or that his life is totally without joy, or that he is always in pain. On the contrary, some patients are troubled by how rapidly and wildly their emotions change at the slightest provocation. The complaint "I'm just not happy" refers to the lack of an underlying stable experience which stands behind the flux of everyday emotions and makes living fully satisfying and worthwhile. A person's degree of happiness refers to his or her baseline experience of living. I like to use the term *baseline happiness* in discussing the growth of happiness for two reasons. Baseline happiness clearly distinguishes this fundamental quality of experience from the flux of everyday emotions. It also helps people conceive of their most basic sense of well-being as an experience that can grow stonger or weaker.

One case of a patient who suffered a minor crisis illustrates the significance of baseline happiness. Dan, a young manager at a large aerospace firm, had seen me four times in two months but had not followed my suggestion to begin the TM program. He "didn't have time." He started seeing me at the insistence of his family doctor, who believed that Dan's ulcer had its origin in anxiety. The day Dan got a memo that his department would receive a 15 per cent increase in workload due to staff cutbacks, he came to my office in a frenzy. "Can't *they* understand that *my* people are already overloaded," he said so angrily that he was about to boil over. "It's easy for *them* to make these decisions and *I'm* supposed to be the fall guy. I'm fed up!" It was clear that Dan would not be able to execute the order effectively and resentment would build up within him and his department. The net psychological result for Dan would be another minus registered in his storehouse of impressions and a weakened baseline happiness.

Several days later, I was giving a lecture at the local TM center on the psychophysiological effects of the TM program. Afterwards, a man in his early thirties came up to me and told me that since he had been practicing the TM program he had noted an increase in his ability to handle pressure. Specifically, he mentioned how he had recently been told that his department would receive an increase in workload due to staff cutbacks. Coincidentally, he worked at the same firm as Dan. I asked him how he handled the situation. He proceeded to tell me about what he called a "very hairy meeting" with all the members of his department. At that meeting, he apparently succeeded in explaining the situation and actually boosting morale to meet the upcoming challenge. The net psychological result for this second executive was the recording of a plus in his storehouse of impressions and a strong reinforcement of his baseline happiness.

What differentiates these two men to begin with is their level of baseline happiness. Due to his weak baseline hapiness, Dan felt the increased workload as the final straw which broke the camel's back. On the other hand, the second executive, secure in his strong baseline happiness, took the workload memo as a challenge. Dan could not feel any challenge because the memo automatically triggered distress which put him into an emotional frenzy. Even if he wanted to, Dan could not take the time to think calmly and creatively. Instead he got caught up in anger, resentment, and the blaming-of-others game. The second executive may have felt some initial concern when he first read the memo, but his baseline happiness sustained his psychophysiological equilibrium. Consequently the memo triggered the flow of creative intelligence rather than distress. He found the inner stability and adaptability necessary to inspire his department. Dan got caught in the stress cycle; the second executive enjoyed the growth cycle. Whether the pressures of living will trigger the stress cycle or the growth cycle depends largely on the strength of a person's baseline happiness.

I find another common experience useful in helping people understand the idea of baseline happiness. Imagine two people at a party; one may enjoy it, the other may not. Why? If a person feels a strong baseline happiness, he is naturally open, relaxed, and able to enjoy the excitement of meeting new people. On the other hand, if a person has a weak baseline happiness, doubts and inhibitions may keep him from enjoying either himself or others. Even before he gets to the party, he may feel anxious instead of excited about meeting new people. The reason alcohol and marijuana are so important at most parties is that few people have a baseline level of happiness sufficiently strong to enjoy either themselves or others without it. The massive ingestion of alcohol, cigarettes, and other mood-elevating drugs is a good index of how much people feel the need for ways of reinforcing their baseline happiness. A strong baseline happiness is important not only to meeting problems effectively but also to an enjoyable experience of everyday living.

Baseline happiness is closely linked with the degree of adaptability, stability, integration, purification, and growth which a person shows in his daily life. The person with a weak baseline happiness depends on his environment for his sense of well-being. He lacks the adaptability and stability necessary to make the best of unexpected or changing situations. If a particularly promising business deal falls through or a week-end does not turn out as expected, he may become angry or depressed. On the other hand, I frequently see in my patients who practice the TM technique how even moderate growth of their baseline happiness enables them to begin taking life's ups and downs in stride.

Accelerating change in all areas of life appears to be the only certainty about the future. Alvin Toffler coined the term *future shock* to denote the impact of this change on the biomachinery of the average person who lacks the adaptability and stability necessary to meet this change comfortably and effectively. The more rapidly humanity races into the future, the more imperative it becomes for each person to develop a strong baseline happiness as an emotional gyroscope to assure well-being in the face of change.

"If I don't keep going, everything is going to collapse" is an unspoken fear of many people with a weak baseline happiness. My patients are typically so caught up in their personal problems that they are incapable of even taking the time to learn what living really means to them and what will make them truly fulfilled. Once a person begins to strengthen his baseline happiness, however, living begins to make sense on its own. I have seen many patients start finding answers to the question "What's the point of it all?" as soon as their psychological integration and baseline happiness begin to increase. Even moderate growth in baseline happiness can enable a patient to begin recognizing his or her talents and value and start setting meaningful goals.

Growth and purification are inevitable results of strengthening baseline happiness. Negative feelings lessen; use of alcohol, cigarettes, and other drugs abates; bodily aches, minor infections, colds, and other health problems tend to disappear. Conversely, a weak baseline happiness tends to invite impurity — colds, need for drugs, anxiety, negative behavior, and so on. I have come to believe that strengthening a person's baseline happiness is the cornerstone of psychological growth. Once baseline happiness begins to grow, relations with others tend to warm-up, self-regard and self-understanding increase, and performance at work or in school usually improves. In contrast, the person with a weak baseline happiness tends to be stilted. Hang-ups and deep-rooted stresses block the natural flow of creative intelligence which would promote maximum growth. Warm relations with others develop slowly because the person feels tight or defensive around new people. Self-esteem remains low because the person does not feel good inside. Performance at work or school is only average because the person does not get fully committed to the task at hand. One way to understand how the TM program promotes such comprehensive growth is to recognize that it strengthens a person's innermost being, his baseline happiness.

Most people believe that the degree of their baseline happiness depends primarily on what they do rather than what they are. Consequently, they chase happiness as if it were a pot of gold at the end of the rainbow. The average middle-class neurotic will have tried almost everything that is supposed to make people happy before finally seeking professional help. A typical patient may have gone through several marriages, changed jobs, bought new clothes, gone on a long vacation, moved to a new city, or any number of things that may have brought some temporary good feelings but not lasting and stable inner happiness. Mere outward changes rarely effect lasting inner growth. One of the first things anyone must recognize is that his baseline happiness depends first on what he is and second on what he does. Of course, what a person does is important to his baseline happiness. If a person fails in trying to do something, or succeeds but can't enjoy it, his baseline happiness will suffer. But a person's degree of baseline happiness at the outset of any undertaking, whether washing the dishes or building a house, will determine whether the person succeeds or fails and whether he enjoys the action or not.

Pleasure

If baseline happiness depends first on what a person is rather than what he does, how can someone go about strengthening his or her baseline happiness? Recent research on the relations between pleasure and baseline happiness sheds some light on this question.

The experience of pleasure and pain is perhaps the dominant factor ruling human behavior. People tend to repeat those behaviors which bring pleasure and avoid behaviors which cause pain. Nearly everyone does things that cause pain to himself and others, but these actions are generally regarded as mistakes. Most people who make mistakes want to correct them. Why? Because everyone has a natural drive to lessen pain and restore or increase pleasure.

Some psychologists, such as the behaviorist B. F. Skinner, would reduce all human behavior to seeking pleasure and avoiding pain. Whether or not human behavior operates entirely according to this simple principle remains in dispute, but it is clear that pleasure-pain plays a major role in establishing a person's baseline happiness.

Baseline happiness depends upon the ratio of pluses and minuses recorded in the memory banks. The limbic system apparently registers the plus or minus of an experience according to the degree of pleasure or pain associated with it. Both long-lasting pleasures, such as achievement, and short-term pleasures, such as eating, reinforce baseline happiness. Similarly, long-lasting pain, such as the loss of a love, in addition to brief pains, such as touching a hot stove, tend to weaken baseline happiness. Deep-rooted stresses are also registered in the storehouse of impressions as long-lasting pains even though a person may be unaware of them. One way to increase the number of pluses would be to increase the frequency of pleasurable experiences. The principle is simple; yet the average middle-class neurotic has lost touch with his or her full capacity for pleasure. What psychophysiologists have learned about pleasure helps explain why.

Human beings show two distinctly different kinds of pleasure responses — excitement and enjoyment. A spine-tingling movie, passionate lovemaking, or winning in Las Vegas are typical exciting pleasures. A leisurely walk in a forest, watching a beautiful sunset, knitting or reading are common enjoyments. Both types of experience can be pleasureable and reinforce a person's baseline happiness, but the physiologies of these two kinds of pleasure are very different. Heart and breath rate speed up during an excitement and slow down with an enjoyment; therefore, a person will normally feel fatigued after an intense, exciting pleasure, but will usually feel refreshed following an extended enjoyment.

Research[4] indicates that portions of the limbic system regulate the two kinds of pleasures. Some parts of the hypothalamus, already discussed in connection with the stress response, apparently mediate exciting pleasure, whereas other portions of the limbic system seem to be involved with enjoyment. What is particularly important is the way in which the limbic system generates excitement or enjoyment and its impact on the autonomic nervous system. I have already pointed out that the autonomic nervous system is at the root of human well-being because it controls a great part of the activity in the body. Physiologists distinguish two main branches of the autonomic nervous system — sympathetic and parasympathetic. While activation of the sympathetic system often tends to mobilize the body and expend energy, the parasympathetic system may serve to calm down the body for repair and restoration. When the limbic system registers an exciting pleasure, it stimulates the sympathetic nervous system, which in turn produces feelings of excitement all over the body. The breath rate picks up, the mouth becomes dry, the heart pounds, the fingers and lips tingle, and the emotions surge. On the other hand, when the limbic system registers a quiet enjoyment, it activates the parasympathetic system. Breathing becomes regular, the heart slows, perspiration lessens, and the emotions ease. In short, excitements expend energy and vital bodily resources, whereas enjoyments conserve energy and tend to restore physiological balance. For this reason, excitements are inevitably short lived while enjoyments can be long lasting.

If a person wishes to maintain good health, he must allow the body to rest after exciting pleasures in order to restore psychophysiological equilibrium. An exciting pleasure actually involves the first stage of the stress response, but because the alarm occurs in a non-threatening environment, a person perceives this alarm state as pleasurable. Nevertheless, an exciting pleasure is inevitably fatiguing because it expends bodily resources. When people do not give their bodies ample time to recover from exciting pleasures, this initial pleasurable alarm, which produced a heightened sense of well-being, can turn into distress and cause feelings of discomfort and depression. The limbic system is capable of promoting physiological changes opposite to the stress response. The quiet enjoyment of a sunset would allow for bodily healing and restoration of energy reserves. A person can sit reading a good book for hours because quiet enjoyments are pleasurable and conserve vitality. This does not mean of course that a person should seek only quiet enjoyments.

To strengthen his or her baseline happiness, a person must have ample opportunity to experience both quiet enjoyments and stimulating excitements. Although excitements add vibrance to living, enjoyments provide a continuity to the flow of pleasure. Walter Cannon showed in his famous book, *The Wisdom of the Body*, how health and well-being require balance between the opposing forces that sustain life. One-sided addiction to any of life's opposite values almost inevitably leads to suffering. To avoid this, a person need merely give himself a chance to enjoy a balance of excitements and enjoyments while minimizing whatever activity might cause pain and suffering.

Strengthening baseline happiness is as simple as ensuring the most rewarding possible day by getting a good night's sleep. In practice, however, millions of average middle-class neurotics find that something as simple and natural as getting a good night's sleep is not always easy. Equally trying for many people has become the chase after excitement and the inability to experience enjoyments. When patients come to my office, they will frequently tell me how much trouble they have been having enjoying themselves. "I've started getting edgy when I read, I can't concentrate"; I'm bored with my relationships"; "I can't enjoy the kids like I used to"; "Nothing turns me on anymore," are typical statements. These statements are evidence that the physiology of the average middle-class neurotic is unbalanced. In having slipped out of tune with the natural, the average middle-class neurotic has lost touch with his or her full capacity for pleasure. Excitements have become boring; enjoyments are clouded by restlessness and agitation. Shakespeare put the matter well when he wrote: "We are not ourselves when nature, being oppress'd, commands the mind to suffer with the body."[5] To regain the full capacity for pleasure, a person must restore psychophysiological balance and stop breaking laws fundamental to the expansion of happiness.

Mental Temperature

An important new theory in psychophysiology suggests that each person has what may be called an optimum arousal level. Just as a machine may have a best work pace, the human biomachinery may have a particular degree of excitation at which it works best. Psychologist Donald O. Hebb believes that tension results when a person becomes aroused beyond the optimum and boredom occurs when a person is insufficiently aroused. Most daily activity takes place somewhere between these two extremes, but arousal levels clearly play an important role in baseline happiness. I find the term mental temperature useful in discussing how levels of excitation in the nervous system affect the capacity for pleasure and baseline happiness. Maharishi points out that optimum mental temperature is the least excited state of the nervous system. In this state the mind is uncluttered, comprehension is broad, thinking is most orderly, and the experience of well-being is greatest. This idea makes good sense in light of current research on the relationship of the stress cycle, capacity for pleasure, and arousal levels.

Psychologist Maynard Shelley at the University of Kansas suggests that the pace of modern life is systematically raising peoples' mental temperatures. This occurs when the stress cycle keeps people in a mild but chronic state of distress. When a person sustains a mild but chronic alarm response over a period of weeks, months, or years, he begins to adapt to it, just as we adapt to an annoying, persistent loud noise so that it gradually fades into the background of our hearing.

His whole physiology and psychology become fixed in this excited state, and the person no longer notices that he is aroused beyond his natural optimum level. Heightened arousal causes a person to feel "keyed-up," a common condition today. More and more studies are showing how work and even recreational activities in our technological society (repetitive work tasks, driving in rush hour traffic, examinations, violent or erotic movies, spectator sports, and. so on) increase the production of adrenaline, keeping the individual hyperaroused and keeping his mental temperature elevated.

This raised mental temperature has a twofold meaning for a person's capacity for pleasure. When a person gets into a chronically excited state, his hypothalamus and sympathetic nervous system work overtime. This hyperactivity of the sympathetic system inhibits parasympathetic activity necessary for enjoyments. The chronic activity of the sympathetic system sustains a constant tension, which underlies all of a person's experience. As long as the person keeps busy, that tension goes unnoticed. But as soon as the person finds himself waiting in line with nothing to do or sitting down to read, the underlying tension surfaces. The result is: *The higher the mental temperature, the more difficulty a person has experiencing enjoyments. A raised mental temperature literally blocks a person's ability to enjoy quiet pleasures.* At the other end of the pleasure spectrum, a raised mental temperature means that a person has difficulty enjoying mildly exciting experiences — starting a hobby such as photography or sailing, meeting a new person with an interesting story to tell, or going out to a favorite restaurant. "I just can't get into it," a patient will say. When a person's mental temperature gets high enough, he becomes almost exclusively dependent on strong excitements as his primary source of pleasure.

Diagram 11 schematically illustrates how an optimum mental temperature makes excitements and enjoyments easily available, and how the raised mental temperature of the average middle-class neurotic obstructs the mental capacity for pleasure.

Diagram 11
MENTAL TEMPERATURE

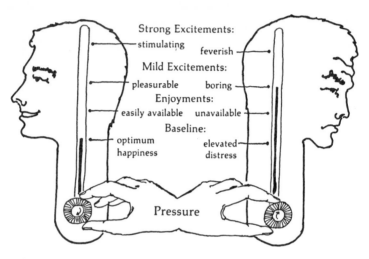

Strong Excitements:
stimulating   feverish
Mild Excitements:
pleasurable   boring
Enjoyments:
easily available   unavailable
Baseline:
optimum   elevated
happiness   distress

Pressure

An optimum mental temperature requires what psychophysiologists call autonomic balance. This means that the person who experiences a strong excitement will almost automaticlly rest afterwards, so giving his parasympathetic system an opportunity to balance the sympathetic system's energy expenditure during the strong excitement. Autonomic stability enables a person to slip back and forth from excitements to enjoyments and steadily strengthen baseline happiness. The average middle-class neurotic suffers autonomic imbalance, meaning he may enjoy a strong excitement, but his hyperaroused sympathetic system interferes with the tendency of the parasympathetic system to restore energy and vital resources. This imbalanced state can last only so long before the sympathetic system finally gives in to the need for parasympathetic activity, resulting in mild depression. The cyclical moods of the average middle-class neurotic range from excitement to boredom and finally to mild depression, which eventually gives way again to excitement. What helps mental temperature return to and remain at its optimum is the growth cycle. When the flow of creative intelligence results in achievement and satisfaction, autonomic balance increases. A person begins to follow a natural rest-activity cycle which permits the healing of old stresses and the strengthening of baseline happiness. What raises a person's mental temperature beyond its optimum and keeps it there is the stress cycle. When a child undergoes a physical or emotional overload, the resulting stress remains stored in the memory banks and raises the excitation level of the nervous system. Just as a physical wound often causes a body fever, the backlog of excess emotional baggage and old stresses causes what may be thought of as a mental fever. Each time a person slips into the stress cycle, he further exacerbates his mental temperature by increasing distress.

Perhaps the most important behavorial result of raising mental temperature is what I like to call the excitement treadmill. Diagram 12 illustrates the excitement treadmill. The futility of our culture's quest for ever greater stimulation has sound psychophysiological reasons behind it. A raised mental temperature would be in psychologist Maslow's framework, a pathological state. Anxiety and tension indicate the average middle-class neurotic's chronically elevated mental temperature. Most people try to obtain pleasure and gain relief from this chronic tension by further elevating mental temperature. The principle at work here is that excitement, for the moment, inhibits anxiety and mild depression. In practice, what this means is a whole culture, millions upon millions of people chasing after increasing excitement in order to feel some degree of pleasure and well-being. This cultural tendency shows up everywhere. Movies must be more violent and

Diagram 12

THE EXCITEMENT TREADMILL

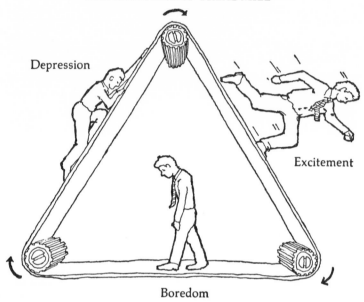

Depression

Excitement

Boredom

spine-tingling.* Rock stars rise and fall with meteoric speed. Vacations must be more exotic and frequent. Cigarettes, alcohol, marijuana, or other drugs have become an absolute necessity for having a good time. There is nothing wrong with increasing excitement

---

*Dr. Lennart Levi, noted stress researcher at the Karolinska Institute in Stockholm has shown that violent and pornographic movies produce a substantial increase in adrenaline secretion. In this light, it is not surprising that Dr. Bozzuto of the University of Connecticut recently reported what he has called "cinematic neurosis." This condition refers to the complex of symptoms (including insomnia, excitability, irritability, and hyperactivity) that develops in some people after viewing violent or terrifying movies. Though some people use these findings to argue the dangers of current trends in cinema, I hold that the danger lies more in people's lack of baseline happiness and psychophysiological stability for absorbing intensely exciting pleasures.

per se, but another important psychophysiological principle turns the chase after excitement into a dead end.

This principle is called habituation. When a person sustains a certain degree of excitement long enough, he gets used to or technically habituates to that state. What had been excitingly pleasurable soon becomes rather unspectacular and finally becomes boring — for example, the big romance that suddenly fizzled out, the "dynamite" record you just "had to buy" but stopped listening to after three playings, the daily wonder of nature that is never seen or enjoyed anymore, the ordinary "miracle" of telephone communication, the jet travel that is taken for granted and no longer appreciated. Dr. Ivor Mills, Professor of Medicine at Cambridge University in England, points out that most people experience brief periods of heightened arousal as pleasurable but become depressed when such a state is prolonged. To overcome depression, Mills explains, many young people attempt to raise their arousal levels still further by taking drugs, listening to rock music at pain-producing intensity, and frantically searching for ever more exciting activities.[6] However, an elevated mental temperature only further increases habituation, which causes the environment to become more dull and drab. Because enjoyments become increasingly difficult, a person must so to speak "up the ante" of what he is willing to go through for exciting pleasures. The irony of this process is that each new excitement fails to strengthen a person's baseline happiness. Eventually the frantic question "What's next?" turns into the morose "Why brother?" In some people, the excitement treadmill may lead to more serious difficulties than a mild depression. If sufficient frustration in a person's private life coincide with enough pressures at work, the person may, depending on ego strength and psychophysiological factors, lose his coping abilities altogether and suffer what is commonly referred to as a

"nervous breakdown." Irritability, hostility, argumen-
tativeness, and irrationality may signal a breakdown in
coping abilities due to chronic hyperarousal and inability
to get off the excitement treadmill.

When a person gets on the excitement treadmill, he is
apt not to understand why he remains unhappy no
matter what he tries to do. Maharishi has formulated a
psychological law that explains why: The mind cannot
maintain a mood on an abstract basis. A person cannot
feel unhappy, angry, depressed, or joyful without his
mind finding some way of explaining why that mood
occurs. Freud identified several mechanisms by which
the mind explains its moods; two of the most important
are repression and projection. By repressing old stresses,
a person remains unaware of why his mental
temperature has become elevated or even that it has.
These repressed memories keep a person in a state of
chronic mild distress, but the mind's tendency to project
leads a person to find external reasons for his discomfort
or unhappiness. For example, a person may start feeling
anxious. Instead of recognizing the origin of his anxiety
in his own elevated mental temperature, he will find
some way to blame it on another person, an upcoming
event, or some immediate problem. The person who
complains that life has no purpose, nothing is
worthwhile, things are not like they used to be, is
projecting his boredom, mild depression, and poor self-
esteem. Long before Freud, Charles Dickens alluded to
the way people perceive when he wrote: "Men who look
on nature and their fellow-men, and cry that all is dark
and gloomy, are in the right; but the sombre colours are
reflections from their own jaundiced eyes and hearts.
The real hues are delicate, and need a clearer vision."[7] As
long as a person continues to project reasons for his
unhappiness, he is likely to remain on the excitement
treadmill. When that person gets into a situation which
triggers distress more than usual, however, the mind's
ability to repress and project begin to weaken, and he

may then recognize that the roots of his unhappiness lie in his own body and behavior. If the symptoms grow sufficiently severe, the person is likely to seek help.

Prescribed and non-prescribed drugs have become the primary way in which people deal with the emotional ups and downs of the excitement treadmill. Alcohol and tranquilizers are consumed to palliate anxiety resulting from a chronically elevated mental temperature. Barbiturates are used in relieving sleep difficulties that may accompany chronic hyperarousal. Amphetamines, marijuana, LSD, and heroin are all used to escape the pitfalls of boredom and depression. Food becomes a drug to provide temporary excitement and security; therefore, overeating is very commonly employed to cope with chronic depression. All these drugs provide temporary relief but have negative side effects, do not enable people to get off the excitement treadmill, and weaken baseline happiness in the long run. If a person finally becomes dissatisfied with relying on drugs to sustain some modicum of well-being, he may turn to psychotherapy. When average middle-class neurotics fail to increase their baseline happiness by the exclusive use of either drugs or psychotherapy, they may start becoming resigned or desperate, depending on the severity of their symptoms. This suffering is usually needless. The solution to increasing the capacity for pleasure and strengthening baseline happiness is simple: lower the mental temperature to its optimum level of least excitation.

Cooling the Mind

Dr. Lawrence Domash, Professor of Physics at Maharishi International University, and Nobel Laureate Brian Josephson, Professor of Physics at Cambridge University in England, point out that the mental temperature concept is analogous to certain laws of physics and provides a useful model for understanding the benefits of the TM program. A basic principle of physics states: As temperature decreases, order increases. A good example of this principle at work in nature is a raindrop becoming a snowflake. When water vapor in a cloud cools to the freezing point, meandering water molecules become exquisitely ordered. The TM technique apparently increases ease and order by lowering the mental temperature or, more precisely, by decreasing autonomic hyperarousal. This in turn permits the entire physical system to settle down and the mental temperature as a whole to shift toward its optimum level of least excitation. Professor Domash adds that in physical systems, cooling also leads to purification. When salt water is sufficiently cooled, the water forms a pure block of ice and the salt separates out into a highly concentrated solution. A similar principle is probably at work in how the TM technique dissolves old stresses, which may be understood as impurities in the nervous system. Simply lowering the mental temperature may explain how the TM technique starts all the purifying mechanisms in the body working to dissolve old stresses thoroughly and efficiently.

A person can strengthen his or her baseline happiness from two angles. First he can increase the frequency of pleasurable experiences. Lowering the mental temperature toward its optimum level of least excitation is essential if this is to occur. Second, a person can dissolve the deep-rooted stresses laid down in the memory banks, which helps permit mental temperature to return to its optimum level. The TM program appears to strengthen baseline happiness from both angles. Each TM session tends to optimize mental temperature, thereby increasing the frequency of pleasurable experiences in one's activities following regular meditation. It also gradually dissolves old stresses, thereby removing the unconscious emotional burden of the past and contributing to a sustained optimum mental temperature.

I am fond of one of Maharishi's analogies which illustrates how the TM program increases capacity for pleasure. Imagine a choppy lake. If you throw a rock into the lake, the rock makes little impression. Now imagine a still lake. If you throw even a tiny pebble into the lake, you will see many ripples on the water. Similarly, even strong excitements have difficulty eliciting pleasure in a person with an elevated mental temperature. This is the habituation process which I described earlier. By lowering a person's mental temperature, the TM program unfolds a person's full natural capacity to experience excitements and enjoyments. When the mental temperature returns to its optimum least excited state, even the most insignificant parts of a person's daily routine can bring enjoyment. Perhaps the single most significant comment which my patients make after beginning the TM program is, "I've started enjoying life more." A man previously very tense began to discover the pleasure of daily chores around the house. Three months after beginning the TM program, a business woman started enjoying her drive to and from work every day. Students so often report increased pleasure in studying that I have come to expect this comment within three to six months after an anxious student begins the TM program. What regularly surprises my patients is how the TM program increases their capacity for pleasure without their trying to change themselves.

Many of my patients are caught up in the strain of trying: trying to do better at work, trying to lose weight, trying to get over personality hang-ups, and so on. When I explain how recent research indicates that comprehensive growth can occur without so much strain, some patients will not even hear me at first. I am not surprised. After all, on the basis of 30, 40, 50, or more years most people are certain that life is a struggle and have abandoned the idea that a realistic person could be happy in just "being alive." The average middle-class neurotic seems to believe that such a state is the province of a few beatific children who will lose this joy of living upon growing up to face the real world. When I explain that the TM program helps a person regain this natural joy of living, some patients become suspicious. Then I must point out how different people may have different ideas about the nature of life, but the TM program allows almost anyone to see for himself through direct experience how natural happiness can be. Some patients enroll in the TM program right away; others think it over for a while. Once a person begins the TM program, however, he or she almost inevitably reawakens to his or her full natural capacity for happiness in "just being, " as well as in "doing."

Recent EEG research on the encephalographic correlates of pleasure and happiness provide some physiological evidence that the TM program strengthens baseline happiness. Neurophysiologist R. L. Maulsby in 1971 reported on the brain wave changes which occur in infants during periods of serene pleasure such as the mother-child interactions of cuddling, tickling, or showing of a favorite toy.[8] Maulsby noted synchronous theta waves (4-7 cps) as the predominant feature accompanying pleasure and serenity. On the basis of his studies with children, Maulsby termed the EEG pattern typical of a child's pleasure, hedonic hypersynchrony. He emphasized that hedonic hypersynchrony may be the most important EEG change related to emotional development.

In adult TM practitioners, Banquet, Glueck, and Levine have found brain wave changes which may be the adult expression of Maulsby's hedonic hypersynchrony in children. Levine suggests that the TM program enables the adult to recover the natural enjoyment response characteristic of children. Synchronized theta waves in TM meditators may be the EEG correlate of the least excited state of consciousness and its regular elicitation may prove to be an important contribution to psychoemotional growth in adults.

By optimizing mental temperature through the TM program, most people can start to notice an increase in the pleasure of day-to-day living. The result is a steady growth in baseline happiness. I have noticed in many of my patients and friends who practice the TM program that their baseline happiness ususally grows so strong that they begin to show what might be called an almost uninterrupted center of inner well-being. The founder of Gestalt Therapy, Fritz Perls, summarized the importance of finding such a center when he wrote, "If you are centered in yourself, then you don't adjust anymore...then you assimilate, you understand, you are related to whatever happens. Without a center there is no place from which to work...achieving a center, being grounded in one self, is about the highest state a human being can achieve."[9] The person who lacks a strong baseline happiness is at the mercy of his environment for his sense of well-being. This is why "coping" and "adjusting" are such popular words among average middle-class neurotics. For the person who regains the natural strength of a stable baseline happiness, living becomes not coping but a delightful and exciting growth process.

It's ironic that Western psychology and psychiatry have been talking so much lately about regaining inner wholeness when nearly all current therapies encourage people to look for this wholeness via processes outside of themselves. After all, psychotherapy is an interpersonal process. In psychoanalytically-oriented therapy, childhood relationships with parents and siginificant others are of utmost concern. In family therapy, relations within the family are primary. In encounter groups, what is going on in the here-and-now of the group is most important. In Transactional Analysis a person learns to analyze his relations with others. It seems obvious, however, that to experience the core of his being a person must turn his attention inward, not outward toward others or the past. Prior to scientific research on the TM program, Western psychology simply missed the fact that every person has the capacity to experience easily and naturally the least excited state of consciousness and thereby unfold a strong inner center of well-being and happiness.

A question I hear frequently is, "How important a scientific advance is the TM program?" To answer it, I like to use a graphic analogy. Imagine a world full of insomniacs. If in such a world someone discovered sleep, scientists would study with amazement this phenomenon of relaxing and losing consciousness. After the physiologists had verified the value of sleep, physicians would begin perscribing it as essential to optimum physical and emotional well-being. The typical response to the doctor's prescription would at first be, "What do you mean, just close your eyes and sleep? Is it safe? Sounds like a cult. None of my friends have done it. And anyway, what do I *do?* You must have to *do* something to sleep." The explanation that sleep is safe and easy because it is wholly natural would probably fall on deaf ears. But eventually, sleep would gain widespread recognition as one of the greatest scientific discoveries in this world full of insomniacs because it enriches peoples' lives in a comprehensive manner. That is what is happening with the TM program. The TM technique permits almost anyone to begin experiencing a fourth state of consciousness, different than waking, sleeping, or dreaming. The regular experience of this least excited state of conscousness is proving to be essential for anyone wishing to live fully and enjoy maximum happiness.

Happiness, Dynamism, and Creativity

One concern which comes up frequently at my lectures on the TM program is the fear that the happy person will lose his dynamism and creativity. People are afraid that the TM program might make them into dull milquetoasts, who just sip tea and live passively. In fact, the opposite occurs. The TM program fosters a dynamic state of *restfulness* and *alertness* in the functioning of the mind and body. An optimum mental temperature is that state in which a person is most awake and alive yet perfectly at ease and very orderly in his thinking and action. This state conserves energy, which is why those people physically and mentally most capable of throwing themselves into a whirlwind of constructive activity tend to be more calm and less stressed than average. The person with a high mental temperature scatters energy and confuses calm with lethargy because he often experiences fatigue whenever his mental temperature falls. The tension of his chronic hyperarousal gives way to fatigue when he relaxes because his strained biomachinery needs a chance to repair and restore itself. However, the whole point of optimizing mental temperature is to get the mind and body working most efficiently, naturally, and happily. The energy of anxiety and distress should not be confused with the energy of true dynamism.

"It is quite wrong," Maharishi explains, "to think that one who has gained this state [of restful alertness] remains slumped in enertia...,"[10] and he uses an analogy to illustrate how the TM program increases dynamism. An arrow may be at rest in two distinctly different states — lying on the ground and pulled back on a bow. In one state, the arrow has no potential dynamism, in the other, it has the maximum. Practicing the TM technique twice daily is like pulling an arrow back on a bow. TM practice enables a person to collect a maximum degree of ease, order, mental clarity, and energy before plunging into activity. From a superficial viewpoint, the archer pulling an arrow back on his bow seems to be confused because he is pulling the arrow away from the target. Similarly, some people believe that taking 20 minutes twice a day for a TM session doesn't make sense because it will reduce their time available for work and play. Actually, the TM technique saves time by increasing dynamism, efficiency, and capacity for happiness just as the archer saves time by pulling an arrow back on his bow rather than trying to hit the target by throwing the arrow.

By increasing a person's ability to enjoy his daily routine, optimizing mental temperature actually increases motivation. Maslow and others have shown how the experience of pleasure both whets the appetite for more and bolsters confidence that more can be achieved. Psychologist David Frew at Gannon College in Erie, Pennsylvania, has published several papers which indicate that the TM program increases dynamism. In two separate studies, Frew found that the TM technique improves productivity among executives as well as blue-collar employees.

Fundamental to a dynamic personality is good health. Strong evidence suggests that optimizing mental temperature contributes to health maintenance because it requires a relative balance between the sympathetic and parasympathetic branches of the autonomic nervous system. Autonomic balance is so important to health that general medicine distinguishes two types of people, labiles and stabiles, according to their degree of autonomic balance. People with a tendency toward autonomic instability, and this includes most average middle-class neurotics, are called labiles. The labile person has a tendency to expend energy without restoring it. He may go to bed early after a hard day's work only to wake up tired in the morning. While the labile rests, the chronic hyperarousal of his sympathetic system keeps the body tense and the mind full of worries. The result is fretful sleep. The resulting bodily wear and tear leave the labile ripe for diseases of all kinds. Autonomic lability may be a precursor of psychosomatic and mental illness. The importance of good health to dynamism and baseline happiness needs little elaboration. Few people will say, "I feel great and rarin' to go," when they are in bed with the flu. Still fewer people who frequently get the flu or colds will talk about how much energy they have or how much they are enjoying themselves. On the other hand, people with balanced autonomic functioning, stabiles, are healthier than average. The stabile person shows greater resistance to disease, less motor impulsivity, a higher degree of mental health, and less susceptibility to conditioning than a labile person. The average middle-class neurotic tends toward autonomic lability while the TM program increases autonomic stability.

The concern that the TM program may dampen creativity has its basis in the popular belief that distress and suffering are a necessary basis for creative expression. The romanticized careers of a few creative geniuses, such as Michelangelo and Van Gogh, may seem to support this idea, but the lives of many other great creators, such as Plato, Bach, and Einstein contradict this assumption. Maharishi has emphasized, "How tragic it is to believe that tension is necessary to improve life! It is said that poets and artists have created their most inspired work under tension. All such statements are due to ignorance and an inability to distinguish between tensions and pressures of time or circumstances. Pressure of time or circumstances can sometimes produce much finer work but only from minds that are free and relaxed, which do not become tense through this pressure."[11] The majority of great creative men and women have not only been free from neurosis, but have also lived happy and fulfilling lives expressing the highest human ideals. It seems far more likely that creative individuals have succeeded in their achievements despite, rather than because of, their distress or suffering.

If a person experiences pressure or pain, he generally wants to get rid of it; so distress does play a role in the drive for tension reduction. But Maslow and his colleagues have shown that tension reduction ranks among the most superficial of motivational processes. Far more basic and presumably at the heart of the creative process is what Maslow called "the drive toward self-actualization." According to Maslow, this drive is the compelling force within every living thing to grow, develop, and express its innate capacities. Tension reduction cannot explain a child's desire to learn or the business executive's ambition to increase his responsibility. Another motivating principle, self-actualization, has proven necessary to explain growth and creativity. By reducing distress and the need for immediate tension reduction, the TM technique apparently enables people to get in touch with this deepest impulse of life.

Stressed individuals tend to get caught up in very stereotyped behavior patterns, lose their spontaneity, and become unreceptive to feedback. The creative person generally shows openness to new ways of handling situations, a natural spontaneity, and an above average ability to integrate inputs from the environment. The stressed individual never has enough time to do anything; internal pressure keeps him on a constant treadmill of tension. Creative people may be involved in hundreds of activities but always seem to find time for more; the pressure of deadlines rarely disturbs feelings of ease and well-being. The stressed person often resents criticism and cannot accommodate the demands of others without tension. The creative person can usually accept criticism and utilizes it to do his best. By increasing spontaneity, receptivity, ability to accept criticism, and feelings of ease and well-being, the TM technique removes some of the roadblocks to creativity. Noted psychologist Arthur Deikman describes this effect of meditation as "deautomatization":

> ...permitting the adult to attain a new, fresh perception of the world by freeing him from a stereotyped organization built up over the years and by allowing adult synthetic and associative functions access to fresh materials, to create

with them a new way that represents an advance in mental functioning.... The struggle for creative insight in all fields may be regarded as the effort to deautomatize the psychic structures that organize cognition and perception.... In this sense, deautomatization is not a regression but rather an undoing of a pattern in order to permit a new and perhaps more advanced experience.[12]

Research has shown that people practicing the TM technique excel on open-ended "pure" tests of creativity, such as the Torrence Test of Creative Thinking, developed to measure the creative thinking process described by eminent scientific researchers, inventors, and creative writers. Using this classic test, psychologist Michael MacCallum at California State University at Long Beach found increased fluency, flexibility, and originality of creative thinking in TM practitioners. He reported that long-term TM practitioners demonstrated much greater freedom of expression within a slightly structured framework than did new meditators. In a longitudinal study at York University, Ontario, researcher Howard Shecter found that meditators practicing the TM technique increased significantly in their ability to find novel solutions on the Match Problem Test while control subjects did not. Psychologist Gary Schwartz at Harvard University also reported that TM practitioners do unusually well on creativity tests, which require fluency of imaginative production. Several psychological studies have confirmed that the TM program fosters self-actualization. Since self-actualization and creativity are closely related, it is not surprising that the TM program promotes creativity.

Maharishi points out that the TM program enhances creativity in two ways. He indicates that the TM program fosters the ability to maintain both wide-angle vision and focused attention at the same time. An essential characteristic of creative thinking seems to be the mind's capacity to entertain free-floating ideas and reveries yet remain able to focus sharply on a particular idea if desired. The average middle-class neurotic tends to block the spontaneous flow of ideas by getting caught up solely in focused attention or losing himself in unstructured thinking out of which nothing tangible emerges. Psychophysiologist Elmer Greene has shown that synchronous theta wave activity is correlated with a wakeful "reverie," the sine qua non of creativity. Regular practice of the TM technique appears to facilitate the conditions favorable for the spontaneous occurrence of this wakeful theta pattern. It is interesting indeed that the brain wave patterns seen in deepest TM practice are similar to those seen in the so-called "Aha" effect in the creative person at the moment of sudden insight into a problem.

Maharishi also states that the least excited state of consciousness is essentially "a field of all possibilities." Psychologist A. H. Murray points out in his essay, "Vicissitudes of Creativity," that creativity requires a "permeability of boundaries, boundaries between categories...between different spheres of interest...[and] between conscious and unconscious processes."[13] The low cortical arousal of the least excited state of consciousness resulting from the TM program seems to foster the permeability which permits a person to entertain a wide range of possibilities in any situation.

Many creative people have described what seems to be the least excited state of consciousness as fundamental to their creative pursuits. For example, the American poet Walt Whitman gave beautiful expression to the ultimate source of life and consciousness:

> Thou transcendent,
> Nameless, the fibre and the breath,
> Light of the light, shedding forth universes, thou centre of
>   them,
> Thou mightier centre of the true, the good, the loving,
> Thou moral, spiritual fountain — affection's source —
>   thou reservoir,

Thou pulse — thou motive of the stars, suns, systems,
That, circling, move in order, safe, harmonious,
Athwart the shapeless vastnesses of space,
How should I think, how breathe a single breath,
    how speak, if, out of myself,
I could not launch, to those, superior universes?[14]

Creativity is not just limited to the arts or scientific discoveries but can be a daily experience of vitality, spontaneity, and responsivenesses. It is as natural to have a continuous outflow of creativity under conditions of high mental health as it is for a current running through a filament to radiate electromagnetic waves of heat and light. By maximizing psychophysiological integration, the TM program systematically unfolds a person's capacity for creative living culminating in the state of enlightment.

The Blossoming of Love

Perhaps no experience is more characteristic of the average middle-class neurotic than the frustration of trying to love or be loved. Trying and loving just do not seem to go hand in hand. Almost every patient who comes to see me expresses concern in one way or another about his or her capacity to love. A housewife might tell me how much she has been trying to love her children, yet she gets angry with them over trifles. A couple will describe how hard they have been working to make each other happy, and later will tell me how frustrated and unhappy they are. A student might bemoan the futility of all his efforts to find a girlfriend before telling me how badly he feels about himself. Among those personality changes which my patients appreciate most as their baseline happiness develops is the growth of the ability to love spontaneously and effortlessly, perhaps because, as Maharishi points out, "lack of love denotes lack of life content."[15] Joanne, 26, the mother of two, began seeing me because of frustration and mild depression. She expressed this sentiment when she told me with a sigh of relief, "Thank God, I don't have to try to be loving anymore."

A classic misunderstanding held by most people is that they have to love or be loved *in order* to be happy. In fact, the reverse is true. Happiness is the foundation as well as the result of loving. Warmth, sharing, and love are natural to the happy person, which helps explain why people like to be around and love the happy individual. But no matter how hard the unhappy person tries to love, his efforts are destined for frustration because he lacks the inner sense of well-being basic to the ability to love. And, as Maharashi states, "the show of love without genuine love is a shame to life."[16]

The key to increasing a person's capacity to love is in strengthening his baseline happiness. With a growing baseline happiness, a person begins to appreciate life more and more, and Maharishi notes that the ultimate development of the ability to appreciate is love. This kind of growth in appreciation helps a person start having warmer relations with others and develops naturally into love for oneself, family, friends, the environment, and all humanity. A loving cycle ensues: the more appreciation a person feels, the more love he gives, and the more love he receives in return.

How full of love can life become? Maharishi explains that people restricted in their capacity to love are "wee small ponds where the love can flow only as ripples and not as waves of the sea...."[17] When a person's full ability to love unfolds, he discovers, according to Maharishi, that personal love for a mother or a father, for a husband or wife, is expressive "of the concentrated state of universal love...."[18] Maharishi adds, "To live this state of concentrated, universal love is the ultimate fulfillment of life. It is an unbounded flow of love at the sight of everything, at the sound of everything, the smell or taste of anything, the touch of anything; the whole of life in its multifarious diversity is nothing but the fullness of life, bliss and contentment...."[19] Apparently, the human capacity for love is inherently unlimited. Psychological research confirms that the TM program reduces the negative feelings — fear, insecurity, anger, depression, and so on — that hinder the ability to love and have intimate relationships. At the same time, the TM program promotes spontaneity, positive self-regard, warmth, and tenderness — all qualities necessary for a person to have the capacity to love. The increased capacity to love resulting from the TM program is due to a genuine growth in baseline happiness and not to artificial attempts to maintain a loving mood.

A sales manager who was seeing me for help with a drinking problem described how hollow was his world of contrived feelings. He told me about a sales convention in which no one really cared about anyone else, yet everyone walked around with pasted-on smiles and pretended to be warm and sincere. "How could I not drink relating to people that way?" he asked. "Alcohol was the only way people even came close to letting their hair down." The need for chemical means to break through one's own contrived feelings disappears once a person genuinely strengthens his or her baseline happiness. Warmth and love become natural expressions of inner well-being.

A characteristic effect of an elevated mental temperature is the inability to sustain rewarding love relationships. Social psychologists have shown that love relationships built upon relaxation are much more stable than relationships based exclusively upon excitement. Excitement breeds short-lived relationships for the same reason that it breeds only short-term happiness. The human nervous system is capable of sustaining only so much excitement before it must switch gears, turn off, and restore exhausted energy reserves. Just as happiness can give way to depression, what appeared to be love can become frustration, anger, and resentment.

Time and again I have seen patients become almost
addicted to the excitement shared with a new lover.
Caught up in such a whirlwind of romantic excitement,
they begin to make tremendous demands on one
another because they believe that they have finally
found the one who magically meets all their needs.
When all the attention and fanfare tapers off and the
initial excitement becomes difficult to sustain, illusions
start bursting, one after another. Due to the laws of
habituation and the excitement treadmill, the relationship inevitably becomes insufficiently stimulating, and
both partners become susceptible to feeling inadequate,
frustrated, hostile, resentful, or just plain "let down." Of
course, this analysis does not mean that every relationship which breaks apart must have been based on
excitement, or that excitement cannot be a wonderful
and life-supporting experience for two people to share
together. However, it does mean that intimacy, the most
profound of interpersonal human pleasures, grows in an
atmosphere of mutual ease.

When relaxation and quiet pleasures are the basic
bond in a relationship, the likelihood of deepening love
and growing emotional rewards is great for several
reasons. First, each partner enters the relationship with
a strong baseline happiness. If a person is already
enjoying considerable pleasure from within, the pleasure derived from a relationship with another person
becomes an added delight. This situation frees both
people from the need to make escalating demands upon
one another to sustain their happiness, and it protects
them from overwhelming disappointment or anger if a
need goes unmet. Second, each has a greater capacity for
what is essential to any relationship — giving. If two
people come together, each expecting the other to
provide lots of excitement, attention, and caring, then
both tend to get more caught up in taking than giving.
When both people already enjoy a significant degree of
inner satisfaction, they naturally overflow in sharing

their happiness with one another, and the relationship blossoms.

People who practice the TM program grow naturally in baseline happiness and a stable sense of self. As a result, they tend to form strong and joyful relationships in which each person feels free to express his or her full potential instead of feeling trapped by an exclusive dependence on one another for feelings of well-being. The seed of love grows in the soil of happiness. The TM program waters the roots of intimacy and love by unfolding a natural inner fullness of well-being and happiness. The fruits of love are the natural result of the expansion of happiness.

5

How a Shrink Became a Stretch

"Are you going to see your shrink today?" a friend asked one of my patients.

Pausing, my patient answered, "Yes, but I don't think of him as a shrink; I think he's more like a stretch."

"What do you mean by that?" the friend inquired.

"Well, his whole approach to helping people get it together is a lot different than the other psychiatrists I've gone to. He doesn't just help you learn to cope but shows you how life can be a lot more than coping. Instead of shrinking your mind he helps you stretch it, to expand to your full potential," my patient replied.

When Ralph, a 37 year-old business executive whom I was seeing told me this story, I laughed out loud. I also started thinking for the first time about how my experience and knowledge of the TM program was changing my theory and practice of psychiatry.

* * *

I began the TM program while in my last year of psychiatric residency training at the Yale University School of Medicine. Little did I know that a very brief interchange at lunch with a fellow physician in 1972 would be the first step to a whole new perspective on the practice of psychiatry. In fact, when my friend first mentioned that he had recently begun the TM program, my comment was "Oh really. I guess you'll soon start coming to the hospital in a turban and flying on a magic carpet. Won't that be cute." When my friend, whom I respected, insisted that the TM program was something he found quite valuable and that it was not weird and did not mean a person would go off to sit on a mountain top or live on brown rice, I became somewhat less skeptical.

About one month later, I was driving with a nurse to an important appointment when we got stuck in bumper to bumper traffic. I became very frustrated while she remained cool and calm; so I asked why she wasn't more upset. She attributed her state of ease to her TM practice. Impressed, I made a mental note that it was time for me to learn more about the TM program.

Later that week I saw a poster reading "Come hear more about the Transcendental Meditation program at the Yale School of Public Health Auditorium, 8:00 P.M." I decided to go to the lecture, still half-expecting to find a white robed guru talking philosophy. To my surprise, a well-dressed married couple gave the introductory lecture. They showed slides of impressive scientific evidence to back up their claims about how the TM program can enrich a person's life.

Two aspects of the lecture most impressed me. First, the scientific research on the benefits of the TM program had been done by reputable researchers at places such as the Harvard and UCLA medical schools and published in reputable journals such as *Science*, *Scientific American*, the *American Journal of Physiology*, *Psychosomatic Medicine*, and the *Journal of Counseling Psychology*. Second, the two people giving the lecture seemed to show in their own personalities a quality of happiness which I had observed in very few people. Trained as a psychiatrist to recognize when people are putting on a facade to cover up their real feelings, I was certain that these two TM teachers were not faking a mood of happiness for the sake of impressing the audience. After speaking with the two teachers at the end of the lecture,

I could not help but think to myself, "Whatever they've got, I'd like some of it too."

Two weekends later on July 1, 1972, I received my personal instruction in the TM technique. When I came out of my first meditation, I could not believe what I had just experienced or how I felt. Never before had I enjoyed such a state of deep relaxation and never before had my mind seemed so sharp and alert. Not that I had thought of myself as a very tense or anxious individual, but this unique state of ease and mental clarity contrasted sharply to what was then my baseline experience of life. I had previously experimented with hypnosis and Jacobson's progressive relaxation, but never had I felt so completely relaxed and rejuvenated. I felt not just good but ecstatic. Colors seemed brighter, and everything and everyone looked better to me. These feelings continued for hours afterwards.

My first subjective experience with the TM technique encouraged me to consider further the objective research. This unique, time honored, and very simple mental technique produced in me such a state of emotional ease and well-being along with mental clarity and order that it had obvious implications for the practice of psychiatry. I could not help but think to myself on that first day how I had a professional obligation to find out more about the program. I even entertained the thought of going through whatever training might be necessary to teach it. "I may not have read about the TM program in medical school, " I thought, "but this technique could become an important part of modern psychiatry."

After completing the TM course, I immediately drove to Boston to attend a symposium at the Massachusetts Institute of Technology on the Science of Creative Intelligence. I met Maharishi and was very impressed by him and what he had to say. One thing was obvious; he was a happy man, at peace with himself and the world. I knew he had something great to offer. I also had an opportunity during the symposium to hear Dr. Glueck present his initial ground-breaking research on the use of the TM program with psychiatric patients. Other presentations by astronaut Rusty Schweikart, East Asian expert, Alfred Jenkins, and astronomer Lloyd Motz, and Maharishi's illuminating comments at the end of each, "stretched" my horizons of knowledge. I returned to Yale enlivened and wanted to know more. Over the next year, I took advantage of every opportunity to learn more about the TM program. I discovered that an introductory course in the Science of Creative Intelligence (SCI), was being taught for credit to undergraduate and graduate students at Yale, and I promptly enrolled in it. In addition, at the local TM center I began an introductory SCI course that consisted of 33 color video-taped lectures by Maharishi.

Both SCI courses profoundly affected my understanding of psychiatry and human development. What I enjoyed most about the Yale course was its interdisciplinary approach to understanding the basic principles that govern the growth of creative intelligence in nature and human life. Like most educated people, I had become so specialized in my own field that I had difficulty understanding the significance of new developments in other fields traditionally unrelated to psychiatry, such as physics, mathematics, or music. There is a joke in academia these days about specialization getting to the point where the hard rock geologist has difficulty talking to the soft rock geologist, much less the astronomer to the botanist, or the chemist to the anthropologist. By showing how all knowledge is structured in consciousness, SCI establishes a common ground and vocabulary for the meeting of all disciplines. On the one hand, nothing should be more obvious than the significance of a person's consciousness to what he can know. If a person's mind is dull, he will have difficulty learning anything. Yet on the other hand, no field of Western knowledge had been more overlooked than that of consciousness itself, until Maharishi founded the Science of Creative Intelligence.

Having completed the prerequisite training in SCI at the local New Haven TM center, I decided to enroll in a six-month course to become a TM teacher at the completion of my psychiatric training. When I left for the course, held under Maharishi's supervision in Switzerland, I must admit that I had been enjoying the TM program so much that I thought I was going off for a vacation in a beautiful country as well as to become a TM instructor. To my great surprise, the TM teacher training course was no idle vacation. In fact, it was one of the most intensive learning experiences I have ever encountered. From early morning until late at night we spent all of our time in a course of study designed to make us highly competent teachers of the TM and SCI programs. One of the reasons for our intensive study was the requirement that all final exams be passed without any errors. Each course participant had to demonstrate flawless knowledge of the course material in order to become a TM teacher. The testing on this course was as rigorous as the testing I underwent during my medical school years. When I graduated from the course, I felt a real sense of pride and a high degree of professionalism, now not only as a psychiatrist but also as a teacher of the TM program. I had felt and seen these same feelings of confidence in professional ability, great respect for tradition, and a strong sense of mission to help others when my colleagues and I graduated from medical school and at the completion of specialty training.

Sometimes people ask me why they cannot teach the TM technique to their friends after learning it themselves. On the basis of my experience, I answer that there is every difference in the world between learning and teaching the TM technique. People vary widely in their initial experiences in learning the TM technique, and the teacher must know what specific instructions to give each person with a different kind of learning experience. Although each person who takes the initial TM course learns the same technique, everyone learns at his or her own rate and requires individualized instruction. I know that I could not have taught the TM technique properly without completing the necessary training. It would have been grandiose and a great error for me to have thought to myself, "Ah, I'm a psychiatrist, a physician of the mind; therefore, I have the training and ability to teach the TM program without attending a teacher training course." The result of such thinking would have been tragic because no one whom I might have tried to teach would have learned the TM technique properly. From a medical point of view, the value of highly trained teachers of the TM program all over the world cannot be overestimated. The practicing physician can only feel confident recommending the TM program if he knows that this time-proven, scientifically validated technique is taught systematically by highly qualified instructors.

I had begun cautiously recommending the TM program to some of my patients during my last year at Yale and was impressed with the initial results. I received much inspiration and guidance in doing so from Dr. Glueck, whose pioneering work on the use of the TM program as an adjunct treatment of psychiatric patients was well under way.

When I returned to my practice after graduating from the TM teacher training course, I felt even more confident and qualified to incorporate the TM program into psychiatric practice. Along with my medical colleagues at the Institute of Psychophysiological Medicine, I began strongly recommending the TM program to many of my patients. As a teacher of TM at the local San Diego World Plan Center, I frequently taught our patients and much of my staff in weekend courses. I began finding that many of my patients suffering from mild middle-class neurosis improved rapidly after starting the TM program. Never before had I seen these kinds of patients, who are generally stable but plagued by anxiety and other symptoms, improve so quickly. It soon became clear to me that the TM program, along with an average of about seven psychotherapy sessions to help a patient through a crisis or to provide necessary support, education, and guidance, was all that many patients needed to begin losing their symptoms and start enjoying happier lives. At the same time, I discovered that severely disturbed patients need very careful supervision based on expert knowledge of psychiatry and the TM program in order for the TM program to prove helpful for them. I did find that when used properly, as an adjunct to psychotherapy, the TM program can add significantly to the recovery of severely disturbed patients. The more I used the TM program with all my patients, the more clear it became that the Science of Creative Intelligence offers a whole new understanding of the mind. This new science, along with its practical aspect, the TM technique, can advance the practice of psychiatry and psychotherapy in many ways.

Will TM Put Psychiatry Out of Business?

Sometimes people ask me whether I worry that the TM movement is going to put me out of business. I enjoy this question because it gives me an opportunity to explain how I see the TM program fitting into new trends in medicine and psychiatry.

Over the past several decades of exciting scientific discoveries and increasing specialization and subspecialization, medicine has focused on the diagnosis and treatment of specific diseases at the expense of promoting total health. Although cardiologists are now highly skilled in handling cardiac arhythmias, the number of people dying from heart attacks at earlier and earlier ages continues to rise steadily. Pulmonary physicians have learned much about managing emphysema and lung cancer, but the sale of cigarettes and the incidence of these diseases grow yearly. Psychiatrists have developed psychotherapeutic and psychopharmacological means of treating neuroses and psychoses, but more and more people are seeking psychiatric help than ever before. I do not mean to be the least bit critical of the medical advances resulting from specialization and sub-specialization, but this trend toward increasing technological sophistication in the treatment of specific diseases is not helping people avoid getting sick in the first place. For this reason, health maintenance must become a central theme for future health care planning and research. The truth in the old proverb, "An ounce of prevention is worth a pound of cure" has never been more clear.

In trying to promote health maintenance, modern medicine is returning to a few ancient and fundamental medical principles. Perhaps the most important of these ideas is the close connection between emotional and physical health. Medical specialization has contributed so greatly to separate treatment of emotional and physical illness that many people think medicine has always distinguished doctors of the body from doctors of the mind. Actually, the belief that mind and body are inseparable and that the patient should be treated as a whole goes back beyond the formal practice of medicine. The Greeks recognized that a sound mind requires a sound body and that a sick person is likely to feel sick in mind and body too. Twenty-four hundred years ago, Hippocrates, the father of Western medicine, recognized that "our joys, delight, laughter...our griefs, despondency and lamentation...the fears and terrors that assail us, some by night and some by day" are inextricably intertwined with changes in bodily functioning. He knew that a violent emotion could trigger an asthma attack, and he put this knowledge to work in his therapeutics. He reportedly used support and counsel-

ing to cure King Perdicas of Macedonia of a gastrointestinal disorder.

The new discoveries of psychophysiological and
psychosomatic medicine are gradually melting the
barrier between psychiatry and medicine. Claude
Bernard, a famous nineteenth-century physician,
taught that the seeds of disease and disorder hover all
around us but whether or not they take root depends
primarily upon the condition of the terrain, the human
body. The most complex physical structure of all known
works of nature, the human body consists of billions of
interconnected cells organized with immeasurable
complexity into tissues, organs, and organ systems. The
ability of this awesome piece of biomachinery to
withstand and adjust to a never-ending flow of pressure
from within and without depends on maintaining a
maximum degree of ease and orderly functioning.
Indeed, life itself depends on maintaining a maximum
degree of biochemical order in the face of a changing
environment.

The stress cycle appears to be the principle means by
which people make themselves ripe for disease.
Emotional and/or physical events can trigger the stress
cycle. In either case, the stress cycle increases susceptibility to diseases of all kinds — from colds and
indigestion to tuberculosis and heart disease. Psychiatrist Holmes found that ten times more widows die
during the first year after the death of their spouses
than other single and married women in the same age
groups. Another remarkable finding of his was that in
the year following the divorce divorced persons have an
illness rate twelve times higher than married people. I
have already explained how distress causes havoc in
both physiological and psychological functioning.
Because distress has emotional and physical causes and
results in physical and emotional symptoms, its treatment requires an approach which takes into account the
unity of mind and body.

Most physicians would agree that chronic distress plays a critical role in undermining health; yet the effective diagnosis and treatment of chronic distress has eluded most doctors. I believe that the barrier between modern psychiatry and general medicine has contributed significantly toward this shortcoming in modern medical practice. If they diagnose chronic distress at all, most doctors will treat it reflexively with a prescription for tranquilizers and some good advice. It's funny that as soon as doctors go into practice they seem to forget their own distress — hyperventilation, headaches, heart palpitations, and nervous tension — during medical school exams. It is estimated that as many as 80 per cent of the patients seeing family doctors are suffering from what basically amounts to chronic distress. These patients may not be seriously ill, but they are certainly suffering and may be on the road to serious illness in years to come. These concerns underlie modern medicine's return to a psychophysiological approach which treats the whole person, both mind and body.

At the Institute of Psychophysiological Medicine, we combine psychiatric and general medical practice. Psychiatrists and family practitioners share their skills in the diagnosis and treatment of people suffering from organic and emotional illnesses. Before my involvement with the TM program, I was among those physicians concerned that medicine had taken a wrong turn in separating the treatment of emotional and physical illness. My experience using the TM program with a wide range of patients suffering from emotional and organic illness greatly strengthened my practice of psychophysiological medicine and health maintenance.

Perhaps the most important contribution that the TM program makes to our practice of psychophysiological medicine is prevention. Systematic reduction of chronic distress is imperative for teaching people how to avoid recurrence of old illnesses and to escape falling victim to new ones. Because the TM program produces physiological changes which help in the recovery from emotional and organic illness, we find it ideally suited to our efforts to treat people rather than diseases at the Institute. It adds a very human touch to the treatment process. We have been very pleased with the feedback that we have received from our meditating patients. They recognize that the TM program is consistent with the need for rest to promote healing.

In my own practice of psychiatry, I feel more strongly identified with the medical profession since I've started prescribing the TM program. Until the advent of the TM program, psychiatrists had relied on psychotherapy as the principle treatment for neurosis. In practicing long-term psychotherapy, however, psychiatrists develop a relationship with their patients that is completely atypical of medical practice. No other doctor will spend hundreds of hours with a single patient over many years. The orthopedist does not spend hours and hours with the person who breaks his leg. He simply sets the fracture, puts the leg in a cast, and watches over the patient to make sure that the leg is healing properly. The internist does not spend hours and hours trying to cure his patient of pneumonia. He puts the patient to bed, prescribes appropriate antibiotics, and watches over the patient to make sure that no complications arise. The surgeon does not spend years treating his patients, but simply performs whatever surgical operation is necessary and watches the patient for post-operative complications. The TM program enables the psychiatrist to prescribe a means whereby a person can promote his own psychological growth and reduce the need for long hours of psychotherapy.

Psychotherapy is based on the assumption that the psychiatrist can provide sufficient corrective emotional experiences to promote healing in his patients. Experience shows that this process takes hundreds of hours for minimal results. With the scientific validation and widespread availability of the TM program, psychiatry has a means of treating mild middle-class neurosis efficiently and effectively. The TM program permits the psychiatrist to prescribe a safe and reliable means whereby the patient can gain corrective experience on his own. The psychiatrist then returns to the role of physician, watching over the patient to make sure that the patient is following the therapeutic routine and that no complications arise while natural healing takes place.

Hippocrates very humbly pointed out that the physician only applies the splint; nature heals the broken bone. Rest has always been a doctor's most fundamental prescription because rest permits natural healing processes to work most effectively. An old Latin addage — *Medicus curat, Natura sanat,* the physician treats but nature heals — applies well to the use of the TM program in the treatment of emotional and physical illness. On the basis of clinical experience and numerous scientific studies, I have become convinced that the TM program represents the most effective natural means available for the treatment of mild middle-class neurosis and the symptoms of chronic distress.

With the growth of individual and social concern about happiness and human potential over the last several decades, the psychiatrist has been called on to play three related but distinct roles. On the one hand, he is a medical specialist who takes care of people suffering from a mental illness. This role is implicit in the classical definition of psychiatry as a medical specialty. On the other hand, today's psychiatrist is spending more and more of his time seeing people who do not suffer from an illness or disease in the medical sense and do not really require the attention of a medical specialist, but are still unhappy and seeking help. This role is implicit in the popular definition of psychiatry as the place to turn to for help with emotional problems. The third role of the psychiatrist has its roots in the ancient meaning of psychiatry, derived from the words *psyche* (spirit) and *iatros* (healing). In his role as healer of the spirit, the psychiatrist grapples with the ultimate questions of identity, the nature of man, the purpose of life, and the highest possibilities for human fulfillment.

Is the TM program going to put psychiatrists out of business? Surely not. But it will provide a shortcut to long-term therapy for millions of average middle-class neurotics and will add significantly to the treatment of severely neurotic and psychotic patients. By relieving the psychiatrist of the need to start his middle-class neurotic patients on long-term therapy, the TM program can free the psychiatrist to give more attention to those patients who really need his professional skills.

Above all, psychiatrists are physicians devoting their lives to helping relieve the emotional suffering that troubles millions today. Because the TM program is proving to be a potent and useful means of improving emotional well-being, psychiatrists in general are welcoming its growing popularity. If more and more people would practice the TM program as a kind of vaccine against distress and emotional illness, all mental health profesisonals would applaud the resulting decline in mental illness.

A GP Psychiatrist

When people learn that I do little long-term psychotherapy in the classical sense, they often ask what I actually do with my patients. My practice is a typical population of psychiatric patients — all ages, diverse socio-economic backgrounds, and a wide range of diagnostic categories including many average middle-class neurotics. Some patients who come to see me need immediate hospitalization; most do well as outpatients. I give all my patients extensive life history questionnaires at the time of their initial evaluation and periodic follow up questionnaires to help me judge the results of treatment. I like to think of myself as a GP psychiatrist, drawing on a wide range of experience and knowledge from medicine and general psychiatry and not just specializing in one psychotherapeutic approach. With each patient, I will usually function in one or a combination of three basic roles: physician, educator, or guide.

When a person complaining of emotional and physical symptoms comes into my office, my first role is that of a physician. Is the person suffering from an organic illness? Is he or she an average middle-class neurotic or a severly troubled individual? These questions guide the diagnostic process that is always the critical first step in setting out to help a patient. A person may show all the signs of anxiety neurosis — severe anxiety attacks, excessive worry, sleep disorders and fatigue — but have a very different illness. For example, hyperthyroidism, hypoglycemia, or pheochromocytoma may all mimic anxiety neurosis. The following case is an illustration of the importance of the psychiatrist's role as physician.

William had been out of the Army two years before coming to see me. Twenty-six years old and in the real estate business with his brother, he was highly agitated during his first office visit. He complained of frequent anxiety attacks and showed signs of growing paranoia. Specifically he believed that his brother was cheating him and trying to take over their business. Though he seemed to love his mother, he reported a complete inability to control the angry outbursts that he frequently vented upon her. The last psychiatrist whom William saw diagnosed him as a paranoid schizophrenic, hospitalized him for a month, and put him on a rather heavy dosage of phenothiazines. The drugs made William groggy but did not adequately relieve his symptoms. At the encouragement of a family friend, William sought my help.

When I first saw him, I took a very detailed history and discovered some important symptoms which he had not reported to his previous doctors. William's anxiety attacks apparently went back to his early childhood, when he would for no obvious reason feel "seized by panic and ready to explode." In addition, he was sometimes very suddenly troubled by what is called macropsia-micropsia, which means that his visual image would become very large (e.g., a chair would seem ten feet tall) or very small (e.g., a person might seem no bigger than a postage stamp). William never reported this symptom to his other doctors for fear of being seen as a "real case for the nut-house." His macropsia-micropsia occurred in discrete episodes often accompanied by a strange smell, severe anxiety, and poor impulse control. He would fear flying into a rage and hurting someone.

I ordered an EEG, and the findings confirmed my suspicions. William showed a seizure focus in the left temporal lobe. I diagnosed him as suffering from temporal lobe epilepsy and started him on anti-epileptic medication. He began psychotherapy with me to help sort out his paranoia and to better understand and accept his epilepsy. Once on Dilantin, he began to improve rapidly. His need for phenothiazines dropped sharply over the next few months. During this time, I started him on the TM program, and his anxiety attacks and temporal lobe seizures further decreased. He began to deal more rationally with his paranoia and to recognize it as the net product of some valid real-life suspicions interacting with his long untreated illness. If a person frequently gets anxious and has such unsettling symptoms as macropsia-micropsia, he can easily start feeling paranoid. Since learning to understand and manage his epilepsy, William has needed neither further hospitalization nor additional psychotherapy. Follow-up after 22 months revealed him largely free of symptoms and making progress in all areas of his life. The impact of the TM technique upon epilepsy shows much individual variation depending on the kind of seizure disorder and whether anxiety or rage play contributory roles. The addition of the TM program to standard medical therapeutics for epilepsy deserves clinical investigation. The psychopysiological approach was critical to William's diagnosis and treatment. Had his epilepsy remained untreated, his condition would have steadily deteriorated, as expected in the "chronic paranoid schizophrenic." This single case does not mean that all or even most schizophrenics have been mis-diagnosed. It does illustrate the importance of psychophysiological medicine in psychiatry. A medical examination to rule out organic disease should always be completed before a patient is diagnosed as suffering from an emotional illness or chronic distress.

Once the possibility of an organic illness is ruled out the task of assessing the severity of the patient's emotional disturbance remains. Because psychiatric patients often go through phases of remissions and exacerbations, diagnosis and treatment of an emotionally disturbed individual requires considerable skill. To diagnose a latent schizophrenic on the verge of a psychotic break as an average middle-class neurotic and just send him off to the TM center would obviously be a serious mistake. Therefore, when a person complains of emotional distress, I look for the signs of severe, regressive, or long-lasting symptoms indicating he or she has more than a mild middle-class neurosis. If the person has the mild emotional problems which characterize the middle-class neurotic, a referral to the TM center and a number of follow-up visits with me are usually sufficient. The person soon starts reducing his chronic distress and enjoying more happiness through his own self-improvement. On the other hand, if the patient shows signs of schizophrenia, manic-depressive illness, acute depression, alcoholism, drug addiction, or

other severe behavorial, emotional, or thinking dis-
orders, a careful three-pronged treatment program
utilizing medication, psychotherapy, and the TM
program must be designed and carefully managed.

An important contribution which the TM program is
making to my practice is the increase in the number of
patients I can treat. I have virtually no long-term
psychotherapy patients. On the contrary, I am losing
patients all the time, and I love it because it means they
are learning quickly how to sustain their own rapid pace
of self-development. Progressive psychiatrists and
mental health planners alike have pointed out the poor
use of resources involved in the physician going through
four years of medical school, a year of internship, three
years of psychiatric residency, and perhaps an additional
five years of post graduate training in psychoanalysis
only to treat less than ten patients a year. If a
psychiatrist regularly sees patients two, three, or four
times a week for one to five years, he can obviously
handle only a small number of them. Group therapy
arose in part to enable psychiatrists to handle a larger
percentage of the people seeking psychiatrist help, but
the call for means to help the psychiatrist expand his
caseload capacity grows stronger each year.

At the Institute, my colleagues and I are able to see or
supervise a very large number of patients. My working
principle is to see patients as little as necessary to sustain
their *optimal* progress. It is a great error, I believe, to
assume that the more years a patient sees his therapist,
the better the results will be. There is no research to
confirm this assumption; to the contrary, I have
frequently seen long-term psychotherapy have
regressive harmful effects. Rather than encourage long-
term therapy, I tailor a therapy schedule for each
patient. One client may need a half-hour visit weekly,
another 15 minutes daily (for example, an alcoholic
or addict during the first few weeks of abstinence). Some
people may need only monthly telephone checkups after

seeing me regularly for a few months. I see many patients for one hour weekly and only on the rarest of occasions see someone for two hours weekly. I see patients more in the beginning, once a week usually, and less after the first two months. Other than patients who need to be followed long-term for medication maintenance, I generally have no patients in therapy for more than four or five months.

Though I have come to rely heavily on the TM program as an adjunct to standard psychiatric practice, I still use various psychotherapy techniques, behavior therapy, couples work, family therapy, group therapy, and medication as needed in an approach adapted to meet the needs of each patient. I have been impressed with the tremendous utility and great value of the TM program across a wide range of diagnostic categories, for people from all walks of life, and as a complement to many psychotherapeutic techniques. Indeed, when practiced regularly by the psychiatric patient under appropriate supervision, the TM program appears to add substantially to any standard treatment approach.

How a Stretch Practices Psychotherapy

Psychiatrists have been colloquially called "shrinks" or "head shrinkers," probably because they traditionally delve into and analyze early childhood experiences. Many people in and out of the mental health profession still believe that psychoanalyzing problems is necessary for insight and progress in therapy and that the "shrinking" process is therefore basic to psychotherapy. Rather than improving the patient's self-image, this process of focusing on problems lowers or "shrinks" self-esteem.

Neurotics typically begin therapy with inflated views about what the psychiatrist can do for them. It's not uncommon for patients to give their therapists the message either overtly or covertly "Doctor, it's up to you to make me better." We psychiatrists will often answer this plea by saying, "You seem to have the idea that I know how you can solve your problems. Let's explore this childish notion." Though patients with unrealistic expectations present real problems for the psychiatrist, I have long questioned whether analyzing the patient's wishes and expectations is the best approach to treatment. I have asked myself how I would feel if each time I brought my car in to an auto mechanic for servicing, he answered my request for help with, "You seem to have some sort of idea that I can fix your car for you. Let's explore this a little." The psychiatric patient has a right to expect that the psychiatrist will prescribe some definitive kind of treatment which will relieve his suffering. The psychiatrist is correct in teaching the patient that he is not a mental magician and that in the long run the patient must take the responsibility for his own growth and problem solving. But the patient needs more than this message. He cannot maximize his own growth without the knowledge and tools necessary to do so.

Prior to the scientific validation of the TM program, psychiatrists had little choice but to shrink the patient's expectations in order to prepare the patient for the lengthy, tedious, and frequently frustrating process of psychotherapy. Helping the patient develop a realistic self-appraisal and reasonable expectations is certainly of critical importance for psychotherapy to proceed. I have found, however, that prescribing the TM program helps my patients come to this point without spending hours and hours talking about past miseries and magical wishes. This happens largely because from the start I put a substantial responsibility for progress in each patient's hands by prescribing the TM technique, which the person practices on his own for 20 minutes twice daily as compared to his weekly visit with me.

When someone comes to see me, I help him understand that no matter what happened in his past, the basic cause of his present misery is the stress impeding the normal functioning of his body and mind. Once the person understands the psychophysiological roots of his suffering, I let him know that there is a direct and effective way out. I explain that the TM program provides a psychophysiological means by which he can systematically promote natural healing processes to dissolve the backlog of accumulated stresses and maximize health and well-being. Growth will take time, I explain, but I assure him that by following the TM program as prescribed, steady progress will follow. On the basis of this mutual understanding, I establish a therapeutic alliance with my patient. At this point, I let him know that I will assist and support him in better solving life problems while the TM program gradually heals the psyche and unfolds his full potential.

This approach to psychotherapy means that I realistically and honestly raise the person's image of what he can do and encourage expectations about what he can get from the TM program. I gently "stretch," not shrink, his self-image and expectations. What this means practically is that I spend very little time exploring the details of past miseries. My therapeutic sessions generally involve three primary activities: teaching the person basic emotional or interpersonal skills which he or she may be lacking, exploring a crisis situation to help someone work out his or her feelings and behavioral options, and helping an individual understand and make maximum use of all the changes resulting from the TM program. As a "stretch," I expand the person's vision of possibilities in concert with the growth in consciousness taking place. As symptoms abate, I help the person channel his increasing energy, vitality, and emotional well-being toward realistic goals in tune with his desires and abilities.

I see my primary role in a patient's overall treatment not as a psychological surgeon who delves into the person's past to somehow unravel old emotional wounds, but as an educator who helps the person make good use of whatever energy, intelligence, and emotional stability he has available to improve and enjoy his life. In growing up, many people have not learned basic emotional, intellectual, or social skills. Psychotherapy, as an educational process, can help a person learn the skills that he or she lacks. For example, a young man may not have learned how to ask a girl for a date and he may feel inadequate and frustrated because of this inability. It may seem a simple matter to the emotionally healthy person, but some men may need to learn systematically how to say to a woman, "I would very much enjoy taking you to a movie Friday night." Psychotherapy can provide the all-important opportunity for this kind of learning to take place. In working with people to help them catch up on whatever developmental lag may be causing them difficulty, I draw on a wide variety of therapeutic techniques. To help the person who has not learned how to express warm feelings, I may use role playing. Another typical therapeutic approach I draw upon is assertive training to help the shy or inhibited person learn to express his or her desires. For example, I might teach a person how to ask his boss for a raise or how to handle criticism without feeling like crawling into a hole. To accomplish the unlearning of bad emotional habits and to increase a person's behaviorial repertoire in specific areas of incompetence, psychotherapeutic techniques such as role playing, modeling, and group discussion can play useful roles.

Sometimes patients ask me whether they will need psychotherapy if they start the TM program. For some of the people who come to see me, the TM program may be all they need; others can benefit from professional assistance in addition to the TM program. Psychotherapy can provide a "course of study" in which the person learns how to express his new-found creative intelligence in new and rewarding behaviors. The need for this kind of therapeutic support in the severely disturbed person who begins the TM program is obvious. In less disturbed people or average middle-class neurotics, psychotherapy can help make activity more strain free. If a person has a specific behavorial problem which he or she would like to overcome but which lingers even after several months or years of the TM program, psychotherapy with an educational focus may be very useful. A case history best illustrates why a TM practitioner might come for therapy and what he can gain from it.

Fred, a 25 year-old engineer at a large manufacturing firm, had been meditating for two and one-half years before coming to see me. During his first visit, he lauded the TM program for "saving [his] sanity" and "getting [him] to loosen up enough so that [he] had the courage to come for help." He described an anxiety-ridden childhood and adolescence with poor self-esteem crippling his social relations, especially with women. "In college, things got so bad," he said, "I considered therapy, but then a friend turned me on to TM." Over the next two years he noted a dramatic reduction in his general anxiety level. His performance anxiety dropped enough that he began to feel confident at work and started planning his future. When it became clear to him that he needed more education to "get where [he] wanted to go," he enrolled in night school. To his surprise and delight, his anxiety before and during exams disappeared almost entirely. Despite these and other general benefits from the TM program, Fred felt troubled by a lingering neurotic fear which he very much wanted to lose and thought he might now have the courage to face. He had never really dated and panicked at the thought of asking a woman out.

During his first visit, I made the following proposals. First, Fred should stop straining so hard to "make it." Along with the anxiety reduction produced by his TM practice, Fred had noted a considerable increase in energy. Because he had never learned to enjoy himself socially or in sports or hobbies, he channeled all this energy into striving to achieve. But he was doing so at the expense of his health and overall growth. To enrich his personality, Fred needed to let some of that energy flow in new directions. My second suggestion was that we work together on opening up new channels for his creative intelligence and that I teach him some of the interpersonal skills he was lacking.

Over the next four weeks, Fred spent an hour a week with me in which we did role playing. I modeled for him conversing with a woman, including asking her out on a date. I then had him practice what he might say comfortably in his own words. Our sessions involved considerable laughter as Fred discovered that it wasn't so hard after all. In one session, I had one of the office secretaries join us to help Fred practice. When he felt ready, I suggested that we look up in the phone book some organizations which had singles activities for him to get involved in as a first step toward dating. He liked the idea of the Sierra Club and began attending some of their meetings.

Each week during the next two months I reviewed with Fred the progress he was making in his "field work." The theme of these sessions was that the time had come for him to take the plunge. He had somehow gotten the idea that he should wait for the TM program to dissolve all the old stresses inhibiting his desire to date before asking a woman to go out with him. I let him know that some anxiety about doing anything new was inevitable as long as a person was not fully enlightened. I also reinforced his self-image by letting him know that he was in fact an attractive and gentle person. Three months after his first visit, he finally asked one of the women whom he had seen several times at a workshop to go out to dinner. She accepted and Fred had achieved a phase transition of sorts. Within a few weeks, he was dating frequently and enjoying a dimension of his personality which had lain dormant for years. He continued to see me for another three months to talk over new issues which arose, the most important of which was the deepening of relationships. Again, this was handled in a forthright and educational manner. The variety of complaints that prompts people to seek my help is enormous. I draw on a wide range of psychiatric methods in designing a specific psychotherapeutic program suited to each person. I have noticed, however, that the TM program consistently enhances a person's ability to gain from psychotherapy. First, it reduces the anxiety which often makes it difficult for psychiatric patients to learn anything and thereby directly increases learning ability. In addition, the TM program seems to strengthen motivation to change by reducing the fear of failure and by increasing stability and self-confidence. Finally, it increases the patient's ability to think clearly in an orderly fashion. When a patient experiences a significant growth in mental clarity, he naturally feels an increase in his personal power to fulfill his desires. This feeling whets the patient's appetite to learn, and the increase in mental clarity enables him to bring more of himself to the psychotherapeutic process.

A Stretch as Spiritual Guide

As a "stretch" I am attuned not only to neurotic symptoms of dis-ease and dis-order, but also to symptoms secondary to a spiritual awakening. Psychiatrists Jung[1], Horney[2], Assagioli[3], and Maslow[4] have discussed the stages of spiritual realization, but their writings have not as yet infiltrated the standard curricula in psychiatric training. Indeed the phenomenon of spiritual awakening has received so little attention in the psychiatric literature that most practitioners are unprepared to diagnose and treat the personality changes resulting from it.

Spiritual refers to the experience of wholeness and integration, irrespective of religious belief or affiliation. It is not a statement of belief per se or a measure of church attendance; indeed an atheist could have a profound spiritual life. Spiritual experiences of an extraordinary as well as of a more general nature have been recorded throughout history and in every culture. There are indications that spiritual awakenings are becoming widespread among Americans today. A Gallup Poll conducted in 1962 asked, "Would you say that you have ever had a 'religious or mystic experience' — that is, a moment of sudden religious insight or awakening?" One adult in five answered "yes" to this question. With respect to the whole adult population, this percentage represents approximately 20 million people. At the National Opinion Research Center of the University of Chicago, Andrew M. Greeley and William C. McCready conducted a survey in 1974 among some 1,500 representative American adults. They asked, "Have you ever had the feeling of being very close to a powerful spiritual force that seemed to lift you out of yourself?"[5] Forty per cent reported having had at least one such experience and half of these had felt it several times, indicating that 40 million adults have experienced the symptoms of spiritual awakening, 20 million of them repeatedly. These surveys suggest that the number of people reporting spiritual experiences has more than doubled in a decade.

An overwhelming feeling of happiness, an ecstatic joy that fills the person with a deep sense of peace, security, understanding, and certainty are what usually characterize a harmonious spiritual awakening. People of all ages, races, nationalities, and occupations report a virtually identical experience of ecstasy, of rebirth, of being lifted out of themselves, of knowing the "way things really are." This experience of "absolute" knowledge gives the person an unshakeable conviction and profound understanding of life's basic goodness and unity and leaves him totally comfortable with his place in the larger scheme of things. Though difficult for many to put into words, this knowingness, what Maslow called "Being cognition," leaves all who have had it significantly changed, never to be quite the same again.

Spiritual awakenings are ecstatic and enrapturing when they occur and have profound significance for the people who have them, but they may also be alarming and disruptive. The vast majority of people who have these experiences never speak of them to anyone, not even a close family member or friend, for fear of being thought "crazy" or because the awakening is do deeply personal that "it cannot be adequately communicated, so why bother." Unfortunately, the attitude of many mental health workers is to see these reports of spiritual awakenings within a pyschopathological model, as a form of regression, an escape, a mini-psychotic episode, or a symptom of schizophrenia. This is unfortunate because many healthy and stable individuals have these experiences but need support and understanding from a knowledgeable guide if they become initially unsettled or confused. The Greeley and McCready survey was doubly remarkable because the most frequent "mystics" were not drug-taking hippies or fundamentalists, but well-educated, disproportionately Protestant, solid middle-America types.

Psychiatrist Robert Assagioli, the founder of Psychosynthesis, has outlined how to recognize and manage disturbances that can arise at the various stages of spiritual realization. Two cases from my practice illustrate the value of the TM program in assisting in the treatment of these spiritual crises.

Anne was a 25 year-old housewife who quite suddenly and unexpectedly had a profound spiritual awakening one morning:

It was incredible. I opened my eyes to find the room filled with light, a golden glow that left everything fresh and radiant. It was like I saw the world again for the first time. It brought me to tears. Everything was so beautiful, so precious. I felt sanctified and made whole. Life was profoundly good; wars, bickering, and complaints seemed silly. Love, universal love, was the only reality. I understood myself, history, my family, the world situation, everything. But I wasn't thinking, I just knew. There was no fear — just light, love, and a peace that defies all description. It was all encompassing; time stood still, each moment seemed infinite and blissful.

But as great as the feeling was while it lasted (it lasted for about eight hours and then gradually receded over the next ten) that's how crushed I felt when it left. It was worse than if I had all at once lost my husband, child, parents, and best friends. I felt like I had been cast out, had the door to the spiritual kingdom slammed in my face. I felt unworthy, more so than I had ever felt before. My existence seemed shallow and futile without that larger loving awareness.

An ecstatic state may last for moments, hours, or even days, but it is bound to cease. When the knowingness and experience of life's oneness, love, and joy begin to fade, a personal crisis may ensue. As Assagioli so poignantly describes:

The personal ego re-awakens and asserts itself with renewed force. All the rocks and rubbish, which had been covered and concealed at high tide, emerge again. The man, whose moral conscience has now become more refined and exacting, whose thirst for perfection has become more intense, judges with greater severity and condemns his personality with a new vehemence; he is apt to harbor the false belief of having fallen lower than he was before.[6]

Anne had never suffered from any emotional disorder or abused drugs. Following the "coming down" from her awakening, however, she became so full of despair that at the encouragement of a friend she sought me out. When Anne first came to see me, she was no longer certain whether her experience had been real, a fantasy, or "just plain crazy."

Anne felt very relieved when I validated her experience. I read her passages from Maharishi, Thomas

Aquinas, Plato, William Blake, and William Wordsworth to help her appreciate the universality of what she had experienced. When she realized that she had glimpsed life's deeper reality, the transcendental field, her spirit began to pick up. But her pressing questions remained: "Why would such a supreme experience come and go, and how can I regain it?"

Our discussion of enlightenment helped her with these questions. I again read passages of Maharishi's that distinguished between temporary experience of the transcendent and the permanent experience of it in the state of enlightenment. Anne had heard of enlightenment but had always thought it a mystical state with little practical value, and whether practical or not, attainable only through many years of effort. A brief discussion of psychophysiology helped dispel these misconceptions. I showed her how enlightenment is simply the normal state of the human biomachinery free from the backlog of old stresses; I explained how the TM program unfolds this state naturally. When she saw that the TM program would bring her back to the heights of pure consciousness in a step-by-step fashion, she became eager to begin. She recognized that the "fall" which she had experienced was natural and that she could now plant herself firmly on the path to total enlightenment.

Anne learned the TM technique the weekend after her visit with me and thoroughly enjoyed it. During her first meditation, she once again glimpsed the transcendent, not quite with all the fireworks of her first experience, but in a stable and rewarding way. After two more visits with me, twice daily TM practice and advanced lectures at the TM center were all she needed. She did beautifully and at last contact was on her way to a TM teacher training course.

Anne's case illustrates the kind of support necessary to help a person through a spiritual crisis secondary to a sudden "awakening." Tom's case illustrates another kind of spiritual crisis which may occur from the lack of any such glimpse of life's deeper reality.

Tom, a 32 year-old married architect, came to me complaining of "depression, low motivation, loss of reality, and acute anxiety attacks." A partner in a leading firm, he was quite successful. He had a stylish home, enjoyed collecting primitive art, was well read, and his recreational pursuits included extensive travel and sports cars. Married to a wonderful woman, he reported no major problems at home and had suffered no major difficulties throughout childhood, adolescence, and early adulthood. In the classical sense Tom had "made it"; yet his history revealed a vague and elusive but growing sense of emptiness, "something missing," which he found difficult to describe. He compared his experience to "being frightened but not knowing the cause" and expressed frustration at his inability "to straighten [himself] out by the power of [his] own intellect." Tom had been living the apparent full enjoyment of health and prosperity when this progressive disturbance of his inner life caught him by surprise; he slipped into a spiritual crisis without knowing it. This kind of crisis typically occurs not in neurotic individuals but rather in those who are in many ways already happy and dynamic people.

Tom fought his growing despair for awhile by throwing himself into his business affairs, traveling with his wife almost every weekend, "going to parties right and left," and experimenting with marijuana. The joy of these activities came and went, but his inner strain always returned. Familiar with some psychological concepts, he began to fear that his "psychological defenses were crumbling" and that he was "becoming psychotic." His persistent inner turmoil produced a variety of symptoms including depression, insomnia, agitation, restlessness, exhaustion, and all kinds of physical symptoms. He went to see his family doctor who told him that he was suffering from a "bad case of nerves" and prescribed Valium and sleeping pills to help him "settle down and take it easy." However, Tom's condition worsened. He started losing interest in his personal and professional affairs and felt what he had valued in life was "vanishing like a dream." He became preoccupied with questions about the purpose of life, the meaning of his despair, and intellectual doubts of many kinds. As his anxiety, agitation, and uneasiness became more and more painful, his dependency on Valium grew.

By the time he came to my office, he was convinced that he was going to "flip his lid." He described himself as "trapped in a box" with his inner self "pounding the walls." Having no idea what he was looking for, he played with ideas such as quitting his job, leaving his marriage, and even taking his own life. His decision-making and reasoning abilities were clearly impaired. He knew he "had everything" but was miserable. As a result, he felt oppressed by guilt and remorse.

How should Tom's condition be diagnosed? Observed from the outside and gauged in ordinary standards of mental health, he had deteriorated mentally and emotionally. His productivity and efficiency had dropped. He was not spared his family doctor's well-meaning but superficial diagnosis of a "bad case of nerves." In many ways, his symptoms resembled the various manifestations of psychoneurosis and a borderline schizophrenic state. His physical symptoms such as a rapid heart rate and anxiety attacks suggested anxiety neurosis; his overall personality integration and his deeply rooted existential concerns suggested that he was not suffering from ordinary pathogenic conflicts but symptoms secondary to a spiritual crisis.

The symptoms of ordinary neurosis are regressive in nature, while those resulting from unconscious stirrings of spiritual potential are distinctly progressive. Neurotic patients generally show signs of emotional immaturity such as inability to express feelings easily and appropriately. The spiritual crisis usually occurs, however,

in the emotionally mature person who is looking for
something more in life. The neurotic person often has
difficulties with parents, mate, or children because he
has not become emotionally autonomous and remains
oppressed by child-like attitudes. On the other hand, the
person in a spiritual crisis has difficulties with friends
and family because his emotional autonomy is so great
that he feels driven to withdraw into himself for a while
until he finds what he is seeking. The neurotic may seek
refuge in illness or invalidism in order to escape the
requirements of ordinary personal and social life. The
person in a spiritual crisis has not previously and does
not during his crisis resort to manipulative, deceitful
ways of avoiding responsibility. On the contrary, he has
usually been very responsible and takes the responsibility for his present crisis squarely upon his own shoulders.
Finally, the personal history of the neurotic reveals
symptoms deeply rooted in the person's past while the
history of the person in a spiritual crisis shows
symptoms emerging for no obvious reason.

Several decades ago, Jung recognized the progressive
nature of the spiritual crisis when he wrote:

> To be normal is a splendid ideal for the unsuccessful, for
> all those who have not yet found an adaptation. But for
> people who have far more ability than the average, for
> whom it was never hard to gain successes and to
> accomplish their share of the world's work — for them
> restriction to the normal signifies the bed of Procrustes,
> unbearable bordeom, infernal sterility and hopelessness.[7]

How to treat a person going through a spiritual crisis
depends first upon understanding its cause.

The origin of a spiritual crisis is lack of spiritual
experience. A person can start feeling empty inside
when he has all the modern comforts of living but lacks a
profound inner experience of wholeness. Without such a
well spring of inner experience, the small ego can start to
feel asphyxiated by the boundaries of everyday living
even though everyday pleasures are many. The TM
program is ideally suited to the treatment of spiritual

crises because it permits the direct experience of inner wholeness. When a person transcends during practice of the TM technique, the small ego throws off the shackles of bounded perception and gains the status of unbounded pure consciousness. This experience, along with knowledge about it, are the means for a person undergoing a spiritual crisis to emerge at a higher level of personality integration.

When I explained the TM program to Tom, he decided to begin the following weekend. His wife took the course with him. From the very beginning, he noticed a reduction in symptoms. His insomnia cleared and his anxiety lessened. He felt reassured that he was not "going crazy." Over the next weeks and months he reported feelings of optimism and well-being much greater than he had ever known before. He decided, after thinking it over carefully, to leave his architectural firm because it had become "too commercial and was cramping his creativity." After taking a month off with his wife to see the latest modern European architecture, he returned feeling refreshed and started his own firm. Whereas he had been losing his ability to enjoy his day-to-day activities, he gradually discovered renewed pleasure and satisfaction in the simple routines of living. He reported a substantial growth in his occupational creativity, "almost like discovering a whole new reservoir of ideas." Finally, he felt his "search was over"; he now knew what he had been looking for and how to find it.

My role with Tom was more that of a spiritual guide than psychotherapist in the classical sense. As a teacher of the TM program, I could play for Tom certain audiotapes by Maharishi which elucidate the process of spiritual growth better than any written material. These tapes often served as the basis for our sessions, helping Tom learn as much about his experience as possible. Several months after beginning the program, Tom felt his growth had slowed. Ups and downs on the path to enlightenment are natural. Tom learned that he need not doubt his progress during a period of apparently slow growth. We discussed how the physiological effects of the TM program assure steady growth even when it may not be immediately noticeable on the surface of the personality. I saw Tom five times over the next two months to help him recover as quickly as possible from his crisis. He then started seeing me on a monthly basis for about six months, not so much because he needed it but because he felt he got a lot out of our discussions. At the end of this period, it became clear to us that taking residence courses and the SCI course at the center rather than more visits with me was the best way for him to accelerate his growth.

Treating people in spiritual crises requires some caution and special skills from the therapist. He must have the dual competence of a trained psychotherapist and spiritual guide. Suffering secondary to a spiritual crisis must be carefully distinguished from a basic ego disturbance, psychoneurosis, or psychosis. It is obvious that treatments appropriate to these two kinds of patients are quite different. The neurotic must be assisted in eliminating fears, inhibitions, and dependency and in developing a mature ego appreciative of self and others. The person in a spiritual crisis needs help in expanding his emotional and intellectual horizons to allow the transcendent its proper place in the personality. The TM program is very helpful to both categories of patients, but the role of the therapist is very different for each.

In my practice, I see many patients who may show both neurotic symptoms and those secondary to spiritual growth. Some people may achieve a high degree of spiritual development but remain handicapped by certain infantile fears or interpersonal "hang-ups." The therapist must be sensitive to such a person's needs for spiritual validation while fostering personality re-education in specific areas. Few psychiatrists presently have the training necessary to treat a person in a spiritual crisis, but I am optimistic that this situation will change as more mental health professionals recognize the significance of applying the Science of Creative Intelligence to their work and take the SCI course.

Doctor, Do You Practice the TM Program?

Even though psychiatrists face the same stresses and strains that affect almost everyone today, people expect them to be free from emotional distress. This expectation may not be unreasonable because an auto mechanic whose car never ran properly would hardly deserve confidence as an auto mechanic.

"It is particularly often noted by laymen as well as professional observers," wrote Dr. Albert Ellis, founder of Rational Therapy, "that most psychotherapy practitioners are themselves hardly the very best models of healthy behavior. Instead of being minimally anxious and hostile as on theoretical grounds one might expect them to be if their own therories work well, they are frequently seriously emotionally disturbed, even after they have undergone lengthy psychoanalytic or other treatment."[8]

Psychiatrists are motivated to alleviate suffering in themselves and their patients, and in quiet moments almost every psychotherapist wishes that he could better reflect the ideals of emotional health and well-being that he tries to foster in his patients. However, there are few quiet moments for a psychiatrist. It is a very difficult and demanding profession and has one of the highest rates of suicide and drug addiction of any group. The general failure of psychiatrists to enjoy a high ideal of mental health does not so much reflect badly on them as people as on the limited efficacy of psychotherapy alone as an efficient means of producing emotionally healthy people. If psychotherapy doesn't cure the patient, it cannot be expected to cure the doctor. In an important article on the TM program as an adjunct to psychotherapy, psychologist Patricia Carrington and her husband psychoanalyst Harmon Ephron point out the usefulness of the TM program for the therapist's personal growth.[9] Psychiatrists who learn the TM technique often take to it immediately because they quickly see its potential value for their personal and professional lives.

The TM program helps psychiatrists avoid two occupational hazards — exhaustion and loss of emotional objectivity. Few people appreciate how strenuous helping people with emotional problems can be. Listening to patient after patient pour out all the miseries of life can be exhausting, which explains the jokes about patients saying "Doctor, are you there?" or "Doctor, are you asleep?" When I began the TM program, one of the first benefits which I noticed was my ability to be more fresh and alert with each person who entered my office. Psychotherapy sessions can be emotionally trying not only for the patient but for the therapist. When the therapist sees another patient just minutes after a very heavy session with a previous patient, he cannot help but carry over some of the emotional stress. I have found that the TM program helps considerably in enabling me to listen attentively without becoming so emotionally caught up with a particular patient that I carry his problems to the next session. The TM program fosters the spontaneous ability to care along with the physiological stability necessary for empathy and emotional objectivity. It promotes the growth of a fully developed heart and mind, so necessary for a therapist.

In his discussion of transference Freud was the first to describe just how intimate psychotherapy becomes when the patient transfers all his repressed feelings about his parents onto the therapist. No matter how much the therapist may wish to remain objective, therapists also transfer some of their wishes and needs onto the patient. This phenomenon of counter-transference may be damaging to the best interests of the patient. For example, the therapist may tell himself that he wants to make his patients more self-reliant while all along he encourages their dependency because he transfers his need for people to be dependent on him to his patients. Because the TM program daily exposes the whole fabric of the nervous system to deep relaxation, it promotes the kind of psychological integration that helps the therapist avoid the pitfalls of counter-transference.

My colleagues and I at the Institute of Psycho-physiological Medicine, as well as physicians using the TM program whom I have met all over the world, are recognizing that the TM program may be essential for a doctor to be at his best personally and professionally. Dr. Clifford Ward, the Medical Director at the Institute, described the benefits he has noted from the TM program:

As a physician and physiologist, I first became interested in the therapeutic use of the TM program when I read the physiological studies describing the way in which the program stabilizes the autonomic nervous system. The concept of a person being able to intervene naturally in stablilizing his autonomic nervous system has boundless potential for optimal health. The overt manifestations of certain major diseases are the result of years of neurophysiological turmoil, harassing, and fatiguing the autonomic nervous system.

After having learned the TM technique a year ago, I began experiencing its benefits first hand. A tranquil efficiency prevails. Dealing with what was the stress of a busy medical practice has become a joy. Achievements come much more easily. In stressful situations, health-promoting rather than health-damaging physiological responses occur. And how? It's all just a matter of optimizing one's neurophysiology through the TM program.

Psychiatrist Robert Hyman spent a year working with us at the Institute. He has been a teacher of the TM program for two years and a meditator for four years. "Using the TM program in my psychiatric practice has made psychiatry a much more enjoyable profession," he wrote, "because it has reduced the frustration of wanting to do more for my suffering patients than I had the knowledge or means to do. Prior to my personal and professional use of the TM technique, psychiatry was frequently fatiguing and non-fulfilling. The TM program has helped me grow as a person and as a psychiatrist, and it is proving to be the most important element in the treatment program for my patients." He has found the TM program helpful to himself and to his patients in gently relaxing psychological defenses which waste energy, cloud interpersonal relationships, and inhibit the natural enjoyment of living. "Defenses dissolve spontaneously through the program," wrote Dr. Hyman, "because the underlying anxiety and conflicts which seemed to require defenses simply disappear." On a very personal note, Dr. Hyman concludes, "Through the TM program I have discovered a wonderful feeling of effortlessness, ease, and comfort in everything I do. I enjoy the beauty of life much more than before I began TM, and I am much more appreciative of the natural tendency of life to progress. The seeming antagonism between the world and myself has disappeared, and I have enjoyed an inner spiritual growth which psychiatry only rarely talks about but generally recognizes as representing an ideal of human grownth."

The entire staff at the Institute practices the TM program. I am convinced that it makes for a much better work atmosphere. Even though our offices are filled with stressed and suffering people, the feeling in the air is one of ease, order, and satisfaction. Our patients often comment on how pleasant the office atmosphere is. I would not be surprised if the general feeling of ease and order in our staff did not contribute in large measure to our patients' willingness to begin the TM program.

Sometimes a patient will say, "Everyone here is so happy. That's what I want!" Indeed, that is what we all want.

At the risk of sounding a bit mushy and unscientific, I would add a human note to how the TM program helps therapists. It enhances their ability to love. Unconditional love is often a patient's most important need because most patients have been love-starved throughout their lives. Patients need to be accepted fully and non-blamefully in spite of their incompetencies, misdeeds, disturbances, and complaints. If the patient feels the doctor's genuine love and compassion, a helping relationship can blossom. Ironically, psychologists and psychiatrists are often just as guilty as many physicians in remaining aloof and cold behind their professional exteriors. I believe that the unloving therapist may often do harm instead of good for many patients despite his best intentions.

In the therapeutic relationship, the psychiatrist lends his own ease, orderly thinking, and emotional well-being to each patient; so he must sustain an ample supply of these qualities. In his 1957 presidential address to the American Psychiatric Association, Dr. Francis J. Braceland emphasized that "the ideal goal of the psychiatrist is to achieve wisdom — to reflect those human qualities most important to helping another person."[10] All aspects of therapy — verbal exchanges, feelings, suggestions — can reflect only as much wisdom as the therapist has. Whereas a surgeon may be a "lousy person" but a "great surgeon" (in the narrow technical sense), a psychiatrist who is a "lousy person" is going to be a "lousy psychiatrist." Psychiatry is not just technique; the human elements remain of paramount importance.

Most patients are surrounded by other stressed people who reinforce dis-ease, dis-order, and emotional chaos. The effective psychiatrist introduces a new element of ease, order, and happiness into the patient's human relationships. In one sense the psychiatrist assumes the responsibility of a lighthouse amidst a sea of darkness. He radiates ease and order which guide the patient toward a strong baseline happiness. The TM program gives the psychiatrist access to his own unlimited reserves of creative intelligence and thereby contributes substantially to effective therapy. Once the patient begins the TM program, he starts drawing on his own creative intelligence and gradually needs to "borrow" less and less ease, order, and happiness from the psychiatrist. Soon, the patient no longer needs the therapeutic relationship. When patient and therapist both practice the TM technique, the termination of therapy is joyful and easy because the patient does not feel cut off from his source of nurturance. He knows that he is genuinely able to keep growing in happiness on his own.

A healing personality is not only necessary for the practice of psychiatry but to most of the health professions — from a dentist helping his patient feel at ease and follow instructions to a physical therapist remotivating a stroke patient. Technical skill may be important, but the health professional's basic attitudes contribute significantly to the outcome of many forms of treatment. Psychologist Carl Rogers emphasizes that emphathetic listening (the ability to feel deeply what another person is saying), caring, emotional ease, and compassion are basic to the healing personality. Unfortunately, the rigors of medical training often squeeze these qualities out of future medical practitioners. As a result, many patients end up running from one doctor to the next because they do not feel really cared for. Because the TM program helps develop personhood in the broadest possible sense, introducing it into medical training may be the best way for young physicians and all health professionals to develop qualities of the healing personality.

An example will illustrate how important the consideration and sensitivity engendered in the physician by the TM program can be in effective medical practice. A doctor does much better when, instead of expecting or demanding patient cooperation, he seeks to earn and retain it. Consider the patient who has just learned that he has essential hypertension. The hurried authoritarian doctor may be tempted to say, "Here's your prescription for hydrochlorothiazide. Take one pill in the morning and one at bedtime. Follow these directions exactly and look for the side-effects I am going to describe to you. Let me see you again...." The physician may be well-meaning and competent but unempathetic to the patient's negative reactions to being told he has a chronic illness and then being ordered to take medication that will probably have unpleasant side-effects. It is no wonder why so many patients fail to follow their doctor's directions, and failure to do so leads to poor patient care. A sensitive physician in this case would directly contribute to better medical care by exploring the patient's fears and telling him about essential hypertension, its course, and what can be done about it. He can become the patient's ally by giving the reasons for prescribing the medication, perhaps noting that the medicine comes in two forms, describing them, and then letting the patient decide which would be the most convenient form to take. This kind of healthy collaboration between doctor and patient does not depend so much on the amount of time that the doctor spends with each patient but the quality of the interaction. Many of my colleagues in their busy medical practices have commented on how the TM program has helped them become more responsive and sensitive to their patients, even when time is limited.

All health professionals are encouraged to practice the TM program. If they meditate regularly, they will start to find that they, their patients, and the practice of their art have changed — that, in fact, everything is more lively, the whole world has changed.

6

Rx for Dis-ease and Dis-order

A simple question posed by one of the foremost professors of psychiatry at Yale, Dr. Walter
Igersheimer, and his answer, deeply affected my
professional development.

"What do all patients coming to you have in common?"
he asked our class of first-year psychiatric residents.

The question left us perplexed. In the past year we had
become familiar with the wide variety of symptoms and
complaints troubling people seeking psychiatric help,
whether the person was hospitalized or an outpatient.
Among those hospitalized were persons plagued by
delusions or hallucinations, while others showed signs
of acute depression and withdrawal. Some patients acted
like children unable to take care of themselves, and
others openly expressed suicidal intentions. Outpatients complained of severe anxieties, guilts, worries,
fears, marital difficulties, work problems, alcoholism,
and drug abuse. Those patients referred to us by general
practitioners usually sought relief from psychosomatic
complaints such as chronic headaches, heart
palpitations, skin rashes, or fatigue. In addition to
learning how to distinguish schizophrenia from manic-
depressive illness, or hysterical conversion from a true
neurological disorder, we had studied the many ways of
treating each of these diagnostic categories.

We reflected on all we had learned, but the answer to

this seemingly simple question continued to elude us. Realizing we were stumped, the eminent professor interrupted our contemplations to ask, "Can anyone venture even a guess as to what all your patients have in common?"

"Maladaptive psychological defenses," one bold resident guessed.

Another proposed, "Inability of the ego to integrate id and super-ego demands."

"You're not treating textbooks," the professor said sharply, "you're treating human beings."

The class fell silent. After a long pause, he looked directly at us and said, "What is common to all your patients is their pain. They come to you because they are hurting, and they need your help in relieving that pain. As a physician, it is your duty to relieve their suffering as best you know how. No matter what diagnostic label you may pin on your patients, you have to ask yourself, 'Am I doing enough to relieve this person's pain?' "

When I first learned the TM technique, I couldn't help but recall my old professor's words about the common factor in all patients. Psychiatrists may differ in their diagnoses, but most agree that their patients suffer because of an accumulation of stress and tension which cripples their emotions, mental faculties, and behavior. This crippling effect shows up in a variety of symptoms and syndromes which have become the basis of psychiatric diagnosis. Over the past several decades, psychiatrists have become dissatisfied with their diagnostic schema, especially for the neuroses and character disorders, because these diagnostic labels have not proven particularly helpful in treatment.

Underlying all of these labels is the basic fact that the suffering person generally lacks ease in his emotional life and order in his thinking and behavior. Anxiety, fear, repressed rage, guilt, or shame are all signs of emotional dis-ease. Worries, obsessions, sexual dysfunctions, compulsions, interpersonal strife, and drug abuse are basically thinking and behavior dis-orders. In treating patients, the psychiatrist aims at relieving suffering by helping to restore ease in the patient's emotional life and order in his thinking and behavior. The first scientific research on the TM program was published in 1970, and as a result a few psychiatrists recommended it to their patients. Ever since then the number of psychiatrists using the TM program in their practices has grown steadily because it provides a new dimension in addressing stress-related problems and promoting psychological growth.

These psychiatrists have reported that the TM program has triggered progress in patients who seemed unresponsive to other approaches to treatment, and that it has even doubled the rate of progress with many patients. Some cases indicate that the TM program may relieve symptoms which are not alleviated by psycho-therapy and often reduces the need for medication. Because disturbed sleep frequently precedes a general worsening of symptoms or an acute psychotic episode, psychiatrists are pleased to learn that the TM program seems especially effective in rapidly restoring normal sleeping patterns.

The following case histories give some insight into how the TM program can help psychiatric patients who are suffering from more dis-ease and dis-order than a mild neurosis. Nearly all of the following cases come from my practice, although several were reported to me by colleagues using the TM technique with their patients. It should be noted that the TM program was not the only therapeutic agent used with any of these patients. Nearly all required medication, psycho-therapeutic support, and professional supervision. A few of the patients learned the TM technique while hospitalized, most as outpatients. The TM program cannot be expected to end magically the patient's need for psychiatric care after a suicide attempt or an acute psychotic episode. As long as a patient suffers from enough emotional dis-ease or thought dis-order to impair his daily activity significantly, psychotherapeutic support remains essential to the patient's progress.

Anxiety Neurosis

Anxiety is the feeling that accompanies the alarm stage of the stress response. The palms sweat, the heart begins to pound, breathing becomes rapid, and a person feels generally tense and uneasy. It is nature's way of calling a person's attention to the fact that something may be wrong in his external or internal environment and mobilizing the mind and body to meet a demanding situation. Mild anxiety while waiting to give an important speech, driving on icy roads in heavy traffic, or waiting for a loved one to come out of surgery may be normal. Many people, however, suffer more than occasional mild anxiety. They may be walking back to work after lunch, reading quietly at home, or about to go to a party when they are suddenly gripped by feelings of tenseness, apprehension, shortness of breath, faintness, and an intense fear of impending doom. This reaction may develop without any apparent external cause and lead these individuals to fear a heart attack, cancer, or insanity. These people are suffering from anxiety neurosis. The symptoms are frightening, and the resultant fatigue is intense; so the anxiety neurotic frequently seeks medical attention.

It has been estimated that between 10 and 30 per cent of Americans seeking medical help are suffering from symptoms related to anxiety neurosis, a disease which troubles people of all ages. Students suffering from anxiety neurosis will typically become nearly incapacitated by anxiety attacks before an important exam. Housewives sometimes find it impossible to get out of the house because of anxiety attacks. Older people and adolescents alike may find that chronic anxiety attacks disturb sleeping, eating, and basic bodily functions. They are forced to seek professional help for relief.

Psychiatrists generally regard anxiety level as a critical barometer of mental health, because anxiety is the common denominator of almost every mental illness. Severe anxiety may precede major depressive or psychotic episodes. Anxiety plays an important role in psychosomatic complaints and is often a contributor to drug abuse. Relatively resistant to curative treatments, anxiety neurosis may be controlled with medications. Long-term psychotherapy has been the major approach to treating anxiety neurosis but has generally proven to be of little value. The steadily rising number of prescriptions that doctors write for mild tranquilizers is indicative of the failure to stem the tide of increasing anxiety in America. At the same time, most patients suffering from anxiety neurosis resent the prospect of taking tranquilizers for the remainder of their lives. Nearly all tranquilizers have some dulling effect, which patients find unpleasant even though the tranquilizers help control the anxiety attacks. In contrast, patients find that the TM program reduces anxiety but at the same time sharpens the mind and enriches the emotions. Many patients also like the TM program because it is natural; they can do it for themselves without ingesting the synthetic chemicals prescribed by traditional treatments.

Sally was 23 when she sought emergency help from me because she "couldn't stand it anymore" and thought she was "going to flip out." She had been raised in an overprotective atmosphere and had never left home. Quite shy and overweight, Sally had long suffered from chronic anxiety. A few weeks prior to her seeking psychiatric help, she had made plans to move away from home and live with a girl friend. Though Sally was working as a salesgirl and was able to support herself, her decision to leave home brought overwhelming criticism from her parents. As a result, she began suffering "panic attacks" in which she would hyperventilate, become dizzy, and have to lie down to regain control of herself. My psychiatric evaluation revealed an immature, baby-faced young lady paralyzed by fears, doubts, suppressed anger, and poor self-esteem, but there was no evidence of an impending psychosis.

I provided support and reassurance during her initial visit, formed a brief-treatment contract with her, and suggested she begin the TM program. A week later, Sally was completing her instruction in the TM program when she came for her second visit. She liked the TM program from the start and showed immediate benefits from it. Over the next month, Sally had two more visits with me. During that period, her tension and apprehension decreased substantially, and she no longer felt herself to be in a crisis. Despite continued resistance from her family, Sally found an apartment and moved into it with a girl friend. Though she experienced some increase in tension when she moved, she did not require any emergency visits. She remained firm and in control of herself. Follow-up after 14 months revealed that her self-reliance had continued to improve remarkably. A very active and enthusiastic participant in the TM program, she no longer suffers from anxiety attacks. She has become slim and attractive. She has made many friends and is dating frequently. Sally is no longer overwhelmed by her parents' criticisms or demands and shows them more compassion and understanding. No psychological testing was necessary to confirm what was obvious; Sally had become a happy person.

The TM technique serves as an anti-anxiety agent, as was evident in Sally's case, by changing the individual's internal physiological response to environmental circumstances, thereby allowing a more adaptive behavioral response to life pressures. During practice of the TM technique, breathing becomes shallower and slower, heart rate and cardiac output decrease, muscles relax, skin resistance increases markedly, the brain achieves greater synchrony, and the meditator experiences a refreshing state of restful alertness. The integrated hypometabolic state produced by the TM technique appears to be the psychophysiological opposite of a maladaptive anxiety attack. The TM program appears to cultivate a degree of physiological and psychological stability sufficient to prevent anxiety attacks. In the face of intense pressures, the meditator feels not so much the impulse of "fight or flight" but instead enjoys his natural capacity to "stay and play."

Hypochondriacal Neurosis

Doctors' offices are overloaded with people who are terrified because of minor pains and who are morbidly convinced that something dreadful is happening to them. These people are suffering from what psychiatrists call "hypochondriacal neurosis." A close relative of anxiety neurosis, hypochondriacal neurosis has its roots in the disturbing bodily aches and pains which can accompany the accumulation of stress. If a person has heart palpitations, abdominal tension, chronic fatigue, or frequent headaches, he will naturally become concerned about possible illness. In the face of such symptoms, a medical work-up is indicated. Yet for many millions of people who discover that their doctor can find nothing physically wrong to explain their symptoms, a natural concern for health can become an agonizing neurosis. Like all neurotic symptoms, excessive concern about health builds on itself. When the doctor gives the person suffering from stress-related symptoms a clean bill of health, the symptoms and the real suffering associated with them do not disappear. A person will then tend to fall into the trap of becoming even more fearful about his health, thereby intensifying the stress response and his symptoms.

The common treatment for hypochondria is the same as that for anxiety neurosis—tranquilizers. Many hypochondriacal patients will refuse to leave the doctor's office without a prescription for some form of medication. The TM program has many advantages over minor tranquilizers in the treatment of hypochondriacal neurosis. First of all, such drugs as Librium and Valium are too frequently prescribed in the treatment of daily stresses and strains, with dependency on these drugs becoming all too common. Furthermore, they produce negative side effects such as a dulling of the mind and a reduction in energy level. The TM program has no such adverse side effect and promotes what the pills do not— a real reduction in the person's accumulation of chronic stress. At best, tranquilizers can help a person avoid accumulation of further stress but do nothing to get at the cause of the symptoms underlying the hypochondriacal neurosis. By dissolving accumulated stress and increasing baseline happiness, the TM program gradually eradicates the roots of hypochondriacal neurosis. I have used the TM program successfully as practically the sole therapeutic agent with many hypochondriacal patients.

Ed was a 24 year-old law student who had suffered frequent anxiety attacks ever since age 17 and who, for the last two years, had begun suffering from a whole series of apparently imaginary illnesses. When his symptoms began to intensify to the point of incapacitating him during his first year at law school, he sought psychiatric help. His chief complaint was chest pain and a fear of impending doom, as if he were "going to have a heart attack at any moment." Ed had many medical work-ups, all of which proved unremarkable. He spent 13 months in analytically oriented psychotherapy when he was 21 but "got little out of it." Though he felt he had made progress after 12 weeks of Primal therapy, he found himself once again crippled by fears of illness and anxiety attacks six months later. Tranquilizers and relaxation exercises provided minimal relief.

Ed initially showed a slow response to the TM program. During his first three months practicing the technique, his anxiety attacks and fears first lessened and then increased in intensity. The TM technique was apparently releasing some of the deep-rooted stress causing his anxiety. Psychiatric support and frequent checking at the local TM center were necessary to keep Ed practicing the TM technique during this rough period. After three months, Ed began to show steady improvement and soon no longer required tranquilizers. Therapy was terminated after five months. During a follow-up interview a year later, Ed reported:

> Before I started the TM program, I really thought I was heading for the hospital. There was just no way out. Pills, doctors—nothing helped. I wasn't sure whether the TM program would do it either for the first few months, but I stuck with it. Now I can see that the TM program has really made a difference. The anxiety is almost gone and so are the fatigue and the insomnia. I'm not such a hypochondriac anymore. Sure, I still get tense before an exam sometimes, but I've never felt so strongly that everything is going to be alright. My mind has gotten sharp, my grades are improving, and I really look forward to each day when I get up in the morning.

How widespread is hypochondriacal neurosis? Contrary to popular belief, it is neither a form of malingering nor simply a disease of eccentrics or little old ladies. The sale of billions of over-the-counter pain pills plus a lucrative industry offering quasi-remedies for an assortment of bodily aches and pains is probably the best index of how widespread hypochondriacal neurosis actually is. It has recently been called the "silent epidemic," because general practitioners refrain from using the term "hypochondriacal neurosis" and prefer to diagnose their patients as simply excessively nervous or overanxious "crocks." Whatever the condition may be called, it is a source of real distress for hundreds of thousands of people who feel very concerned about their health but whose symptoms do not stem from an organic disorder. To think that hypochondriacal neurosis has only psychological causes is to overlook the real physiological and psychological consequences of accumulated stress. The TM program is especially helpful in the treatment of hypochondriacal neurosis because it is self-administered. The patient begins to relieve the chronic stresses underlying the multivariate symptoms causing excessive concern about personal health, but also feels secure in the knowledge that he is correcting the dis-order or dis-ease, be it physical and/or psychological, for himself.

Phobia

Many people feel uncomfortable around spiders or snakes, some people feel uneasy looking over a cliff, and children often fear darkness and thunder. All of these fears, which may be called mild phobias, are of little concern either to the people having them or to psychiatrists. When a person grows deeply incapacitated by one of these or by any other fear, he suffers from a severe phobia that requires psychiatric intervention. Severe phobias may or may not be accompanied by generalized anxiety but often accompany other psychiatric symptoms.

The psychoanalysis of a phobia involves trying to get the patient to accept sexual and aggressive wishes, the disowning of which is thought to underlie his fears. Behavior therapy attacks a phobia by trying to decondition the automatic fear response to whatever object or situation was triggering it. The behavior therapy technique of systematic desensitization in-volves having the patient practice relaxing in the presence of the object of his phobia or while imagining phobic scenes in a graded fashion. Behavior therapy has had greater success than has psychoanalysis in the treatment of phobias, but even this method has a 40 per cent relapse rate within one to three years after treatment.[1]

Whether understood from a behaviorist or psychoanalytic perspective, the phobic person suffers emotional dis-ease and a behavior dis-order. The following cases illustrate how restoring ease and order through the TM program can help relieve phobic symptoms.

George was a 46 year-old merchant in a large Eastern city. Married with three children, he had suffered general anxiety and intense fear of traveling in cars, buses, boats, trains, and airplanes. In the past seven years, he had never once left his city. He walked to work and would only rarely leave his neighborhood. His general anxiety was becoming an ever greater burden to himself and his family; he had very recently become impotent; and he felt that, "If things keep up the way they're going, I'm not even going to be able to leave the house." Having spent 13 years, off and on, in a variety of therapies, George had very little confidence that anything could help him. In any case, he had decided to spend no more money on therapists; he had already spent over $20,000.

At the urging of a friend, George acceded to seeing one more therapist for one visit. When asked what therapy had helped him most, George explained that his experience with behavior therapy had provided some relief. Recognizing George's absolute reluctance to start another program of long-term therapy, the psychiatrist recommended the TM program almost as a last resort. Because the cost of taking the TM program was minimal and he could do the TM technique for himself without relying on a therapist, George decided he had "nothing to lose but another $125" and took the TM program. One month later George wrote his therapist to share his experience with the TM program:

You're not going to believe what has happened. I can't myself. The fear that has gripped me for so long just began to disappear the very first time I meditated. My headaches come less often now, and I stopped being so nervous. I go for regular checking; the instructors in the TM center have been so helpful. Last weekend, I drove 200 miles to attend a weekend advanced course in the TM program, and I had no problems. I can't explain it, but I've got this new inner feeling of confidence. My wife says I'm a new man. She may be right. She's learning the TM technique this weekend. Thank you, Doctor, for telling me to do something that worked. You've restored my confidence in the medical profession.

A follow-up interview after 18 months revealed that George was still free from his phobic symptoms and still enthusiastic about the TM program. He is no longer impotent, and he travels out of town regularly on weekends with his family.

Obsessive-Compulsive Disorder

The least common of the neuroses, the obsessive-compulsive patient is frequently resistant to treatment. He suffers from a great deal of anxiety but keeps much of this anxiety blocked from his awareness through the process of repression. Though many people struggle against feeling anxious, this struggle becomes strong enough in some people to result in the thinking disorder called "obsession," in which certain thoughts continually grip the mind.

Obsessional thoughts may often be quite meaningless, as the unending recall of phone numbers or multiplication tables, or they may be very disturbing, as when a person continually hears himself thinking, "I am no good," or "Shame, shame, shame." Obsessions may also involve ruminations about a particular event in the past or an anticipated problem in the future. What typifies obsessional thinking is the person's inability to shut it off.

Though the obsessive-compulsive neurotic is at the mercy of his own uncontrollable thinking process, he generally does not tumble into psychosis. He counters his massive anxiety by exercising rigid control over his personality. This iron grip on feeling and thinking requires that the obsessive-compulsive neurotic dispel the energy of his obsessive thinking in ritualized, harmless actions called "compulsions."

Compulsions may be thought of as obsessive actions. Typical compulsions may be the need to wash the hands 10 or 15 times a day, to dress and undress in precisely the same way, or to search the house repeatedly for strangers every night before going to sleep. The need for control imprisons the obsessive-compulsive in a gloomy experience of living. Spontaneity, creativity, and easy, relaxed pleasure remain out of reach for most obsessive-compulsives. Though they remain functional their chances for achievement are limited by rigid thinking and their inability to relate to others in a warm, natural way. Marital relations become mechanistic, rigid, and dehumanized; they may become occasions for the most elaborate rituals, with minimal pleasurable reward.

To treat obsessive-compulsive neurosis, the psycho-analytically oriented therapist might try to help the person begin feeling the aggressive impulses that he is desperately controlling and begin learning to express those impulses in rewarding ways. The behavior therapist might treat obsessive-compulsive neurosis by teaching the patient thought-stopping and by prescribing relaxation exercises to help reduce the need for compulsive acts. Role playing might be used to help the patient become more assertive. By gradually expanding the patient's repertoire of behaviors, the behavior therapist hopes that the patient's obsessions subside. Though these approaches to treating obsessive-compulsive neurosis may have some validity, the problem in the treatment of these patients is their resistance to every form of treatment. They resist the exploration of their pasts and are afraid to let go of their rigid behavior patterns. In this light, the TM program is a unique approach to treating obsessive-compulsive neurosis because the patient is not asked to probe his past or to change his behavior patterns in the present. Instead, it systematically reduces the tension in the obsessive's metal "pressure cooker" and allows for the gradual easing of controls.

The obsessive-compulsive generally finds his first experience of the TM technique to be very delightful and quite moving. He discovers, for the first time, that his mind can settle down, his body can relax, and he can experience a degree of inner pleasure without having to try to do anything. Though obsessive thoughts may be troublesome during meditation for the first few months, patients generally report an inner stability which reduces the significance of the obsessive thinking. Regular practice of the TM technique over a period of time seems to lesson the grip of obsessive thoughts and gradually reduce compulsive behaviors. The TM technique enables the obsessive-compulsive to relax his rigid personality and begin enjoying increased ease and spontaneity. Some psychiatrists have wondered whether the obsessive-compulsive might have great difficulty learning the TM technique because it involves an easy attitude toward mental activity, and the obsessive-compulsive tends to control his thinking and attention rigidly. Experience with patients seems to indicate that this fear is generally unwarranted. Obsessives usually learn to "let go" at a self-regulated pace in the TM program, as illustrated by Greg's case.

Greg was a single 32 year-old accountant who had suffered from obsessive-compulsive symptoms since his early adolescence. He complained of becoming very tense around other people, especially in public places. He was troubled by the compulsion to recite multiplication tables and repeatedly adjust his clothing. He resented the tendency of his mind to become absorbed in nonsensical thoughts that confused him or arrested his attention. Greg had a very authoritarian personality, was hypercritical, and suffered from poor interpersonal relationships.

Two previous years of psychoanalytically oriented psychotherapy revealed that he had always been very dependent on his mother and that he had a great deal of difficulty in separating from her and individuating. Psychoanalysis also unearthed his repressed anger and hostility toward his mother but did little to relieve his symptoms. He had great difficulty developing any kind of intimacy with women. After cutting short his psychotherapy, Greg briefly tried behavior therapy, which he disliked intensely, and later a group therapy program, which helped him some in learning relationship skills but did little to relieve his many symptoms.

Greg first learned about the TM program when he began individual psychotherapy with me. He saw me once weekly for four months and approximately once monthly for several months thereafter. During his first five months of the TM program, he improved very slowly but steadily. Psychotherapeutic support was essential to keep him meditating, but by the end of the first five months he was saying, "I'm finally learning what it means to just be, without my mind racing a mile a minute." Follow-up after 14 months revealed that Greg was much less troubled by obsessional thoughts. His relations with other people had improved, and he had a girl friend with whom he felt very close. "It's so amazing," said Greg, "that, by not trying so hard, as I'm learning through the TM program, life can improve so much."

Obsessive-compulsive behavior is an extreme case of being locked in boundaries, of being caught up in rigid, stereotyped thinking and behavior. The regular experience of unboundedness through the TM program reduces rigidity and gives the practitioner an increased sense of personal freedom. Obsessions are a dis-order of thinking. By reducing stress and increasing the orderliness of the mind, the TM program spontaneously eliminates this weakness. In his twice daily practice of the TM technique, the individual learns to take it as it comes, in a pleasurable way, and to neither anticipate nor resist change. Gradually he loses his need to manipulate and control himself or others. As a result, the authoritarian individual becomes more open, more at ease in his relationships. Life becomes more effortless, more natural.

Depression

Depression ranks with anxiety among the most often reported psychological symptoms troubling people today. According to a recent National Institute of Mental Health Survey, approximately 20 million people in our country suffer some medically significant degree of depression. Over 250,000 people annually are hospitalized for depression. Depression is the major contributor to suicide, which ranks as the tenth overall cause of death, despite evidence that it is grossly under reported in many areas of the country. Studies have shown that millions of people suffer from depression which too often goes unrecognized and untreated. Particularly the somatic symptoms of depression—insomnia, restless sleep, early morning awakening, loss of appetite, compulsive overeating, fatigue or tiredness, loss of interest in relationships, and bodily aches and pains with no organic basis—are so common in everyday life that they often go unrecognized as characteristic of illness. Chronic fatigue is a major precipitant of, and contributor to, depression. Eighty to 85 per cent of people who complain of chronic fatigue suffer depression frequently.

As a symptom, depression refers to a painful subjective mood. It may be described by such terms as *sad, low, down, blue,* or *discouraged.* Often patients will not describe directly a depressed mood but instead will complain of emptiness or simply not caring about anything.

Depression may develop in a number of ways. Some research indicates that severe episodic depression may run in certain families. Abuse of drugs such as alcohol, barbiturates, or amphetamines may also result in depression. A major emotional loss can trigger a prolonged or pathological grief reaction. Perhaps the most common contributant to depression is chronic stress and anxiety, which sap the body's energy and vital resources. As fatigue accumulates, life becomes "a drag," and the individual loses his motivation. The "final straw" occurs, and a retarded depression ensues.

When a person sits around all day doing nothing, as in a retarded depression, he gives his mind and body a chance to rest and recover. For this reason, most depressions are self-limiting. As long as a depressed person does not get so hopeless that he tries to kill himself, he is likely to recover from his depression just by taking it easy. Though most depressions are self-limiting, severe depressions are very disabling. The symptoms which accompany depression make life very unpleasant for the patient and his family. One of the reasons why people become hopeless during depression is their almost complete inability to mobilize themselves.

Various schools of psychotherapy offer different theories upon which they rely in prescribing ways to resolve the root cause of frequent depressions. Psychoanalytically oriented thereapists typically regard depression as stemming from repressed rage. They argue that if a person turns in on himself the anger which he felt early in life when his basic needs were not met, the person becomes prone to depression. The psychoanalytically oriented therapist would help the depressed patient to get in touch with and work through this repressed anger. Behavior therapists understand depression differently. They argue that depression results simply from too much negative reinforcement and not enough positive reinforcement. They might treat a depressed patient by putting him in an environment such as a psychiatric unit, where the patient could be carefully rewarded for each simple task performed. By being rewarded for simple tasks such as making his bed, bathing, or talking more, the patient would presumably begin to get more and more interested in becoming active and taking responsibility for himself. This increase in activity would, it is hoped, dispel the depression.

Each of the traditional approaches to handling depression may prove useful with certain individuals, but nearly all of these approaches are primarily psychological in their method. The efficacy of certain medications in alleviating depression indicates that depression has an important physiological basis as well. Just as anxiety corresponds to the alarm stage of the stress response, depression corresponds to the third stage, exhaustion. The TM technique catalyzes the body's natural ability to recover from depression. It provides the rest necessary for the body to replace chemical resources depleted by fight-or-flight responses, excessive anger, fear, and chronic distress. The TM program apparently helps eliminate the fatigue which sustains depression, and then goes on to let the steam out of repressed rage gradually by enabling old psychic conflicts to heal themselves. Patients who are suffering from more serious depressive symptoms, while able to learn the TM technique fairly readily, may require daily supervision and encouragement by a TM teacher in order to meditate comfortable and regularly. This is not surprising because these patients are generally unable to perform even simple daily tasks because of their lethargy and complete absence of motivation. The more serious the depression, the

longer it may take the patient to notice obvious benefits
and the more support he may require to meditate
regularly. Nevertheless, when the TM program is added
to traditional approaches to treating depression—be
they behavioral, psychoanalytical, or psychopharmacological—patients tend to improve at a rate
much faster than usual.

When Laura, 26 years-old and married, finally
concluded there was no escape from her despair, she
took an overdose of aspirin and ended up in the
emergency room. In her initial interview, she said that
she had been "struggling with feelings of depression all
her life, but things had gotten a lot worse in the past few
months." Family and school pressures had become
"unbearable." She made her suicide attempt because she
"didn't want to struggle anymore; life is too full of pain
and cruelty." Though Laura had no history of sleeping
problems or bodily aches and pains, she found it hard to
relax because the moment she stopped her frenzied
activity, she became depressed. "I haven't been at peace
with myself," she said, "for as long as I can remember."

Laura had been in intensive psychotherapy on two
previous occasions, with reportedly little or no benefit.
Anti-depressant medication had also provided little
relief. From the emergency room, Laura was admitted to
the hospital psychiatric unit for four days of crisis-
intervention and subsequently was followed as an
outpatient. All signs indicated that she was likely to
show a poor response to psychotherapy and that her
condition would probably worsen over the years. With
psychotherapy offering little promise of help and
anti-depressant medication putting a dangerous means
for another suicide attempt into her hands, I suggested
that Laura begin the TM program as soon as possible.
She began the TM program on her last day in the
hospital. Over the next six months, Laura not only
recovered from her severe depression but also stated,
"Thanks to my TM practice, for the first time in my life I

know what it means to be really happy." She felt that she had become much more effective as a teacher and better able to handle students with less strain. After three months of watching the welcomed progress in his wife, Laura's husband began the TM program. Whereas, prior to the TM program, Laura felt inadequate and "left out" in her marital relations, she now felt "more in touch with myself, much closer to my husband." She was especially pleased with the TM program because, as she said, "it is something I can do for myself. It calms me down, gives me more energy, and lets me feel happy naturally."

When Laura was initially tested on the hospital psychiatric unit, she appeared to be an angry, sullen person who blamed others for her difficulties. Her interpersonal relationships were impaired; she was likely to be argumentative, tactless, and unpleasant. She showed marked depression, irritability, suspicion, and poor judgment—all indications of the possibility of a psychotic or pre-psychotic break.

The improvement that Laura demonstrated after only six months of the TM program was unexpected. The TM program apparently counteracted the chronic anxiety that preceded her depressive episodes, while gradually resolving her pent-up rage and resentment. Over her first six months of the TM program, Laura shed her angry attitudes and blossomed into a warm, friendly person. By decreasing her stress level, the TM program apparently opened up new sources of energy and increased her ability to experience pleasure. Laura's baseline happiness grew substantially.

Laura had been prone to depression all of her life. Another case, that of Jolynn, illustrates how the TM program can help with depressions secondary to the loss of a loved one. A 29 year-old art dealer and free-lance writer, Jolynn best expresses in her own words how the TM program helped her:

> My brother was my closest friend. From a very early age, we had a sense of a very strong connection—call it

karma if you wish—and a very deep love for one another. At 24 he committed suicide. Suicide was never proven in fact, but I knew, and his best male friend at the time knew that it was. During the course of the funeral, I was unable to express my grief and was unable to cry at all, partially because I felt totally alienated from my parents (who in my mind were primarily responsible for the development of my brother's psychological problems), and from any religious/ritualistic mode of expressing my grief in a socially acceptable way. Also, I still felt such a deep connection of love with my brother that, to me, he was not dead, nor would he ever be.

However, because I had kept my initial feelings of shock inside, I had a very severe stress attack while I was lying in bed the evening after the funeral. I felt that my body was going to explode and that my mind was going to crack at any second. It was only through a concerted effort of talking to myself and trying to be rational that I was finally able to overcome this attack, thinking that when I returned home I could then release this stress. Although I did release some stress on a superficial level on my return, the deeper stress remained without my realizing it. For months after, I suffered from a kind of numbness but found it impossible to cry. I had early-morning awakening, weight loss, and guilt. Everything about my life was getting worse and worse.

Finally, a friend told me I should start the TM program because he was concerned about me and thought it would help. I figured it wouldn't hurt, so I signed up for the course. During my first meditation I felt in touch with myself and my inner core and had feelings of great joy and love or the first time in years. These feelings triggered the memory of the joy and love I felt for my brother, and the thought crossed my mind that if I had only known about this technique sooner, if I had been able to pass it on to my brother, then perhaps he would have wanted to live. At that moment, I began sobbing and weeping uncontrollably and continued weeping off and on during the course of that meditation. Afterwards, I realized that I had released a great deal of the stress caused by my deep grief, which had been stored up for several months. I felt cleansed and renewed and was no longer afraid of expressing my feelings of grief.

I have been meditating about 17 months and I have consciously experienced this release two times since then. I now feel that I have cleared out almost all of the stress that was held in on the night of the funeral.

The rage I felt for my parents is gone. Three months after I began the TM program, we were able to talk about our shared tragic loss and support each other in our grief. I doubt that this would have been possible for me without the TM program.

In addition to restoring Jolynn's depleted bodily resources, the TM program helped her recover from the profound emotional loss she had suffered. She was able to dissolve her reactive rage for her parents, which undoubtedly had earlier antecedents than her brother's death, freeing her to mourn and recover. Her case illustrates how the relief inherent in the deep inner experience of well-being can allow a natural purification process to unfold mentally and physically. The ability of the TM program to strengthen baseline happiness naturally may be its most important contribution to the alleviation of depression.

Psychosomatic Disorders and Heart Disease

Psychosomatic diseases are those caused or heavily influenced by psychological tension. The classic psychosomatic diseases include essential hypertension, peptic ulcer, bronchial asthma, rheumatoid arthritis, migraine headache, neurodermatitis, and ulcerative colitis. It is estimated that from 70 to 80 per cent of the patients seen by family physicians are suffering from psychosomatic diseases; but their mild complaints— aches and pains, diarrhea, constipation, skin rashes, heart palpitations, heartburn, fatigue, etc.—frequently have a psychogenic cause. Because all of these symptoms may accompany a wide variety of diseases, a physician is always obligated to make a thorough search for any possible organic basis for his patient's symptoms. When a thorough medical work-up proves negative, the probability is that the symptoms have their origin in chronic stress and tension.

To say that a psychosomatic illness has a psychogenic rather than an organic cause is somewhat misleading. Chronic distress and deep-rooted stresses cause significant changes in how the body functions. When prolonged, these organic changes give rise to psychosomatic symptoms and, eventually, to diseases. The principal physiological change underlying psychosomatic disease is hyperactivity of the sympathetic branch of the autonomic nervous system. When this energy-expending branch of the autonomic nervous system becomes too active for too long, the weakest point in a person's body will begin to break down due to overwork. Different people will develop different symptoms and diseases depending on hereditary, constitutional, and environmental factors. One person may have a touchy stomach, another may have sensitive skin, and yet another may have a vulnerable circulatory system.

Of the many diseases in which chronic distress plays an important role, essential hypertension (high blood pressure of unknown cause) attracts the most attention in the medical field, and with good reason. It is the silent killer. It is the most common circulatory disease, yet it produces virtually no symptoms, gives no warning in the over 24 million Americans—one-third of the adult male population—suffering from it and its serious complications. Hypertension predisposes one to the disease of atherosclerosis (hardending of the arteries), which is thought to be the major cause of heart attacks and strokes. The higher the blood pressure, the greater the risk of developing atherosclerosis and its terrible consequences, which account for over half the deaths in the United States annually.

There has been much research to show that hypertension is related to chronic distress through the inappropriate eliciting of the fight-or-flight response. Psychiatrists have observed that most people suffering from essential hypertension tend to be defensive and to view their environment as hostile. This attitude may be basic to the disease. Anti-hypertensive drugs act to reduce the hyperactivity of the sympathetic nervous system, thus lowering blood pressure. Prescribed drugs are a very important therapy for decreasing blood pressure, but they frequently have uncomfortable side effects such as diarrhea, dry mouth, muscle tremors.

The regular practice of the TM technique is another way to lower blood pressure. People regularly practicing the TM technique will generally have low resting levels of blood pressure. A controlled study at Harvard revealed that, when used in conjunction with anti-hypertensive medication, the TM program significantly reduces high blood pressure in hypertensive patients. At the Institute of Psychophysiological Medicine, we now regularly prescribe the TM program for patients suffering from hypertension, in addition to providing the standard medical treatment for this disorder. Patients who learn the TM technique to lower blood pressure often get more than they bargained for. A 49 year-old business executive noted:

> The TM program has helped to bring down my blood pressure, which is great, but it's done a lot more than that. After just six months of meditation, I find that I am much more patient with Maggie and the kids. We're all doing the TM technique, and it has brought more joy, warmth, and understanding into our family life. Work doesn't seem like work anymore. I'm not trying as hard, but I'm getting a lot more accomplished. I've got energy to spare. I used to be hostile and angry, now I take things in stride. I've learned how to relax and take it easy without losing any of my drive.

This personality change, which often occurs in people who learn the TM technique, may account for the lowering of blood pressure. It is unlikely, however, that the regular practice of the TM technique alone will be adequate therapy for severe hypertension. The TM program does serve as a very useful adjunct to anti-hypertensive drugs and often allows for a steady reduction in dosage. It is possible that the TM program alone may replace drug thereapy in the case of mild hypertension because it has none of the pharmacological side effects, but this judgment should always be made by the patient's physician. Regular visits to the doctor are a must to ensure that blood pressure is adequately controlled.

Undoubtedly the most exciting possible use for TM in relation to hypertension and its serious complications lies in its preventive value. The damaging effects of excessive stress and tension on the heart and circulatory system were recognized as early as 1897 by one of the greatest physicians of all time, Sir William Osler:

> In the worry and strain of modern life arterial degenera-tion is not only very common, but develops often at a relatively early age. For this I believe that the high pressure at which men live and the habit of working the machine to its maximum capacity, are responsible rather than excesses in eating and drinking. . . . Angiosclerosis, creeping on slowly but sure, *"with no pace perceived"* is the Nemesis through which Nature exacts retributive justice for the transgression of her laws—coming to one as an apoplexy, to another as an early Bright's disease, to a third as an aneurysm and to a fourth as angina pectoris, too often slitting *"the thin spun life"* in the fifth decade at the very time when success seems assured. . . . A man who has early risen and late taken rest, who has eaten the bread of carefulness, striving for success in commercial, professional or political life, after twenty-five years of incessant toil reaches the point where he can say, perhaps with just satisfaction, *"Soul, thou has much goods laid up for many years; take thine ease,"* all unconscious that the fell sergeant has already issued the warrant.[2]

It wasn't until 77 years later that cardiologists Meyer Friedman and Ray Rosenman reported on their research in *Type A Behavior and Your Heart*, indicating that personality type is a critical factor which determines a person's likelihood of a heart attack. Over the past 15 years, these medical researchers at the Mount Zion Medical Center in San Francisco have been able to detect by behavior pattern alone the man likely to have a heart attack (Type A) and the man unlikely to have a heart attack (Type B).

What are the characteristics of Type A behavior? Fundamentally, it consists of those feelings and their respective motor expressions displayed by an individual possessing an exaggerated drive, ambition, aggressiveness, competitiveness, and above all, sense of time urgency—even at supposed times of leisure. Most people have some or all of these attributes, but the young executive likely to be stricken with a heart attack possesses them to an unusually high degree. He appears to walk, talk, and even eat to the pace of a stop watch. In contrast, the easygoing Type B personality is much less likely to suffer from a heart attack. In one study, Type A men showed eight times the narrowing of the coronary arteries due to build-up of fatty plaques than did a similar group of Type B men. "Hard facts from dozens of retrospective studies by investigators worldwide," writes Dr. Rosenman, "have shown that the majority of coronary patients under the age of 60 are Type A. In their massive California study of 3,182 men in 11 corporations, Friedman and Rosenman showed that most of the high-level executives in these firms were relaxed Type Bs—not the hard-driving Type A men. Apparently, the Type B is more likely to attain the highest levels of executive leadership than the aggressive Type A, perhaps because calm, creative, and dynamic thinking is primarily a Type B rather than Type A characteristic.

Friedman and Roseman have learned much about the role which chronic distress plays in the evolution of cardiovascular disease. The biochemical changes of the alarm stage include the release of free fatty acids from the body's fat deposits to be used as fuel for the body's coming energy expenditure. High concentration of fatty acids in the blood is associated with hypertension, heart attack, and stroke. Fatty acids, along with cholesterol, are what clog the coronary arteries. Diet was once thought to be very important in regulating the blood cholesterol, but subsequent research has shown that changes in diet generally lower cholesterol level no more than five per cent over a one-year period. However, the stress response seems to be critically important in determining cholesterol levels. Under chronic tension, the hypothalamus releases hormones that discharge cholesterol, increase clotting elements in the blood, and even produce an abnormal blood sugar state—all of which significantly contribute to the development of heart disease.

Smoking is also an important risk factor in heart disease, but Type A personalities are much more likely to smoke than Type B people, and Type A smokers are much more likely to have heart attacks than are Type B smokers. Lack of regular exercise is another risk factor in heart disease, but Type As are much less likely to follow a moderate exercise routine than are Type Bs because Type As never seem to have enough time.

Type A behavior may be the critical factor accounting for the two deaths every minute, or 1,000,000 deaths annually that result from heart disease. But how can the ambitious, aggressive, competitive, hard-driving Type A person, who often holds a demanding executive position, develop a healthier Type B personality?

Drs. Friedman and Rosenman devoted one third of their best-selling book to practical guidelines for helping the Type A learn Type B behavior. Their suggestions include: "Remind yourself daily that *being* is more important than *having*"; "Learn to hold opinions loosely"; "Become more intimate with your friends"; "Stop and start to really take in the wonders of the universe"; "Slow down"; "Stop interrupting and start listening." Any physician or psychiatrist knows all too well that this is good advice for self-improvement but that patients often hear this advice as quite platitudinous and even a bit sophomoric. Besides, it inadvertently falls on deaf ears. The patient nods; he knows he needs to relax; the doctor knows the patient needs to relax; but behavioral prescriptions do little to ease the driving inner tension at the core of the Type A personality. The question remains how a person can naturally develop an inner ease that will help him to interact freely with others, to avoid constant unnecessary strain and tension, to enjoy the blessings of life, and, perhaps paradoxically, to achieve more as a result.

Clinical observations at the Institute of Psychophysiological Medicine indicate that the TM program naturally changes the Type A individual into a happier, more relaxed, and more effective Type B person. Psychological research on the TM program supports these observations. Extensive studies show that the TM program decreases nervousness and irritability, increases spontaneity and creativity, and increases self-acceptance and capacity for intimate contact. Furthermore, two studies have shown that executives practicing the TM program show less worry about promotion but an increased likelihood of promotion due to improved performance. The decline in cigarette smoking among people who practice the TM technique also indicates that the TM program helps transform the Type A into Type B. Apparently, people who practice the TM technique no longer need to reach for a cigarette to relax or to help them through a demanding situation.

The TM program has two basic advantages over all the behavioral prescriptions and other methods of helping Type A individuals develop a healthier Type B personality. First, the TM technique works, while most other methods do not. Trying to follow behavioral prescriptions to reduce tension can often increase frustration. Because the TM technique works physiologically, it does not require that an individual try to change himself. The natural physiological changes occurring during the TM program automatically relieve chronic stress and dissolve the psychic tension that fuels the Type A personality. At the same time, the increased psychophysiological integration resulting from the TM program systematically improves the individual's ability to perform. Approaching the problem of changing personality through the purely psychological methods of behavioral prescriptions of psychotherapy will rarely, if ever, produce significant results.

The second advantage of the TM program over other means of fostering Type B personality growth is that it is acceptable to patients who reject other methods. Friedman and Rosenman point out clearly how the Type A will balk at behavioral prescriptions and refuse a psychiatric referral. On the other hand, the TM program neither threatens nor clashes with the Type A personality defenses. A person can start the TM program to increase his energy and productivity rather than to relax. If the Type A finds himself accomplishing more as he begins to strain less and take it easy, then he will have no objections to continuing the TM program. The likelihood of improving performance makes the TM program much more attractive from the outset than any other programs to develop a Type B personality.

The TM program is also attractive because people find that, in the long run, it saves time. The added energy they get from the afternoon TM session effectively doubles the number of hours they have for productive activity. Finally, the TM technique is enjoyable. People tend to look forward to meditating twice a day, while they easily forget to follow behavioral prescriptions.

The TM program may prove to be among the most effective ways to reduce high blood pressure and the incidence of heart disease, but it also seems to be very effective in helping to alleviate a wide variety of less serious tension-related symptoms. The following case vignettes from the Institute of Psychophysiological Medicine illustrate how the TM program helps people with psychosomatic complaints.

A 23 year-old secretary had been suffering from insomnia for years. Having begun taking sleeping pills very regularly, she finally sought psychiatric help because she feared becoming addicted to the medicine. After three months of the TM program, she no longer required any medication. Now she falls asleep easily and sleeps soundly. In addition, she reports that the TM program has helped her feel less tense and more energetic. Insomniacs frequently benefit from the TM program. One research study has shown that the TM program reduces the average time necessary for a group of insomniacs to fall asleep from 75 to 15 minutes in just 30 days.[3]

A 38 year-old corporate accountant suffered from severe dermatitis, which had been treated by dermatologists with little success. His condition resembled neurodermatitis and primarily involved the upper extremities, the back, and the face. Despite taking 5–10 milligrams of Valium three times a day, he still felt apprehensive and anxious, especially at work. After the first six months of the TM program, his anxiety decreased and his dermatitis showed improvement. During periods of marked stress, the dermatitis temporarily flared up. After one year of the TM program, however, he is completely without symptoms. The skin rash is gone, and he reports a steady increase in his job performance and satisfaction.

A 35 year-old woman had been suffering from an irritable colon for almost six months. There was reason to fear that she might be devloping ulcerative colitis.

After six weeks of the TM program, she no longer complained of gastrointestinal symptoms. She gained weight, improved her general health, and, in addition, became more self-assertive.

A 24 year-old medical student had suffered from severe tension headaches for over a year. His headaches became especially severe during exams. Since taking up the TM technique, he no longer gets tension headaches and is improving his academic performance.

A 65 year-old widow came to me complaining of anxiety, depression, difficulty making decisions, severe stiffness in the muscles of her neck, a very coarse tremor of her hands, and numerous aches and pains. After six months of the TM progaram, she no longer had the hand tremor and was almost completely free from symptoms. She stated, "I no longer am afraid of growing old thanks to the TM program. It's opened up new possibilities in my life. I am not as preoccupied with my bodily complaints and no longer wasting time running from one doctor to the next. I have taken up gardening and become more active in civic activites."

A number of teenage patients suffering from bronchial asthma have reported improvement which their treating physicians confirmed. Dr. Archie Wilson and Ron Honsberger at the University of California, Irvine, conducted a study which confirmed that the TM program has beneficial effects in relieving asthma, a disease whose severity has frequently been correlated with the level of distress.

It should be emphasized that TM is not a miracle cure or panacea. Though the TM program is proving helpful in curing psychosomatic diseases, it must be noted that the TM program should never be considered a replacement for anti-hypertensive medication, an ulcer diet, or anti-epileptic drugs. The TM program does, however, promise a means of stemming the rising tide of psychosomatic complaints which confound physicians and cause real suffering for millions of people.

Drug Abuse and Alcoholism

Current psychiatric research suggests that drug abuse remains a very widespread and intractable mental health problem because drugs fulfill genuine needs felt by abusers. People turn to drugs for relief from tension, boredom, and despair, and to gain a few hours of pleasure in their otherwise humdrum lives. Insomnia leads people to barbiturate addiction; anxiety and frustration fuel the need for alcohol; loneliness and alienation pave the road to heroin; and idle curiosity, a genuine desire for spiritual insight, or boredom may be causes for taking LSD and other hallucinogens. None of the current approaches to reducing the drug abuse problem — law enforcement, community education, psychotherapy—have proven even minimally effective in curbing the rising abuse of legal and illegal drugs. Two years after the establishment of the Federal Narcotics and Drug Abuse Administration, all forms of drug abuse remain on the rise. It appears that drug abuse will continue in epidemic proportions until abusers have an effective alternative method of fulfilling the deep psychological needs which compel them to take drugs.

Considerable scientific evidence suggests that the TM program may dramatically reduce a person's need to take all kinds of drugs ranging from alcohol and cigarettes to marijuana and heroin. Five separate studies have shown that the TM program leads to an immediate reduction in drug abuse within the first few months after a person learns the technique and usually to a complete cessation of drug abuse within two to three years of regular TM practice. Rapid reduction in anxiety levels and gradual increase in baseline happiness are probably basic to the mechanics of how the TM program relieves the need to take drugs.

Though the abuse of heroin, "downers," and "uppers" still capture headlines, alcoholism is the most widespread, costly, and crippling drug abuse problem in the United States. Alcoholism ranks third as a cause of death; half of all automobile fatalities and half of all homicides in this country are directly related to the use of alcohol. Each year, over 13,000 individuals die of cirrhosis of the liver caused by alcoholism and one-fourth of all suicide victims have a significant amount of alcohol in their bloodstreams. Steadily on the rise (it now affects one out of every ten American families), alcoholism has proven highly resistant to psychiatric treatment. How the TM program can help in the treatment of alcoholism is well illustrated by the case of Peggy, a 46 year-old woman and an alcoholic for 24 years.

When Peggy began treatment with me, she had already suffered three broken marriages, been through many hospitalizations for detoxification, and was on the verge of her fourth divorce. She had tried individual psychotherapy, group psychotherapy, marital counseling, Alcoholics Anonymous, and had also taken Antabuse, which causes nausea and other uncomfortable symptoms if a person takes alcohol along with it. Antabuse is helpful for the patient motivated to take it regularly, but like many alcholics, Peggy found it all too easy to forget to take her Antabuse and start a week-long binge whenever she began to feel "down in the dumps."

Peggy began the TM program while hospitalized for alcohol detoxification. Pleased with the TM technique from the start, she completely abstained from alcohol for the first six weeks after learning it. When she finally "slipped" and took a drink, she found, to her amazement, "it tasted bad and gave me a headache." This reaction is not infrequent among alcoholic patients who regularly practice the TM technique. Over the next six months, Peggy would intermittently meditate regularly and stay sober, then stop meditation and binge. During this period, she required much psychiatric support and often daily attention from her TM instructor, but she became very regular in her practice of the TM technique. For the last eight months, Peggy has completely abstained from alcohol. She is taking creative writing and swimming classes. Her marriage is taking a "slow turn for the better." Her husband has begun the TM program and both attend regular weekly meetings at the TM center. They are in couples therapy together, and, in addition, Peggy regularly attends Alcoholics Anonymous meetings. For the first time in her life, Peggy is really making use of these other modalities of therapy.

Betty, another patient of mine who had suffered from severe alcoholism, recently wrote me the following:

> I am so happy I took the TM program. I enjoy meditating regularly. Even with the A.A. program you sent me to, I was feeling very nervous and edgy. With the TM program now I feel so much better and relaxed. My TM and A.A. programs keep me busy and happy. I haven't had a drink since I was last in the hospital fourteen months ago.

Patients like Betty and Peggy, who have a long history of severe drug dependency, require a very broad, eclectic approach to therapy, but the TM program appears to make a vital difference. Their instruction in the TM program and the follow-up require careful timing and design. Such patients greatly benefit from frequent checking and advanced meetings to provide them with further understanding about the TM program and the importance of regularity in practicing the technique.

No battle against a major public health problem can gain a significant victory if it only attends to the casualties. Too much of the work in the field of alcoholism has been focused on treating end-stage victims of the disorder and not enough upon the prevention of alcohol abuse, the primary condition that gives rise to alcoholism. While the TM program certainly has much value as a therapeutic technique in the treatment of alcoholism, of far greater significance is its potential as a preventive tool in alcohol abuse.

A study reported in the September 1975 issue of the *American Journal of Psychiatry* by psychiatrist Mohammad Shafii and his co-researchers clearly demonstrated the great value of the TM program for decreasing or discontinuing the automatic and socially sanctioned use of alcohol in the young and middle-aged. These investigators surveyed the frequency of alcohol use in 126 individuals identified as practitioners of the TM technique and a matched control group of 90. No control subjects reported discontinuation of beer and wine use while 40 per cent of subjects who had practiced the TM program for more than two years reported discontinuation within the first six months. After 25–39 months of TM practice, this figure increased to 60 per cent. In addition, 54 per cent of this group, versus one per cent of the control group, had stopped drinking hard liquor. The researchers concluded that the TM program "can be a significant tool in helping an individual to lessen or end dependence on alcohol" and, more importantly, serve as "an effective preventive method for use with potential abusers of alcohol."

Often more difficult to treat than chronic alcoholism is heroin addiction. The National Institute of Mental Health estimates that there are more than 250,000 heroin addicts in America. There is every indication that the decades of law enforcement designed to stamp out opiate addiction have accomplished little. Particularly distressing about the figures on rising heroin addiction are the signs indicating that the greatest increases are occurring among adolescents in the middle-class white drug scene. A survey in a Phoenix high school indicated one student in ten was using hard narcotics. The principle treatment for heroin addiction is methadone maintenance, in which the addict takes a drug called methadone, which satisfies his craving for heroin. Critics ask whether substituting one addiction for another can be called treatment and argue that detoxification followed by rehabilitation in a half-way house setting should be the treatment of choice. Even in the best of treatment settings, however, better than 90 per cent go back to using heroin again. The TM program may prove a useful addition to any current treatment as illustrated by Tom.

Having started "fooling around" with heroin at age 17, Tom got addicted for the first time before he went to college. Because he had wealthy parents who "didn't care how [he] spent [his] money," he found it easy to get more and more "hooked on the habit." By age 22, he had completed only two years of college with very poor grades and had three times submitted to voluntary detoxification. After remaining off heroin for six to nine months, however, he would inevitably feel lonely, depressed, and anxious about his future. When these feelings grew strong enough, he was back on heroin. He had his own apartment and saw his parents infrequently because he "couldn't relate to them." He rarely worked and would usually "sit around all day doing nothing." His few friends also took drugs, and he found it increasingly difficult to have any kind of relationships with women.

Psychotherapy revealed a very immature young man who never had a strong feeling of self-confidence or self-worth. He was very attached to his mother, with whom he was quite angry because she never let him "grow up." He showed very little identification with his father, who had been "traveling all over the world" for as long as Tom could remember.

While hospitalized for his fourth heroin detoxification, Tom learned the TM technique. During his first six months with the technique, he had considerable difficulty with unpleasant sensations and troublesome thoughts while practicing it. Psychotherapeutic support was necessary to help him continue meditating regularly. Over that first six-month period, Tom began to deal with his hostile feelings for his parents and to think rationally about what he wanted out of life. He decided to return to school and to see if he could find part-time work.

Tom continued in therapy for another 12 months during which he had his ups and downs but managed to stay off heroin. He gradually made new friends, none of whom were heavily involved in drugs. He also began to establish a new relationship with his parents, got to know his father for the first time in his life, and maintained a 3.8 grade point average during his final two years of college. Two years after starting the TM program, Tom graduated from his state university and was accepted by a very good business school. At a follow-up interview, he said,

> I think what the TM program has done is let me get in touch with my own strength. That's basically it. I've always had it in me to do well. I'm not unintelligent, but my own feelings of not being worth anything made me too scared to even try to prove myself.... Heroin is a vortex that can swallow a person's life.... I think the TM program should be available to as many people as possible trapped in that vortex.

The TM program has also proven very effective with teenagers who are weekend drug abusers. High school drug education classes seem to have done little to discourage teenagers from taking LSD or smoking marijuana, and some studies indicate that school drug education programs may have added to the drug abuse problem by explaining how to take drugs with caution. Few weekend drug abusers seek psychiatric help on their own, but they often end up in the psychiatrist's office after they get caught by parents or police. Teenagers seem especially pleased with the TM program because it gives them what they call a "natural high." This report by a 19 year-old girl is typical:

> I began smoking marijuana daily and taking speed, acid, and cocaine every weekend, in an attempt to free myself from all of the confusion of the world. Instead, I discovered even greater frustration and felt even more directionless and empty. The TM program made sense to me. Since starting to meditate, my life has begun to come

together. With the TM program, it was easy to give up drugs. I've enrolled in school again and raised my average to 3.6. My life keeps taking increasing shape and direction. The TM program is the greatest.

People with addiction problems tend to be left-hemisphere dominant; they rely too heavily on their analytic and time-bound thinking of the left cerebral hemisphere while suppressing feelings located in the right hemisphere. By increasing inter-hemispheric integration, the TM program increases emotional freedom. As a result, boredom, emptiness, and tension diminish, and emotional life becomes richer and intensified. The TM technique makes life more enjoyable thereby relieving the problem of addiction at its core.

Passive-Aggressive Personality Disorder

Sometimes a person is his own worst enemy, and none more so than the passive-aggressive individual, who blames everyone but himself for his misfortunes. He unconsciously feels great anger and hostility for everyone and everything around him. He would like to explode in rage against his enemies and friends alike but can express his aggressive feelings only by thwarting other people's efforts through mistakes, delaying tactics, excuses, apologies, and accidents whenever someone else relies on him. Because he is too inhibited to express directly his pent-up aggression, he attacks people passively by standing in their way whenever possible — hence the name "passive-aggressive personality disorder."

In unconsciously choosing this weakest of ways to vent his anger and frustration, the passive-aggressive person enslaves himself to failure. Neither his boss, his co-workers, his wife, nor his friends may understand why, but whenever he is involved, things do not work out as planned. Through his repeated failure, he becomes the object of criticism, which stokes the coals of his repressed hostility.

A passive-aggressive individual often suffers from depression, anxiety attacks, and somatic symptoms, which are especially useful in making excuses for breaking commitments. If he seeks psychiatric help, he does so to relieve his anxiety, depression, or other symptoms. In his first therapeutic interview, he will begin with how terrible everyone else is, how they treat him unfairly, and how he cannot understand why he must suffer such injustices. As soon as the therapist begins to point out that others may not be at fault, the passive-aggressive person will begin feeling hostile toward the therapist and start laying every possible roadblock in the way of therapy. This situation often becomes very trying for the therapist because the passive-aggressive person will neither quit therapy and give up the safe doctor-patient relationship nor make real progress in therapy and come to terms with his own behavior. These patients are sometimes not so affectionately referred to as "therapist killers." Behavior therapy tries to shortcut this stagnant therapeutic relationship by teaching the passive-aggressive person to become more assertive through assertive-training exercises. This kind of person can, however, find ways to thwart even the simplest and most direct therapeutic programs. In this light, the way in which the TM program catalyzes rapid growth in the passive-aggressive individual is particularly intriguing.

Jane was a 37 year-old elementary school teacher who complained of a miserable marriage and an unappreciative supervisory staff at work. When her recently widowed and very demanding father moved in with Jane and her husband, she began to be "more and more depressed each day." Though she knew her husband treated her thoughtlessly and sometimes cruelly, she was extremely dependent on him. Whenever he would go away on a business trip, she could not sleep at night, had crying spells, and became quite depressed. His return brought a few hours of happiness until he began

to treat her as he always had. Jane compounded her
troubles by constantly irritating her husband and father.
Dinner burned not infrequently, the house was always
untidy, she could never quite hear her father's call until
he finally got up and came to where she was. When her
depression finally started to worry her, Jane began
individual psychotherapy, toward the end of which she
learned the TM technique at her therapist's insistence.
Jane made little progress prior to the TM program.
She never ran out of reasons why everyone else was at
fault for making her miserable, but she finally found
enough strength to change her life about 12 months
after learning the TM technique. Her first few months
with the program were difficult; she required considerable attention from the instructors in the TM
program to make sure she meditated properly and to
adjust how long she meditated each sitting. For several
two-week periods during her first three months, she
practiced the TM technique for only ten minutes twice a
day in order to slow the rate of stress release caused by
the technique. She did find, however, that her depression gradually lifted during this first three-month
period, and she began to feel more comfortable and
satisfied with her work.

Over the next 12 months, she grew from a meek,
passive-aggressive, dependent girl into a lovely, self-
reliant, and happy woman. To everyone's surprise,
including her friends, neighbors, and husband, she
finally got the courage to insist that her husband join her
in marriage counseling. When three months of
marriage counseling finally revealed that her husband
did not want a wife but a kind of human doormat he
could walk all over and mistreat, she asked for a divorce,
which she got despite great protest from her husband.
Four months after learning the TM technique herself,
she had encouraged her father to learn the technique,
which proved very helpful to his getting over his grief
for his deceased wife. To Jane's amazement and delight,

her father became very close to a widow whom he met at church, and the elderly couple decided to get married. Jane feels she "has had enough of men for awhile," but she also noted in a follow-up interview:

> Before I started the TM program, I couldn't do anything but make myself and people around me miserable. I let people push me around and then I felt angry inside but too frightened to do anything about it. I was a prisoner of my own weakness. The TM program broke the chains of that prison and I'm not even sure exactly how. I guess I just began to lose my fears and just feel stronger inside. I can't really explain it because the change I've experienced in my feelings about myself and my life have been so great. I think for the first time in my life I've become capable of really loving. Before this, I was looking for someone to lean on, to hold my hand, not to love. If the right man happens to come along, I'll be able to be a real woman for him. The little girl has grown up.

Criminal Behavior

The distinction between a person who has a disease or psychological disorder that causes suffering to himself and the person whose psychological make-up leads him to cause suffering for others by engaging in criminal behavior is, from a larger perspective, somewhat artificial. In both cases, the person is dis-ordered. Perhaps for this reason, psychiatrists have become increasingly active in criminal rehabilitation over the last two decades.

The American prison system is notoriously ineffective at rehabilitation. According to the 1971 Congressional Record, two-thirds of the 200,000 inmates incarcerated in federal and state prisons are "alumni" of other institutions. Of the 100,000 prisoners released from confinement each year, 75 per cent again commit crimes and return to prison. Supreme Court Justice Berger has described the present criminal justice system as a revolving door—crime, trial, convictons, prison, release, crime, and back again. As a prisoner whom I saw in psychiatric consultation once told me, "If you want to make a person into a hardened criminal, send him to prison." This statement summarizes all too well the sorry state of our prison system. By increasing psychological dis-ease and dis-order, prisons cause more behavior problems than they cure.

Poverty, poor family life, and drug abuse are three of the most often cited causes of criminal behavior. Though these factors are undoubtedly important, Maharishi cites a simpler and deeper cause when he writes, "Crime is evidently a shortcut to satisfy a craving—a shortcut which goes beyond normal and legal means.... Crime, delinquency, and the different patterns of anti-social behavior arise from deep discontent of... a weak mind."⁴

In this light, the TM program may have a lot to contribute to criminal rehabilitation. Most criminal rehabilitation programs try to change behavior by imposing external rules and reward-punishment regimens, while the TM program changes behavior by increasing internal ease, order, and strength at the depth of the psyche. The principle shortcoming of the external approach is that it changes behavior without changing the person and consequently only rarely results in lasting improvement. By reducing distress and promoting comprehensive psychological growth, the TM program may prove to be the key which opens up a person's receptivity to rehabilitation. A letter to Governor Brown of California from a prisoner who started the TM program while in maximum security at Folsom prison poignantly conveys what it can add to rehabilitation.

Dear Governor Brown:

At the time I am meditating in accordance to the program set up by the Science of Creative Intelligence and its founder, Maharishi Mahesh Yogi.

First of all let me tell you a little about myself. I feel like I have always had problems and have been in trouble all my life. Prior to 1963 I had been arrested for only checks, theft and fraud. The only treatment I had received was a short interview with a Navy psychiatrist prior to discharge. In 1963 I was sent to San Quentin with convictions for kidnapping, robbery, escape and cop shootings. During the following seven and one-half years I saw a total of twenty-two psychiatrists, psychologists and counselors. I spent hundreds of hours in group therapy, group counseling and individual therapy and was finally able to con the psychs into giving me clearance. I was subsequently released on parole in June 1970. In November of 1970, after shooting one cop and assaulting several more I was again arrested. Besides the above, I also picked up convictions for robberies and one convicition for first degree murder. Immediately upon my return to Folsom I became involved in smuggling and trafficking in drugs and escape attempts. All the above is true and can be verified by a telephone call to the institution.

In view of the above it goes without saying that I was housed in the maximum security section and was going nowhere. I felt like I was buried, that I was dying. I felt like I was slowly burning out with each passing day and had nothing to look forward to but death; and with the confusion, misery, hate and frustration that I felt each day, death and the release it promised started looking good to me.

I seriously doubt that I would be alive today if in September of 1974 I had not enrolled in a philosophy class and met the instructor, George Ellis. It is hard for me to describe George because the first time I met him I found it hard to believe what I saw and felt. When he walks into a room he fills it with light and warmth.

After the class I went up to him and just told him that I wanted to be where he was at and how do I get there. George then explained to me that he was but one of Maharishi Mahesh Yogi's many students and a qualified teacher of Transcendental Meditation and that he had reached his present plateau through meditation. After that initial meeting I started reading all the literature I could find on TM, besides having numerous conversations with George Ellis. Then in June of 1975, after saving up enough money to pay the initiation fee, George came to the prison for four days in a row, on his own time and at his own expense, and instructed me in the technique of Transcendental Meditation.

From the moment I received my mantra to the present time, there has been nothing but change within and it has all been positive. The confusion and frustration are gone and the hate and misery I am able to cope with easily. For the first time in my life I know where I am at and more important, I know where I am going. I have direction! Another equally important thing is that I no longer feel the need to use narcotics. I may be living behind forty-foot high walls but I have never felt more free in my entire life.

I spoke with George Ellis today after he had attended a meeting with the Supervisor of Education, Mr. H. Chamblis, and the Associate Warden of Care and Treatment, Mr. R. Thomas. George was advised that he was finally able to secure official permission to hold classes in TM. However, George was also advised that the State would not supply the funding necessary to implement the classes.

Governor, an extremely small number of men here are as lucky as I am in having funds available to pay the initiation fees and this is what this letter is all about. I personally feel that TM is so good for the men here that I am going to pay the initiation fee for my best friend so he can receive the benefits that I have.

There are literally hundreds and hundreds of men here who are aware of TM and want to get involved but will be unable to do so because of the lack of funds. To me, *this* is criminal. All that current programs being funded by C.D.C. do is teach a man to be a cross between a robot and a parrot: act right and talk right and you will be paroled. TM is the only program that starts inside the man's head and has immediate results. In all honesty I can say that after twelve and one-half years in San Quentin and Folsom, with all their psychs and groups, Transcendental Meditation, as taught by Maharishi Mahesh Yogi, has been the only thing that has ever helped me and I know that it can help the rest of the men here.

The beneficial effects of TM are well-documented. The tests conducted at two federal prisons, La Tuna in Texas and at Lompoc here in California, showed nothing but positive gain.

The men here at Folsom are at the end of the line and any funds that you could make available for classes in Transcendental Meditation would be deeply appreciated.

Sincerely yours,

E. J. C.

Despite the general tendency for an individual to seek positive reasons to justify whatever he happens to be doing, this letter reflects a genuine growth in consciousness, a prerequisite for rehabilitation. As Maharishi pointed out, this man had a long history of concern for himself at the expense of others, but after learning the TM technique he showed a striking shift toward concern for others in wishing that his fellow inmates could also begin benefitting from the TM program.

Very shortly after this letter was written, 109 inmates at Folsom petitioned the Governor to appropriate funds for a TM program. The inmates pledged 65 dollars each toward the program in hopes that the State would make up the balance. When Maharishi heard this, he said that the inmates should not have to wait for the technique and could learn for free. A program is now under way. Because it is inexpensive and easy to implement, the TM program is ideally suited for widespread use. Of course, the final solution to dissemination of the TM technique throughout the prison system lies not in the TM organization trying to provide their services free of charge (which it can do on a very limited basis), but in government support for large numbers of prisoners to learn the TM technique.

In his book *Crime in America*, Ramsey Clark redefined rehabilitation in terms of fulfillment. He pointed out that violence becomes almost unthinkable as soon as a person grows inwardly happy and fulfilled. Expanded awareness permits the person to fulfill his own desires without losing sight of the larger social interest. By promoting happiness and expanding awareness, the TM program not only accomplishes the most basic inner changes necessary for rehabilitation, but also prevents the development of the criminal personality in the first place.

Brain Damage

Impaired neurological functioning is often only half the cost of brain damage. When a young person suffers brain damage in an auto accident or a vigorous man in his mid-fifties has a stroke, the emotional shock accompanying the realization that the brain has been permanently damaged can be extremely difficult to absorb. In some patients with brain damage, the discovery of their loss of function puts them into an emotional tailspin that seriously complicates recovery and rehabilitation. Depression, withdrawal, shame, and guilt are among the overpowering emotions that may keep the brain-damaged patient from getting back into activity and learning to compensate for whatever neurological functions might have been lost or impaired. If patients wallow in their depression and self-pity, their inactivity may lead to further loss of mental and physical abilities rather than rehabilitation.

The psychiatrist often called for consultation in cases of brain damage faces a difficult diagnostic dilemna. To what extent are the patient's emotional distress and sometimes childish behavior results of organic damage and to what extent are they results of emotional shock? Because the psychiatrist cannot readily answer these questions, he may have difficulty helping the patient come to grips with the cause of his emotional distress, and he may also have difficulty communicating consistent expectations to the patient. If the psychiatrist expects more improvement than that of which the patient is capable, the patient's failure to meet those expectations can compound the patient's feelings of low self-worth.

Clinical observation suggests that the TM program can be very useful with some brain-damaged patients regardless of whether emotional distress and childish behavior have organic or psychological causes. Because the TM program works physiologically and requires very little from the patient, it can be practiced without expectations and without fear of failure. The ease and order gained during the TM technique provides a direct experience that increases the patient's feelings of well-being and provides a stepping stone back into activity.

It must be understood, of course, that the brain-damaged patient must be capable of communication, a precondition for learning the TM technique. The TM program cannot replace destroyed brain tissue (neurons are apparently not capable of regeneration) and the irreversible loss of function that results from it, but it does appear to help the rest of the brain recover from an acute trauma and to maximize the potential for functioning that still remains. By promoting integration of various parts of the brain, the TM program may help open up new neuronal pathways.

Phyllis was a 31 year-old teacher and graduate student about to receive her master's degree in education when she had an auto accident and suffered brain damage. During her initial hospitalization after the accident, it became clear that her physical wounds would heal quickly but her emotional wounds would require much longer to heal. From the day she learned that her difficulty in coordinating her movements was probably the result of brain damage, she became increasingly withdrawn and began to show more and more childlike dependency. When she refused to converse with friends who came to visit her, her neurologist called for a psychiatric consultation. Six weeks after her accident, she had recovered much of her physical abilities, but required admission to a psychiatric hospital for further treatment of her worsening depression. It was unclear how much of her depression and childish behavior was due to organic damage and how much to psychogenic overlay.

Nine months of psychotherapy produced discouraging results. She had become shy and withdrawn, her emotional tone was flat, she could not leave the hospital grounds because she was "afraid of what could happen," and her behavior resembled more and more that of an eight year-old girl. The suggestion by one of the hospital residents that she learn the TM technique was received as a harmless experiment worth a try. The results of the TM program in this patient were extraordinary. Within weeks after learning the technique, she emerged from her shell and began to show an unanticipated degree of mental clarity. Her depression lifted; she began to make friends with other patients; and she started getting passes to leave the hospital and go to movies, museums and shopping. Within three months, she was discharged from the hospital to return home and pick up her life where she had left off. Though she still had some loss of her remote memory and impairment of other mental functions, she left the hospital optimistic about her future and understandably enthusiastic about the TM program.

Stan was a 43 year-old executive, married, successful, and on his way to becoming the president of one of America's largest corporations when an auto accident left him with brain damage. When he first got out of the hospital, he showed marked loss of memory and ability to concentrate, and he could not speak. Showing a strong determination to get better, he began a rehabilitation program which included psychotherapy to help him with his depression and emotional adjustment. He had already regained his speech when he began the TM program about a year and a half after his accident.

Though his progress prior to starting the TM program had been substantial, he began to recover by leaps and bounds afterwards. A year later, he was back at work in the same job he had held at the time of his accident. He totally recovered his speech, significantly regained his memory, and found his mind sharper than it had ever been before. Neither he nor his doctor can measure how much the TM program contributed to his overall rehabilitation, but both were certain that it helped. "I can do business better now than I could before the accident," Stan said. "I'm sure the TM program has been important in that; I recommend the TM program to anyone who wants to hear about it."

Schizophrenia

Schizophrenia usually indicates a greater degree of disability than any other mental illness. Approximately one-quarter of the nation's hospital beds are occupied by schizophrenic patients. The cost of schizophrenia has been estimated at 11.6 – 19.5 billion dollars annually. About two-thirds of this cost is due to lack of productivity by schizophrenic patients (only about 25 per cent of all discharged patients work) and about one-fifth to treatment costs.

If the neurotic may be said to build dream castles in the sky, then the psychotic may be said to live in them. Schizophrenia is the most common of the psychoses and is characterized by loose, at times incoherent, magical thinking as well as either very anxious, angry, or flat emotional states. A collapse of a coherent sense of self apparently permits the schizophrenic to become absorbed in delusions and fantasies and at times to regress to early childhood behavior patterns. The schizophrenic may feel flooded with stimuli and often has a rapid metabolic rate. Typical schizophrenic delusions include a person thinking that he can derive cosmic meaning from random events such as the number of cars honking in the street at a certain time, or believing that he can control other people's actions through his thoughts, or feeling he is the only one who knows about bizarre sinister plots to destroy mankind. Over the last 25 years, psychiatry has made great strides in treating schizophrenia with psychotropic medication and supportive psychotherapy. Many schizophrenics who would have remained locked in state mental hospitals only three decades ago are now able to function reasonably well in society as long as they continue to take their medication. Psychotropic medication seems to help maintain sufficient psychological equilibrium to permit the schizophrenic to remain reasonably in touch with the world about him. Because schizophrenia is a state of maximum dis-ease and dis-order, and the practice of the TM technique produces ease and order, reports in psychiatric journals that the TM program may be a useful adjunct in the treatment of schizophrenia should not be too surprising.

Twenty year-old Peter was hospitalized following his arrest by the police for throwing a brick through a large store window. When he entered the hospital, he was highly confused and incoherent; he told the police that the window had asked him to break it. Peter was enrolled in the local university as a junior and had evidently had a terrifying LSD experience from which he did not recover. Investigation revealed that Peter had often taken LSD and other drugs to cope with school pressures, but following his last LSD experience, his ability to function deteriorated steadily over a three-week period until he was arrested by the police. When he entered the hospital, his most coherent statement was, "I was somebody important, Saint John, Planet of the Apes, Father Time." He was hospitalized but despite treatment remained psychotic. Over the next three months, he lived at home with his parents, where, even with medication appropriately increased, his overall mental health deteriorated steadily. His sleeping pattern became very erratic and he began to develop an elaborate delusional system in which he could talk to dogs and hear what people were saying in cars by listening to the exhaust. Peter's parents finally brought him to see me, and I had Peter hospitalized again directly from my office.

Peter initially resisted therapy and insisted that I was not a physician but a friend whom he had met in Jamaica. Over the next month, however, the combination of appropriate medication and supportive theapy began to bring Peter's psychosis under control. He became sufficiently coherent to learn the TM technique, expressed interest in starting the TM program, and took the course while on passes from the hospital. His parents also took the TM course. Two weeks later, he was discharged from the hospital but continued individual psychotherapy and medications.

Over the next month, Peter's condition steadily improved. Though he was still quite disturbed, he was becoming somewhat less withdrawn. Peter was then not seen by me for four months, during which time he continued to take his medication as prescribed but discontinued practicing the TM technique ("I can't really think of a good reason."). His psychosis once again worsened considerably. When I saw Peter again, I encouraged him to resume meditating regularly. He did so, and also began attending weekly advanced meetings at the TM center. Since then, he has once again made slow but steady progress. Peter will be attending school in the fall, but, at my suggestion, will be taking a reduced number of credits. He now feels that, with the TM program, he will not want to go back to hallucinogenic drugs; he also feels he will be better able to handle school pressures, which played a role in his first psychotic break. His need for medication has decreased moderately, and he has shown some progress through psychotherapy in sorting out the various social and emotional pressures that continue to trouble him. Though the TM program was certainly not a miracle cure for Peter's psychosis, it evidently added an important stabilizing influence to his day-to-day life and contributed to his overall improvement. In addition, Peter undoubtedly benefitted from his parent's meditating regularly. His father reported felling more at ease while working on his Ph.D. thesis, while his mother made a smooth recovery from a depressive reaction to her son's illness.

This case illustrates how, in conjunction with traditional modes of treatment, the TM program can be used with severely disturbed individuals. However, use of the TM program with such cases requires careful supervision by the psychiatrist and a specially trained TM instructor as well as a carefully designed TM program. After their discharge from the hospital, it is often difficult to keep schizophrenic patients meditating regularly, just as it is difficult to keep them on their medication regimen.

In presenting new methods of psychiatric treatment, almost all authors tend to leave the impression, albeit inadvertently, that the new method works spectacularly for all patients all the time. This impression is almost unavoidable because the new method deserves attention for its successes, not its failures, and the author's intent is to show how the new method can be used properly, not improperly. Though research suggests that the TM program produces varying degrees of improvement in a number of cases, it should be noted that the TM program is sometimes subject to the same problems that stymie other methods of helping severely disturbed patients.

7

TM and Therapy: Facts and Fantasies

Many questions raised at my lectures require that I clarify facts and dispel fantasies about the TM program, its effects, and its relation to the treatment of emotional and physical illnesses.

Can the TM program cure schizophrenia, cancer, or other serious illnesses? Can it precipitate psychosis or an emotional breakdown? Does the TM program have any negative effects? How long must a person practice the TM program to notice results? Do psychiatric medications interfere with TM practice? Why would someone stop practicing the TM technique? Are there ways to accelerate the benefits of the TM program? These questions are but a few which seem to cause confusion.

How significant is this confusion? I have found from patients and people who attend my lectures that it is having two important effects. First, some people are depriving themselves of the full benefits of the TM program because of their misconceptions. Second, other people may be unnecessarily prolonging their own suffering due to illness because they expect the TM program to accomplish what is better achieved through specific medical therapeutics. Two examples will illustrate.

Judy, a 35 year-old housewife and mother of three, had been practicing the TM program for over two years.

She consulted me because she wondered why the TM program had not yet cured her migraine headaches, which had troubled her ever since age 19. In my evaluation, I asked where she had gotten the idea that the TM program cured migraines. Evidence suggests that the TM program helps relieve tension headaches, but this fact has somehow grown into the popular fantasy that it cures migraines. Actually, a new temperature biofeedback technique appears to be the best treatment for migraines. Judy underwent ten sessions of hand temperature regulation at our Institute's biofeedback clinic and noticed a significant reduction in her migraine headaches. Had she done so earlier, she might have saved herself considerable suffering. She might also have enhanced her benefits from the TM program because long-standing health problems and physiological deficiencies can slow the pace of growth.

Howard was a 32 year-old accountant who sought my help with his anxiety and mild depression. Evaluation revealed him to be a classic average middle-class neurotic, and I urged him to begin the TM program. At that suggestion, he balked. "My friend tried TM and all he got out of it was nausea and a headache," he said. When I inquired further, it turned out that Howard's friend had not learned the TM technique from a TM instructor but had picked up some technique from a book claiming to teach TM. Because Howard had heard that the TM technique was simple and easy, he was convinced that his friend had given it a fair try but that the TM technique frequently produced negative effects. I pointed out that his friend had not learned the TM technique because it could only be learned in a specific course. "A course?" Howard replied. "Why should that be necessary?" Again, a fact — the TM technique is easy to learn — had grown into a fantasy that the TM technique can be learned by mail order or from a book at bargain prices. This fantasy in turn supported the further misconception that the TM program frequently produces negative effects.

With the increasing popularity of the TM program, confusion of facts and fantasies about it tends to grow as well. This chapter aims at reducing that confusion by sorting out facts from fantasies in answering several common questions about the TM program and its effects.

Is the TM Program Traumatic?

One concern common to many people about to begin the TM program, especially if they have had some psychotherapy, is that the TM technique might be emotionally traumatic in stirring up unconscious conflicts. The basic concepts of psychoanalysis have become so widely known that many people seem to be familiar with Freud's idea that the unconscious is a "cauldron of seething excitations." The psychiatric term, "complex," which denotes a set of very deep-rooted stresses often requiring years to resolve in psychotherapy, is also well known. A few years ago when sensitivity groups became popular, a surprisingly large number of participants in these groups became psychological casualties because they were overwhelmed by old stresses brought out by intense group pressures. There seems to be little doubt that the TM program does permit the resolution of deep-rooted stresses, frustrated wishes, and old emotional traumas which make up what Freud called the unconscious. Yet, the usually comfortable way this occurs during the TM technique contrasts sharply with the slow, painstaking, and tedious process of analytic psychotherapy.

Most people who are concerned that TM practice may be traumatic seem to get this idea from what they know about psychotherapy. Because it involves trying to get in touch emotionally and intellectually with old, painful memories in order to vent them, analytic psychotherapy is often hard work that causes considerable emotional unheaval. "You've got to work it through" is a favorite expression of analytic psychotherapists for encouraging their patients to persevere in the face of emotional turmoil. The analytic psychotherapist provides some degree of security and guidance which helps the patient come to grips with unconscious conflicts. Yet, the whole process is tedious because a person can handle only so much emotional unheaval at a time, and most patients have not just a few but thousands of mini-traumas at the root of their symptoms.

In contrast, the TM program involves neither hard work nor emotional upheaval for two basic reasons. First, it promotes the resolution of deep-rooted stresses and conflicts through wholly physiological means and therefore involves no struggle to excavate or grapple with the past. At most, a person might note long-forgotten memories passing through the mind during the TM technique, but these thoughts and feelings disappear just as automatically as they arise. Second, deep-rooted stresses tend to dissolve during the TM technique when a person is enjoying a maximum degree of inner stability and well-being. I have frequently seen, within six months after a patient begins the TM program, a disturbance such as a painful lack of self-confidence disappear without our even talking about it in therapy. By strengthening the mind before allowing stresses to dissolve, practice of the TM technique cushions the person from the potentially disturbing impact of the stress release process.

Analytic psychotherapy embraces the premise that hard work is the key to psychological growth. The TM program, on the other hand, accepts that, because so much of what people do has unconscious origins, trying to promote psychological growth is much like struggling to get out of quicksand. The futility of trying to grow is evident in the unsuccessful results of millions of people's efforts to stop smoking, lose weight, be more friendly, get rid of headaches, overcome fears, be more loving, or be happy. It's not uncommon for psychiatrists to see people who have become exhausted and tense in the name of self-improvement. By reducing stress and unfolding new reserves of energy, the TM program allows for growth to take place naturally and comprehensively. TM practitioners tend to smoke less; their weight normalizes, often without conscious dieting; they become less anxious and more outgoing; tension headaches tend to disappear; fears melt away; loving fellings grow; and happiness becomes a day-to-day experience of living.

Resistances to Growth

Because analytic psychotherapy is frequently painful, patients often show what therapists call resistance, which refers to an unconscious refusal to keep delving into past miseries. Resistances show up in many forms. A person may "go blank" or keep changing the subject when the therapist touches on a painful memory. Freud at one point noted that resistance to psychoanalysis was inevitable because people automatically seek pleasure and avoid pain. Thus he suggested that psychoanalysis would in all likelihood have only limited results.

I have found that the TM program, in contrast to psychotherapy, dissolves psychological resistances. Sally, a 22 year-old married woman suffering from anxiety and depression, showed a typical resistance to help. She incessantly complained of anxiety, insomnia, and problems with her husband, how everything was "all wrong," and that nothing could really help her. She took the child-like stance of saying to me and everyone else in her life, "I'm helpless, take care of me." Yet, in every possible way she resisted recognizing that the main cause of her problems was her failure to stand up and take care of herself. Her history revealed that she probably developed this life-stance as an over-protected child who never learned autonomy and had few chances to test out her desires and abilities. Sally went right from her parents' home into her marriage, where she established the same kind of child-like relationship with her husband, whom she held responsible for her happiness and well-being.

If I had taken the traditional psychotherapeutic approach with Sally, I might have tried to help her gain insight into her dependency stance and recognize that she would be happier if she began to take responsibility for herself. This process could have gone on for years with probably few results because Sally was highly resistant to change. Instead of dealing head on with Sally's resistance, I suggested that the TM program might help her feel better. She agreed to take the TM course. To her surprise, over the next six months she started to change. Her insomnia disappeared and her anxiety subsided, but more importantly she began to do things which she enjoyed on her own. She started taking guitar lessons, enrolled in a cooking class, and began making her own friends instead of relying exclusively on her husband to introduce her to people. Though her husband was generally pleased with the changes in his wife and also began the TM program, I invited him to join Sally and me for a few therapy sessions to help him adjust to the fact that he now had a wife, not a little girl.

The TM program was particularly successful with Sally and seems to be very useful in overcoming resistances to growth in many such child-like complainers. This case should not signify that the TM program is a panacea for all resistances to psychotherapy. In fact, resistance to the TM program itself can become a problem with some patients.

A small percentage of patients resist the TM program by simply refusing to learn it. These patients may fear losing control of themselves, or in the extreme, being overtaken by hostile unknown forces. I have found that gentle encouragement and systematic education about the TM technique is the best way to help a patient through this resistance. It is very important that the resistant patient not feel he must begin the TM program in order to continue in therapy. I had one patient who felt I was trying to get rid of her by sending her to the TM center. In cases of such severe dependence, I have found it useful to let the patient know very directly that the TM program will be an aid to growth but not a replacement for the therapeutic relationship. A few patients may initially resist the TM program because they feel it conflicts with their religion, lifestyle, or values. These resistances usually disappear once the person has adequate information about the TM program.

The second way patients may show resistance to the TM program is by refusing to continue to practice the TM technique. If symptoms which the patient had incorporated into his ego structure begin to disappear, a patient may stop meditating because he fears adapting to life without his "old dependable" symptoms. One patient complained, "The TM program made me feel so calm that I couldn't feel angry with my parents anymore." Severely repressed patients have also discontinued the TM program because they felt embarrassed, ashamed, or guilty about the pleasure which they experienced while practicing the technique. Some patients, who enjoy the TM program initially but run into difficulty with the technique, will stop meditating rather than go to a TM instructor for checking, which would immediately remove their difficulty, because they fear failure. All of these cases pose problems, but I have found that my support along with the attention of the local TM instructors is sufficient for most patients who stop meditating to resume regular practice.

Whereas most people thoroughly enjoy the surge of growth resulting from TM practice, a few people need support in integrating it. Rose, a 42 year-old married woman who consulted me about her anxiety and depression, took the TM course the week after I recommended it. Over the next few weeks, she noticed a steady decrease in her anxiety and an increase in energy. Though she was experiencing immediate benefits, she started becoming irregular in TM practice after about two months. In our sessions, it became clear that she was having difficulty assimilating her personality changes into her life situation. Her activites had always centered around her husband's expectations, but now Rose was feeling an urge to pursue some interests on her own, specifically returning to college. She had dropped out of school 20 years before to help her husband through law school.

Her old fears of failure and abandonment began to disappear, permitting her substantially increased freedom. Every day started becoming "a fresh new experience full of possibilities," while she had been used to doing "constantly the same old thing." Amidst this surge of growth, however, crept a panic about becoming autonomous at the cost of growing apart from her husband. This subtle panic led her to start missing meditations.

I first helped Rose appreciate the positive aspects of the growth she was undergoing and to trust her natural inclinations. I suggested that she and her husband, who was also a new TM practitioner, see me to discuss her emerging autonomy. Rose had feared that her husband would react negatively to her taking courses at the local state college but was surprised when, in our sessions, he openly encouraged her to do so. Over the next several months their relationship did go through changes, but all Rose's fears proved to be unfounded.

At my suggestion, both Rose and her husband took the SCI course at the local TM center. In cases such as this, I strongly recommend weekly advanced lectures and the SCI course to balance the experience of rapid growth with an understanding of this process. Many people require only this additional knowledge to lose unnecessary fears about their personality development and to begin enjoying the TM program to the maximum. With her husband's encouragement, Rose has returned to school and is planning to go on for a graduate degree. Both she and her marriage have benefitted from her new-found interests.

How Long for Results?

Most people notice benefits within the first few days, weeks, or months after taking the TM course. Comments such as "I have more energy," "I'm getting along better with the people at work," "The tension in my neck is gone," "I'm getting more work done," "My mind is sharper," "I don't fall asleep watching the evening news anymore," and "I'm happier," are common among TM practitioners of only a few weeks. Because the technique is so easy and natural, almost everyone notices its immediate effects — deep physical relaxation and more mental clarity from the first TM session. If a person practices the technique regularly and notices these immediate effects, then the cumulative benefits of the TM program are bound to accrue because they result automatically from the technique's immediate effects. Psychologists Nidich, Seeman, and Banta, at the University of Cincinnati, showed that two months of the TM program are sufficient for people to demonstrate significant personality growth in the direction of self-actualization.

When people ask how wide is the range of the TM program's benefits, I point out that it can improve every aspect of a person's life because it increases ease and order at the roots of individual life — the nervous system. Maharishi often notes the effects of the TM program are so far-reaching that the 300 scientific studies done on it to date only *begin* to measure its full significance.

Despite the reliability of the TM program's physiological effects, about 25 per cent of the people who take the TM course report that they do not notice its benefits. They cease meditation or do not meditate regularly, saying that they either do not have time or just aren't "getting anthing out of it." How could a person not get results from the TM program if the technique works as well and reliably as physiological tests indicate?

In prescribing the TM program over the last several years, I have had an opportunity to learn why some people do not notice benefits and what is necessary for them to begin doing so. There are many reasons why, ranging from a particular cognitive framework blocking the person from seeing benefits which are taking place to incorrect TM practice inhibiting the physiological effects necessary for cumulative benefits to occur.

One reason why people may not notice benefits is their tendency to look for spectacular changes to occur during their TM sessions. There is no doubt that when correctly practiced, the TM technique produces the psychophysiological state of restful alertness. Important to correct practice, however, is a passive attitude toward experiences which may come and go during the meditation session. If a person is looking for something special to happen when he sits down to meditate, he is in all likelihood straining to notice what's going on rather than meditating properly. Physiological studies show very clearly that, while practicing the TM technique, a person cannot subjectively judge the depth of that meditation. Physiologist R. Keith Wallace reported to me a story illustrative of how in his initial ground-breaking study, a meditating college student came out of a TM session and claimed it was the worst he had ever had and that the researchers should "throw away the records." In fact, the physiological measurements indicated that this young man had experienced the state of restful alertness; the physiological changes that occurred were

252 HAPPINESS

no less than spectacular. Some people become disappointed when they do not have "flashy" experiences while meditating and so discontinue the practice. This decision shows a misunderstanding of what the TM program is all about. Maharishi and his instructors try to make very clear that the purpose of the TM program is not to produce dramatic experiences during the meditation period but to enrich and enliven a person's activity in his daily living.

Another reason why people fail to notice results may be due to their expecting a magical transformation within days after learning the technique. The natural growth fostered by the TM program does not progress by leaps and bounds; rather, it is an evolutionary process, such as that of a child's growth. Even a child's mother does not usually notice his daily growth, but almost anyone will note the dramatic development of a child in six months or a year. If a person is looking for the TM program to produce instantaneous and spectacular changes, he may overlook simple benefits such as increased energy or generally increased feelings of well-being. Some people do notice dramatic changes within days after taking the course, but these cases are not the rule. Most people note that the technique does produce pleasant immediate effects (e.g., restful alertness) and enjoy a steady strengthening of their baseline happiness through regular practice.

What may happen to the person with unrealistic expectations about the TM program is that he or she may stop meditating within a few weeks after completing the course. This decision is regrettable because the person does not really give the program a chance to produce results. When I prescribe the TM program, I usually tell my patients that they should go into the TM course willing to give the program a good chance for a minimum of six months. I explain that this means practicing the TM technique twice a day every day and getting checked regularly to assure its correct practice. I

am convinced that an important reason why few of my
patients (under 10 per cent) complain of no results or
stop meditating is that they begin with the clear idea of
giving the program a fair try. If a person follows the TM
program for six months, substantial results are almost
inevitable.

Lois, a 28 year-old systems analyst and wife of a fast-
rising corporate lawyer, had difficulty noticing results
from the TM program for yet another reason. Having
heard that I am a psychiatrist and a TM instructor, she
sought my help saying, "All my friends started getting
great results within a few weeks after taking the TM
course, but not me. I've been meditating for five weeks,
but I'm still tense, insecure, and unhappy. What's wrong
with me?"

I first asked Lois whether she found the technique
enjoyable and easy to do and whether she was getting
checked regularly. To both questions, she answered
affirmatively, allaying my doubts about whether she
was practicing the technique correctly. I then took a
detailed history. Lois had no history of emotional
disorder, but it did not take long for the source of her
distress to become clear to both of us. Tension and
anxiety became problems for her soon after she was
married. In telling me about her marriage, she described
three years of a grueling relationship. Her husband Ed
grew up in a disturbed family; his mother was often in
and out of the hospital for treatment of severe
depressions. Perhaps as a result he developed a rigid and
controlling personality which dominated, to the point of
suffocation, every aspect of their marriage. They had a
beautiful new house with elegant antique furniture, but
Ed refused to have friends over for fear of "spoiling the
rugs." He owned a Ferrari but didn't drive it because he
didn't want to get a scratch on it or wear it out too
quickly. If Lois disagreed with Ed on even the smallest
matter, she would be subject to a tirade of name calling.
Though she was intelligent and attractive, he often

called her "stupid" and told her she was "ugly." Cold and controlled, Ed was unable to give or receive any tenderness and their whole relationship was impoverished. He preferred to put all his energies into work and winning golf tournaments. He frequently yelled at her to be more independent, but insisted that she accompany him wherever he went and only see his friends. One afternoon when she wanted to visit one of her friends rather than go with him to a golf tournament, he got so angry that he smashed the car window with his fist. When she told him she was growing more and more unhappy, he insisted that "nothing is wrong," called her "ungrateful," and told her to "try harder." Ed did not want Lois to seek outside help because they had a "perfect marriage with a few problems which could easily get worked out."

After Lois described her oppressive marriage, I pointed out to her that she should not expect five weeks of the TM program to make her suddenly feel gloriously happy and at ease as long as she was living under such trying circumstances. When I inquired further about what effects she might have noticed since taking the TM course, she did note feeling more energy throughout the day and less debilitating anxiety when Ed yelled at her. "Perhaps my courage to come and see you is due to TM," she added. Having helped her recognize that the TM program was in fact working, I suggested that she would have to deal with her marriage problems directly in addition to meditating regularly. She had tried to get Ed to take the TM course and begin marriage counseling. He thought the TM program was "hogwash and a rip off," and refused to consider marriage counseling.

It was clear from the inital interview that Lois loved her husband and did not want to leave him. I agreed to see her regularly for a few months to help her start making changes in her marriage if possible. Her marriage has started to improve slowly. At her last visit, she mentioned that her husband was considering taking the TM course and joining her in marriage counseling. Having begun to take her life in hand, Lois has become an enthusiastic meditator. She now recognizes that taking the TM course does not magically change a person's life situation. She has also learned that to experience the full benefits of the program, she must put her new-found creative intelligence and sense of self to use in improving her life.

Another case illustrates yet a different reason why a person might not notice results. George was a 26 year-old organic chemist and researcher who had been practicing the TM program for two years when he came to see me because he felt "depressed and tired all the time." He complained of "always falling asleep in afternoon meditations" and "not feeling well-rested in the morning." At one point he believed that his symptoms might be due to the TM technique dissolving deep stresses too quickly. Presumably to slow down the stress-release process, he stopped meditating for three weeks, but "things only got worse."

In taking his history, I discovered several factors which explained why he remained depressed and fatigued after two years of the TM program. First, he had a rough childhood and an extremely depressed mother; many painful memories of depression had collected in his memory banks. Second, at age 23 George suffered a case of severe hepatitis, which kept him ill for over nine months. Soon after getting over this liver disease, he took a night job, which disrupted his regular patterns of rest. Finally, in his desire to work up the ladder in his company, he began taking on extra responsibilities, which had him working very long hours and often on weekends.

A physical examination and lab studies revealed that George had no lingering hepatitis, but I was convinced from his history that his illness had triggered the onset of his depression and physical weakness. I explained to George how the physical effects of the hepatitis, followed by inadequate rest and strain at work, could open the gates for his backlog of old depressed feelings to come into play. George was surprised when I explained that the physiological basis for depression involves the exhaustion of certain important chemicals in the brain. When I showed him how his strain and overwork prompted his depression, which then caused him to strain further, he asked, "Why isn't TM getting me out of this cycle?"

George had noticed some benefits from the TM program, but mostly in terms of keeping him "from falling apart completely." In our discussion, it became clear that he had so thoroughly strained his biomachinery that the TM program was allowing him to sustain some degree of equilibrium in his hectic schedule but was not permitting him to grow rapidly toward enlightenment. To start enjoying the full benefits of the TM program, George needed to give his body and mind a chance to recover in a concentrated fashion from the psychophysiological effects he had suffered.

I recommended that George take a uniquely restful vacation by going to a one-month residence course in the Science of Creative Intelligence. Under careful supervision available at these courses, participants practice the TM technique three or four times daily to accelerate their growth. I was optimistic that the extra meditations, good food, valuable knowledge, and easy pace of such a course would allow George to dissolve the backlog of strain that was keeping him caught up in the stress cycle.

When George returned from the course, he appeared transformed. He looked cheerful, the circles under his eyes were gone, and he no longer sat with a slumped posture. Follow-up after one month showed no further depression and plenty of energy during the day. He stopped falling asleep in his afternoon TM sessions and enjoyed the technique more than ever before. He had begun the TM program because he had wanted to improve his performance at work but had failed to notice any such effects prior to his SCI course. When he finally found himself accomplishing more at work with less effort, he lost all doubts about whether or not the TM program was effective.

Some people require a dramatic experience of personal growth soon after they take the TM course in order to practice the technique regularly. Deloris is a perfect example of such a person. A 34 year-old mother of two, Deloris came to see me because of anxiety, depression, low self-esteem, extreme lonliness, and poor self-confidence. Throughout her childhood, she rarely received affection or praise and was "criticized by [her] parents all the time." While still a teenager, she married to escape her oppressive household but wound up jumping "from the frying pan into the fire." Many years of trying to make a miserable marriage work further lowered her self-esteem. Finally, she left her husband and obtained a divorce. Deloris had to go on welfare to support her family while she finished secretarial school. All the while, her emotional distress grew, and at the urging of a friend, she eventually sought professional help.

I put her on anti-depressant medication, started seeing her in psychotherapy on a weekly basis, and suggested she begin the TM program. She was quite skeptical that the TM program could produce all the benefits discussed in the introductory lectures, but out of her trust for me she took the course. Though she had pleasant initial experiences, she remained quite doubtful that "getting deep rest for twenty minutes twice a day could help." She began to make progress but attributed her gains in emotional well-being to our psy-chotherapeutic sessions rather than the TM program. She began praising me at every opportunity for how much I was helping her.

Several months later I left for a one-month lecture

tour. Upon my return I saw Deloris again, at which time she began telling me that she had not done well in my absence and that our sessions were very important to her. To my inquiry about her TM practice, she answered that she hadn't been getting much out of its practice, had started missing meditations, and finally quit altogether. I decided that Deloris required a direct approach to reinforce her meditating regularly until she could appreciate its benefits for herself. I gently pointed out that she found me such a wonderful person because she was borrowing my ease and orderliness to structure her life, but such an arrangement was not a permanent solution. She had to begin drawing on her own creative intelligence if she was ever to become a truly healthy and happy person. To motivate her and underscore my confidence in the TM program, I made the following agreement with her. She would start meditating again twice a day, would get checked weekly for the first month and monthly for the next three, and would attend a three-day residence course sometime within the next eight weeks. If she did not notice tangible benefits within five months, I would not mention the TM program to her again.

She resumed meditating regularly, but the real turn around in her progress came when she took the residence course. She came back from the course literally beaming. Her happiness and laughter were contagious. I pointed out to her that she now looked like an autonomous and happy person. Her need for medication and psychotherapy sessions lessened dramatically and instead of going around praising me, she started praising the TM program. Her twice daily TM sessions started to have a steadily greater impact on her well-being as she got out of the stress cycle and into the growth cycle. Several months after the residence course, her long-standing depression cleared. She now attends residence courses regularly to get the most from her TM program, and she has become a lighthouse for the people around her.

Some people come to me with the complaint that the results of the TM program have "worn off." Such a person will typically experience significant benefits with the first few months after taking the TM course and then hit a plateau in which it appears that "nothing is happening." For example, a person might notice an initial reduction in anxiety and cigarette consumption but will not quite give up cigarettes, or another person might notice much better relations with family and friends but find some old tensions surfacing again several months later. The basic reason behind this experience is simple: growth is cylical. Alternating periods of apparently slow and fast growth during the TM program are natural. If a person hits what he feels to be a long-lasting plateau, I usually recommend a residence course. Residence courses are one of the best ways for the person who feels few results from the TM program to begin experiencing significant benefits and start realizing all that the program has to offer. I also suggest that the person get checked by a TM instructor just to make certain that the practice of the technique is absolutely without strain or effort. After six months or a year of meditating regularly, most people become accustomed to the cyclical process of growth and no longer worry about it.

An important reminder for the person who feels he or she is not getting good results from the TM program is to be an aware consumer. When a person completes the TM course, he has the right to take advantage of many follow-up services free of charge at TM centers. If a person has difficulty with or a question about his meditation and does not go to the TM center for assistance, he is not taking advantage of a service for which he has already paid. Weekly advanced lectures and group meditations are helpful and enjoyable. The TM course also qualifies a person to attend TM residence courses, which are the most inexpensive, comfortable, and enjoyable short vacations I know.

Negative Effects?

A frequent question that I hear at my lectures and from colleagues at professional meetings is "Can the TM program have harmful effects for some people?" Concern about possible negative effects from any self-improvement program or medical therapy goes all the way back to Hippocrates, who told his young doctors: "Above all, do no harm." I think today's concern has its origin partly in public knowledge that sensitivity groups, many new psychotherapies, and even classical psychoanalysis have had a significant number of "casualties." Therefore, carefully examining a new growth program for deleterious effects is certainly justified.

Whether or not the TM program produces negative effects is debated among some TM researchers. One camp points out that unpleasant or distressing experiences occur in connection with the TM program largely because some people fail to follow instructions given during the TM course and as a result incorrectly practice the technique. The other camp argues that unpleasant or negative experiences constitute a major reason why some people stop meditating regularly. The question of whether the TM program can produce negative effects may remain a point of dispute, but it is clear that some people do have unpleasant experiences in conjuction with TM practice. I have found that when handled properly by the meditator, TM instructor, and when necessary a mental health professional, these unpleasant experiences do not turn out to have harmful consequences but, on the contrary, may result in great strides in personal growth.

Perhaps the most common reason why some TM practitioners report unpleasant experiences is their failure to take enough time to come out of each TM session gradually. Because the TM technique triggers a drop in metabolic rate much greater than that occurring during sleep, the body naturally needs two or three minutes after the person stops practicing the technique to return to its normal metabolic rate. Suddenly jumping up from a TM session strains the physiology just as does jumping out of bed at 3 A.M. The effects of this strain can include irritability, headache, nausea, dizziness, dissociation, anger, disturbed sleep, "crying spells," and mental confusion. TM instructors emphasize repeatedly during the TM course that two or three minutes of not meditating but just sitting quietly are necessary at the end of a TM session before resuming activity.

Some people do not take this quiet period at the end of TM practice because they feel they "don't need it." They base this false conclusion on their feeling of mental clarity and readiness for dynamic activity at the end of each session. Although the mind may feel ready to go at the end of the TM session, the body needs a few minutes to adjust to the physiology of normal waking consciousness. A case underscores the importance of following this instruction.

Mike was a 36 year-old married construction foreman who had been doing the TM program for a little over three months when he came to see me. He complained of chronic severe headaches with a dull pressure in his forehead and behind his eyes. Prior to consulting me he had seen his internist, who diagnosed him as having either severe sinusitis or a psychosomatic condition. His internist recommended that he have a series of elaborate sinus X-rays and, if these turned out negative, he should consult a psychiatrist.

Mike came to see me the day before he was to have spent $200 on sinus X-rays. I took a detailed history and discovered that his headaches began within a few days after he completed the TM course. When I asked him how much time he was taking to come out of meditation, he answered, "Oh, maybe a minute. That's all I need." He had a vague recollection of having been told to take three minutes to come out of meditation slowly, but he did not think that "a minute or two, one way or another, would really matter that much." Mike had never gone back to the TM center to have his meditation checked since completing the course. I suggested that I check his TM practice right there in my office. To make certain that he gave his body enough time to adjust to the shift from the TM state to activity, I insisted that he sit for five full minutes with his eyes closed at the end of meditation.

When he finally came out of meditation, his headache had vanished, which surprised him but not me. I suggested he put off going for his sinus X-rays for a few days and start taking five minutes to come out of each meditation slowly. I pointed out that he could always have the X-rays if necessary and asked him to come and see me again in four days. When he came back, he reported with delight, "I'm cured! My headaches are gone!" Six months later, he was still free of headaches and enjoying the benefits of the TM program to the maximum. Had Mike gone for regular checking at the TM center as instructed during the TM course, he could have saved himself three months of headaches plus medical bills from his internist and me.

The second common cause of unpleasant experiences during or after TM meditation involves the sudden release of "large blocks" of deep-rooted stresses. From a psychiatric point of view, it is evident that the TM program allows significant repressed memories and feelings to come into conscious awareness relatively rapidly and comfortably. Many of these memories and feelings might otherwise remain unavailable or might take long periods of intensive psychotherapy to be uncovered. In most instances, this emotionally charged material surfaces comfortably because the deep relaxation resulting from the TM technique cushions the person from the unsettling effects of the stress release process. Occasionally, however, a deep stress can dissolve quickly enough to cause some emotional distress or physical discomfort. These periods of abrupt stress release usually last no more than a few seconds or minutes but sometimes persist after the meditation period is over.

During the initial TM course, new meditators learn how to handle periods of intense stress release to minimize unpleasant feelings. A person simply treats the process of intense stress release as passively as a dream during sleep. He refrains from analyzing or resisting any thoughts or feelings that might appear and continues the effortless practice of the TM technique while the "big block" of stress dissolves. If a person forgets to apply these instructions and starts analyzing the stress release process before it is over, feelings of psychological discomfort can carry over into activity.

Unpleasant feelings resulting from the stress release process are easily remedied through consultation with a TM teacher. Trained to help people cope with periods of intense stress release, TM instructors are willing to spend whatever time may be necessary with a person having "rough" meditations. This service is available free of charge at all TM centers. An important reason why physicians can prescribe the TM program with confidence is the widespread availability of well-trained TM instructors to help people resolve any temporary difficulties with the technique.

For the psychiatric patient, and on rare occasions the average middle-class neurotic, an overpowering thought or feeling (e.g., rage, lust, guilt) during TM practice can be frightening. Such an experience can lead a person to question whether the TM technique may be causing personality disorganization or literally "driving him crazy." The individual may then wrongly conclude that the TM program is not only unhelpful but actually harmful and consequently stop meditating. The treating psychiatrist should not reinforce this conclusion but should refer the patient back to the TM teacher for frequent checking until this "big block of stress" dissolves. In some instances, the TM instructor will shorten the person's meditation period to slow down the process of stress release. I have found, however, that only very rarely have problems that required a shortening of meditation time arisen among my meditating patients. In the vast majority of cases (better than 98 per cent), the TM program has promoted psychological growth with few, if any, complications.

Dr. Ivor Mills at Cambridge University in England reported that some people experience mild depression soon after completing the TM course.[1] These people have typically been driving themselves to hold down two jobs, study for exams, or achieve a promotion, and are taking a variety of drugs to ward off anxiety and depression. Caught in a state of chronic hyperarousal, such a person may experience temporary boredom or mild depression after starting TM practice because his arousal level must drop on the way to its optimum level. During this process, the person may go through a period in which old exciting activities have lost their glamour, but he has not yet begun to enjoy his full capacity for pleasure as a result of an optimum mental temperature. For some average middle-class neurotics starting the TM program, a brief period of mild depression may cause consternation and alarm. Generally it is not serious, but psychiatric supervision may be helpful in some cases. On the other hand, the chronically and more seriously depressed patient, as noted earlier, needs a special TM program combined with pharmacological and psychotherapeutic support to gain maximum benefit from TM practice.

One further possible cause of psychological distress in conjunction with the TM program is over-meditating. Some people, mostly adolescents with a history of drug abuse and psychiatric problems, mistakenly get the idea that if ten minutes of TM practice is good, then five hours must be better. Such abuse of the TM technique can produce disturbing psychological effects that can in the extreme include manic or depressive states, auditory or visual hallucinations, or psychosomatic bodily complaints. A few individuals who have abused the TM technique have required hospitalization for treatment. In these cases, reduced meditation time, psychotropic medication, and psychotherapeutic support can generally bring about rapid recovery of psychological stability with no lasting negative effects. However, the addictive tendency of these individuals must then be further treated with strong limit-setting and education.

An Unusual Case

Psychiatrist Alfred French at the University of California, Davis-Sacramento Medical Center, and two colleagues at UC, Davis, reported in *The Journal of Nervous and Mental Disease*[2] a case of a 38 year-old woman who had a "psychotic-like" reaction to the TM program. This report is significant for two reasons. It is the first case of any "negative effects" of the TM program to appear in the psychiatric literature, and the authors offer some excellent insights into the diagnosis and treatment of such cases.

Mrs. M had no history of emotional distress or thought disorders when she enrolled in the TM course. Within days after completing the course, she noted a profound increase in her general feelings of well-being. "Sustained optimism, moderate euphoria, and a strong sense of the inherent goodness and value of her experience" characterized her mood, according to French. In a letter written to her teacher one month after completing the TM course, she described "mental and creative energy at a peak...soaking up creative energy like earth drinking rain. Beautiful people everywhere. Life is so rich. I have to keep expanding to hold my portion." She later noted, "When, through meditation, I began reaching new areas of myself, I was delighted."

Two weeks after beginning the program, she started having compelling fantasies which were euphoric in quality and occurred after but not during the TM period. Soon she started actively encouraging these fantasies, which she later described as waking dreams, in which she experienced "fantastic cosmic and inner adventures." French points out that her pursuit of these fantasies began leading to behavior which "would have been clinically described as psychotic."

Three months after Mrs. M completed the TM course, French and his colleagues interviewed her. Psychological tests indicated that she had a mild thought disorder, was moderately anxious, and was actively seeking help. The mental status examination during her initial interview revealed:

> She was an attractive, neatly dressed and young looking woman who was immediately congenial upon our arrival. She displayed substantial use of intellectual processes, particularly abstractions and analogies, and seemed clearly above average intelligence.... She spoke freely about herself and her unusual experiences. She seemed to be experiencing a fixed level of euphoria reflected in frequent laughter, a virtually constant smile, and an attitude of cheerful optimism toward all events, including her recent experiences. The unusual finding was the lack of variation in her effort and general manner over the three hours we interviewed her. She later explained, "I was not totally there. I was operating also on other levels and couldn't completely return to the here and now that you were experiencing."

Over the next two months, Mrs. M's experience began to change dramatically She started feeling negative moods so intensely that she felt her experience becoming "unbearable." At the same time, she started losing self-control. "The process took me over," she later wrote. "I was on such a precarious balance that it would have been dangerous to change direction or stop." On her own, she experimented with shortening her meditation and stopping it altogether, and her agitation intensified. She sought psychiatric help to ascertain whether she was in her "right mind." Although her psychiatrist did not feel she was "mentally ill," he suggested medication and counseling.

Financially unable to begin psychotherapy, Mrs. M turned, again on her own, to psychological and religious literature. She read Assagioli's theories of psychosynthesis, Maslow's individuation, and Maharishi's writings on the evolution of consciousness. These readings comforted her when she began to realize that her experiences were not "totally crazy," but linked with a process of deep psychological growth. Her whirlwind experience finally subsided when "in a state of complete physical and emotional exhaustion" she knew she "had reached her limit." Her emotional discomfort began to subside and she started sleeping again. Psychological testing several months later indicated that she no longer displayed a thought disorder, showed a substantial decrease in her felt need for outside help, and enjoyed increased feelings of autonomy and comfort.

How should Mrs. M's experience be diagnosed? How should such cases be managed? Grave errors could result from trying to understand Mrs. M's experience solely within the confines of traditional psychiatric diagnoses and pathological states of awareness such as dissociation, mania, depersonalization, or hysteria. She appears to have shown some classical signs of the "psychosis-like" state accompanying a profound spiritual awakening. To force such an experience within the confines of traditional diagnostic categories would be to risk describing the growth to enlightenment as a pathological phenomenon. Treating people going through a period of "rough" spiritual development as if they were truly psychotic can turn a temporary and essentially progressive experience into a chronic pathological state.

Mrs. M started showing her "psychotic-like" behaviors when she began encouraging her "waking dreams." These fantasies probably began as a result of stresses dissolving at the deepest levels of her psyche. A very important principle taught to all novice TM practitioners is: do not encourage the creation of fantasies within meditation and do not make a mood of "spiritual experiences" outside of meditation. If a person does not abide by this principle, he can promote personality disequilibrium by prolonging experiences resulting from the release of stress and starting to live in a fantasy world. Mrs. M apparently got so caught up in her initial euphoria after taking the TM course that she failed to recall this principle. Probably afraid that her euphoria would soon disappear, she began manipulating her mood to sustain her "high." As a result, she slipped gradually into a "psychotic-like" state in which her fantasies took control.

French and his colleagues offer several sound insights into how such cases can be managed in the best interests of the patient's safety and growth. First, they point out the need for the patient to have frequent contact with a TM instructor, who could perform three functions: assure correct practice of the technique, adjust meditation time appropriately, and give some knowledge about the mechanics of growth through the TM program. Second, they note that interaction with a mental health professional who could served as a "spiritual guide" would be preferable to indiscriminate use of medication. Finally, they point out that moderate use of medication to facilitate sleep and anxiety reduction, if necessary, would be helpful. I agree with all of these suggestions but would add the possible need to help the patient set up a structured schedule of daily activity in order to facilitate integration of new heightened awareness with everyday reality testing.

What is the danger of such a "psychotic-like" episode occurring? Extremely few people who take the TM course have such experiences. Indeed, exploratory psychotherapy appears to precipitate periods of intense emotional upheaval far more frequently than the TM program. Because the TM program strengthens the mind at the same time that it promotes stress release, individuals going through such intense experiences usually show an unexpected degree of stability and capacity to take care of themselves. However, the early recognition and proper management of an unusually intense period of stress release can save the TM practitioner considerable discomfort.

Earlier recognition of the type of process involved in Mrs. M's case might have considerably decreased her suffering over a period of several months. Nevertheless, her experience took its own natural course, and she returned not just to a state of psychological equilibrium, but to a state of sustained and heightened well-being. Fully recovered, she states, "My faith in my own system's ability to guide and safeguard my sense of identity and my mind/body system is greatly strengthened. Life has a depth it didn't have before. I am operating at new levels of knowledge and understanding and I have not yet discovered the boundaries of my mind."

The TM Program for Inpatients

Can a hospitalized psychiatric patient with a long history of emotional distress and behavior disorder benefit from the TM program? I often hear this question from people who would like to arrange for a friend or relative in a psychiatric hospital to take the TM course. With half of the nation's hospital beds occupied by psychiatric patients, this question is an important one.

A recently completed large-scale study of the TM program as an adjunct to the treatment of psychiatric inpatients indicates that it does contribute significantly to improvement or recovery in many cases.[3] The study began in mid-1972 under the direction of Drs. Bernard Glueck and Charles Stroebel at the Institute of Living, a large private psychiatric hospital in Hartford, Connecticut. Over a period of three years, a total of 237 patients started the TM program while hospitalized. Patients with all types of psychiatric illnesses participated in the study and even severely disturbed patients were able to learn the technique easily. Only 12 per cent of the patients stopped meditating while in the hospital, a small percentage by comparison to the drop-out rate of other programs involving voluntary participation.

Glueck and Stroebel started the project in part because they felt the two current strategies—insight psychotherapy and tranquilizers—for reducing the chronic and inappropriate "emergency response" were proving inadequate. Intrigued by research indicating that a variety of techniques can produce various states of relaxation that counter chronic anxiety, they decided to investigate three well-known techniques: autogenic training, alpha EEG biofeedback, and the TM program. Two TM instructors joined the hospital staff for the duration of the project.

To equalize the amount of personal and group attention that each patient received, the learning regimes for all three groups were standardized around that of the TM program. Because hospitalized psychiatric patients require more attention than the average person to learn and practice the TM technique comfortably, the TM instructors designed a special follow-up program for patients in the project. Each patient took the standard TM course but then came for daily checking of his or her meditation for the first three weeks after learning the technique. In addition, each patient attended a weekly group session with a TM instructor for the full 16 weeks they participated in the initial evaluation period of the project. The purpose of these meetings was to answer questions and boost motivation to meditate regularly.

"Autogenic training, originally described by Luthe and more recently formalized by Wolpe and Lazarus," Dr. Stroebel explains, "consists of gradually attempting to relax the voluntary musculature in a progressive fashion, starting with the toes and feet and seeping upward to involve the whole body." Despite claims that this exercise reduces general.anxiety when practiced regularly, Dr. Glueck reports that it did not prove helpful to patients in the study. Two groups of six patients each began the muscle relaxation program. For the first two weeks, the novelty of the program held the patients' interest, but it soon became apparent that the patients were not experiencing much reduction in general anxiety. By the end of the fourth week, all the patients had asked to stop the program because they found the exercises quite boring. Some of the patients asked to switch to the biofeedback or TM groups. After this initial failure of the autogenic training program to hold patients' interest, this phase of the project was discontinued.

Alpha EEG biofeedback also proved to be of no significant benefit in reducing patients' general anxiety levels. Although they showed some ability to control alpha production after 15 hours of training, nearly all had difficulty in applying that training to achieve any degree of relaxation when not getting the biofeedback signals. They did not find the alpha state particularly pleasant or relaxing, and some patients reacted to it with a "so what" response. For a significant number of patients, efforts to achieve the alpha state resulted in increased tension and anxiety because of uncertainty about the results. After 26 patients had completed biofeedback training, Glueck and Stroebel concluded that it was doing little to promote relaxation or tranquility and terminated this phase of the project as well.

In contrast to alpha biofeedback and autogenic training, the TM program sustained patients' interest and promoted significant reduction in anxiety levels and an overall improvement in psychological well-being. One of the most striking measures of this improvement was the TM patients' "condition at discharge." When leaving the hospital, each patient received a final psychiatric evaluation and a rating of either recovered, much improved, moderately improved, slightly improved, or unimproved. The TM patients who had participated in the project for a minimum of eight weeks showed a much greater degree of improvement at discharge than a matched group of patients who did not receive the TM program. Standard psychological tests also showed that the TM patients felt a significant reduction in their symptoms. Computerized nursing notes for evaluating daily progress further corroborated the improvement in the TM patients. A final index of the program's benefits was the reduction in the need for medication, especially night sedation, among patients in the TM group.

In a follow-up study of discharged TM patients, the researchers found that approximately half were meditating regularly, another 20 per cent were meditating somewhat regularly but reported plans to continue meditating, and nearly one-third had stopped meditating. An important factor distinguishing the regular TM patients from those who had stopped meditating was contact with a TM center once the patient returned to his or her home community. All of the regular TM patients had visited their local TM centers for checking and support, while only three of the patients no longer meditating had done so. Many of the regular TM patients reported that the TM program was a valuable addition to their lives, frequently far beyond their initial expectations.

This study maps fairly clearly what components are necessary for a hospitalized psychiatric patient to benefit from the TM program. First, the treating psychiatrist and hospital unit staff must understand the basics of the TM program and encourage the patient to meditate regularly. At a minimum this means the patient must have two periods free from interruption each day. Second, a TM instructor must be available for the first three weeks to provide daily checking of the patient's TM practice; thereafter, weekly checking is advisable for as long as the patient remains hospitalized. Finally, because psychiatric patients are apt not to follow any post-discharge treatment regime, the patient needs clear instructions and strong encouragement to contact his or her local TM center. This contact seems to be a critical factor in whether or not a patient will continue the TM practice regularly after discharge.

In summarizing what kinds of patients respond best to the TM program, Dr. Glueck notes that it "seems to affect most immediately and dramatically those psychiatric patients showing considerable amounts of overt anxiety, manifested by symptoms such as hand tremors, perspiration of hands and feet, 'a knot in the pit of the stomach'.... "4 He adds that these individuals are often relieved of anxiety symptoms after their first TM session. The symptoms usually return soon afterwards, but if the patient practices the TM technique regularly, the symptoms gradually subside and eventually disappear over an eight-week period. Dr. Glueck also notes that even patients with overt psychotic symptoms will respond, though more slowly than non-psychotic patients, to the anxiety-reducing impact of the TM program. Patients with severe depressive symptoms appear to need strong encouragement from the treating psychiatrist and the TM instructor in order to meditate regularly, probably because the depression so thoroughly undermines the patient's motivation to do anything. Finally, Dr. Glueck reports that across a wide range of diagnostic categories "no serious side effects or complications have been reported from... TM, providing the

patient is adequately supervised until he becomes
familiar with the technique....Even the most severely
psychotic psychiatric patients can learn to meditate
successfully, although they may require much
assistance and supervision during the early stages."⁵

Major research projects such as that conducted by
Glueck and Stroebel are important to discover all the
medical and psychiatric applications of the TM program
and to establish appropriate clinical guidelines. At the
Institute of Psychophysiological Medicine, we are
initiating a large-scale study of the therapeutic and
health maintenance effects of the TM program on our
medical and psychiatric outpatients. Over a two-year
period, we will be looking at such factors as general
psychological health, regularity of basic biorhythms,
frequency of colds and infections, anxiety, blood
pressure, weight, and cigarette and alcohol consumption. We also plan to investigate how EEG brain wave
synchrony correlates with other measures of psychophysiological balance and health maintenance. Drs.
Glueck and Hans Selye are contributing technical advice
in setting up the project. We are also receiving valuable
assistance from the MIU Institute for Social Rehabilitation. The steadily growing number of major projects
applying the TM program to meet the health care needs
of modern America is greatly encouraging to all who
have witnessed the benefits.

Medication and TM Practice

Many people ask me whether tranquilizers are still
necessary now that the TM program is widely available.
An equally common question is whether prescribed
medication will interfere with TM practice. Both
questions reflect the natural desire to enjoy good health
without depending upon pills. Few people like taking
medication because most drugs produce side effects and
the pills themselves are a reminder of ill health.

However, the fact that the TM program naturally promotes total health should not become a fantasy which excludes the important contribution medications of all kinds are making to health and well-being. Maharishi is very explicit about the relationship between medication and the TM program. In response to a person who complained that a particular drug dulled his TM practice, Maharishi stated, "Remaining ill will spoil the meditation more than the use of medicine. If we have to choose between illness and medicine, it is more useful to decide for medicine and against sickness. The effect of medicine, even if it overshadows clear meditations, is in the final analysis, useful even in the cause of meditation."

Most people can readily understand that the TM program does not magically eliminate the need for medication to control dangerously high blood pressure, antibiotics to combat severe infections, insulin to control diabetes, or other drugs to help a person recover from or control a physical illness. Yet confusion often prevails as soon as questions arise concerning the need for psychotropic medication to help people with emotional distress.

This confusion arises in part because most physicians over-prescribe minor tranquilizers (i.e., Miltown, Valium, Librium) and sedatives (barbiturates, sleeping pills), while few people understand how important are the major tranquilizers (Thorazine, Stelazine, Trilafon), anti-depressants (Tofranil, Elavil, Sinequan) and lithium carbonate for helping people in psychotic or severely depressed states. The major tranquilizers are very useful in combating hallucinations, delusions, thought disorders, marked withdrawals, severe insomnia, and other psychotic symptoms. An acutely psychotic patient could not even learn the TM program without receiving appropriate major tranquilizers. Anti-depressants and lithium carbonate have been a great boon to the treatment of manic-depressive illness. On the other hand, minor tranquilizers can be useful in helping reduce a person's suffering during a temporary crisis such as hospitalization for major surgery, loss of a loved one, or withdrawal from alcohol addiction. In this capacity, these drugs have a definite place in medicine. But when a person begins relying on minor tranquilizers as a primary means of coping with anxiety, use borders on abuse. Most doctors tolerate an excessive dependence upon minor tranquilizers because they are unaware of other ways their patients can significantly reduce anxiety.

In many cases, the TM program reduces the need for tranquilizers. Schizophrenic patients usually require large doses of major tranquilizers to control their symptoms, but these large doses also produce lethargy, apathy, and other unwanted side effects. I have found that by prescribing the TM program for these patients, I can put them on smaller doses of maintenance medication and minimize or avoid side effects. Of equal if not greater significance, the TM program *eliminates* the need for reliance on minor tranquilizers because it cures mild middle-class neuroses by dissolving deep-rooted stresses, optimizing mental temperature, and strengthening baseline happiness. It alters the nervous system's style of functioning from a labile one prone to neurosis to a stabile one geared for self-actualization.

If a person is on prescribed minor tranquilizers or sleeping pills when taking the TM course, he should not try to change his medication regime abruptly. The reduction in need for these medications should be allowed to occur naturally, and the medication intake should be tapered slowly and *always under the doctor's supervision.* A spartan attitude about reducing medication is not helpful. If a person needs minor tranquilizers or sleeping pills, he should take them. The resultant emotional ease will support progress through the TM program. Two cases will illustrate how psychotropic medication can contribute to growth through the TM program. Jane was a 36 year-old TM practitioner of two years when she consulted me because of chronic depression. "The TM program seems to be working so much better for my friends than for me," she exclaimed. "I can't understand what's wrong!" When I took her history, it became clear that she had suffered low-grade depression all her life and occasionally had bouts of severe depression. In addition, several members of her family also had episodic depression. I put her on a course of anti-depressant medication and within a month she started feeling "like a new woman, better than in years." Her TM practice became clearer and smoother, she started to notice increased energy after meditation for the first time, and she began enjoying what she has "always hoped to get from the TM program—more happiness." Jane will be on maintenance doses of anti-depressant medication for at least a year. If she continues to do well, we may try gradually tapering her off the medication. I follow her progress in monthly visits and am optimistic that she will not need to remain on medication indefinitely. However, the importance of her staying on medication for the time being in order to continue enjoying maximum benefits from the TM program is clear.

Mr. S, a 42 year-old postal worker, had been in the TM program for eight months when he came to see me. He complained of severe anxiety, insomnia and depersonalization and showed some signs of paranoia. His history revealed that he had long led a withdrawn existence with few friends and no interests. Twenty years earlier, he had been in a VA hospital for what sounded like paranoid schizophrenia. He started the TM program to help him cope with his anxiety, but the results were not up to his expectations. After completing a mental status exam, I concluded that he suffered from chronic schizophrenia. I put him on phenothiazines and suggested he begin seeing me for short visits. The medication substantially reduced his anxiety and other symptoms, and he began to make progress in becoming a somewhat more active and outgoing person. The TM program added to his psychiatric treatment by increasing his mental clarity and general feelings of well-being, especially since his anxiety level was no longer reaching psychotic proportions.

A type of case I am seeing frequently among young meditators deserves mention at this point even though treatment does not require medication. In these cases a change in diet is required for the person to start benefitting fully from the TM program. Sarah, a 23 year-old senior in college, came to me complaining of anxiety and fatigue even though she had been in the TM program for two years. Her history revealed no previous psychiatric disorder and a rather happy childhood and adolescence, but she did mention that for the last three years she had been a vegetarian. When I inquired about her diet, she showed very little knowledge or concern about her protein intake. I ordered a six-hour glucose tolerance test to determine whether Sarah might be hypoglycemic (suffering from low blood sugar). Anxiety and fatigue are the classic signs of hypoglycemia, which can become a chronic syndrome in a susceptible person on a low protein, high carbohydrate diet for a long period of time. The test corroborated my suspicion that Sarah was indeed hypoglycemic. I explained hypoglycemia to her and pointed out that vegetarianism is not a part of the TM program. I then put her on a high protein, low carbohydrate diet, with frequent small meals throughout the day. Within a few weeks, she noted a dramatic decrease in her anxiety and fatigue. One year later she was still on the diet and had no further symptoms. She was enjoying the benefits of the TM program to a maximum degree.

The TM Program–Psychotherapy Interface

How can the TM program and psychiatry best complement one another? Of all the questions I am asked, I find this one among the most intriguing. The TM instructor and the psychiatrist are experts in two separate but mutually supportive domains of knowledge. The TM instructor specializes in teaching a program that promotes the natural dissolution of deep-rooted stresses, or what I like to call *subtle states* of dis-ease and dis-order. The psychiatrist, skilled in helping people suffering severe emotional distress, is expert in treating what I like to call *gross states* of dis-ease and dis-order. Subtle dis-order underlies what I have called mild middle-class neurosis; gross dis-orders constitute the severe neuroses, psychoses, and other major psychiatric illnesses. This distinction should help dispel the fantasies that the TM instructor can cure the schizophrenic and that the psychiatrist holds the key to happiness.

Since subtle dis-orders obstruct most people's full enjoyment of living, the vast majority wishing to increase their share of happiness can begin the TM program and enjoy much greater growth much more quickly than they could ever achieve through psychotherapy. The prospect of enlightenment, the complete normalization of subtle dis-ease and dis-order, beckons on the horizon of the TM program, but does not even appear at the furthest reaches of traditional psychotherapy. However, a substantial portion of the people seeking psychiatric help are troubled by both gross and subtle dis-ease and dis-order. For these people, psychiatric treatment is necessary, but the TM program makes an excellent adjunct to therapy. When the psychiatrist prescribes the TM program, he remains legally and professionally responsible for the diagnosis, treatment, and total health care of the patient. The TM instructor assumes responsibility for teaching the person how to practice the TM technique and providing adequate follow-up to help the person get the most out of meditation.

Several factors in addition to the benefits of the TM program make it especially attractive as an adjunct to psychiatric treatment. Patients are pleased when they learn that the TM program is not a therapy for "sick people," but a self-development program practiced by many of the most dynamic people in the world. A physician must have confidence in the uniformity and quality of what he prescribes. For example, in prescribing the antibiotic tetracycline, I must feel certain that the patient will receive from the pharmacist those capsules containing the right amount of the drug with the necessary potency. I feel just such a confidence in prescribing the TM program because of the standard of excellence and the systematic manner in which the initial TM course and the follow-up programs are conducted. Standardization of the program assures the patient and therapist that a person going to a TM center will learn the technique comfortably and properly. Finally, the TM program is attractive because it seems to help almost everyone despite the person's diagnosis. Little of what medicine and psychiatry have to offer can match the TM program in universality and scope of beneficial effects.

All the psychiatric textbooks talk about the need to increase self-reliance in patients to achieve significant and lasting results through psychotherapy; yet the process of long-term psychotherapy itself can undermine the patient's development of autonomy. Psychiatrists have learned over the past decade that keeping a patient hospitalized for a long period after an acute psychotic break can actually lessen the chances for optimal recovery. When a patient comes to the emergency room acutely psychotic, appropriate medication and crisis intervention will often permit the patient to be discharged within three or four days. The longer the patient remains in the hospital after the acute episode is over, the more he begins to abandon whatever tendency toward self-reliance he may have and behave in regressive ways that further prolong his hospitalization.

Despite their awareness of the general value of shortening therapy as much as possible to preserve the patient's maximum sense of autonomy, most psychotherapists inadvertently weaken self-reliance in their patients by keeping them in long-term psychotherapy. Certainly a good psychotherapist can eventually wean his patient from therapy, but just as long-term hospitalization is undesirable for a person having a psychotic break, long-term psychotherapy is generally undesirable for most psychiatric outpatients. Outcome studies simply do not support the value of long-term psychotherapy.

Another contribution of the TM program to psychiatric treatment is the promotion of patient autonomy. The TM program shortens therapy and increases autonomy in two ways. The patient feels self-sufficient because he does the TM technique himself, without assistance after he has learned it properly, and the experience of pure consciousness during TM practice itself promotes feelings of self-confidence and self-sufficiency. Once my patients understand that the innermost natural resources tapped by the TM program, and not me, have been and will continue to be responsible for their healing and growth, we establish a much healthier relationship. They begin to see clearly how I can help them and what they need to do to help themselves, instead of just sitting back and expecting a magical cure for their troubles. In my mild middle-class neurotic patients, this realization frequently marks the end of their need for therapy. These patients see that they, not I, can solve their problems and that they can find the energy, intelligence, and emotional stability to take their lives in hand just by continuing the TM program. In my more severely troubled patients, this understanding marks the beginning of an effective and realistic therapeutic alliance and an acceleration of progress in therapy.

Ending psychotherapy is often a painful and difficult task for the patient who has come to rely on the therapist as a trusted and wise friend. Prior to my use of the TM program, rarely had I seen patients feel genuinely excited about their future growth possibilities at the end of psychotherapy. The termination phase of traditional psychotherapy is characteristically stormy and all too often does not leave people capable of continuing to promote their own growth. Most of my TM patients demonstrate an extraordinary yet very realistic optimism at the end of therapy. Termination is not painful but joyful, almost like a graduation, because the patient leaves therapy with an expanded vision of his own potential and possibilities for happiness, and he has a technique that he knows from experience will continue to propel him toward ever higher stages of psychological integration and well-being to enlightenment.

In noting the impressive contributions of the TM program to relieving subtle dis-order, it is important not to lose sight of the tremendous progress psychiatry has made in reducing gross dis-order. After a major psychotic break, a person may enter the hospital paranoid, hallucinating, and unable to communicate coherently. The mental apparatus may be completely fractured. Through careful diagnosis, appropriate psychopharmacological treatment, and supportive hospital milieu therapy, such a patient may be helped to reconstitute and return home in a matter of days. This kind of success with such patients would have been unheard of two decades ago. Through continued research into the genetic and biochemical processes at work in major psychiatric dis-orders, psychiatry will continue to make progress in treating gross dis-orders quickly and effectively. Much remains to be learned about how the TM program and psychiatry can interact most usefully for the well-being of patients and the collective mental health of the nation. In order for this interface to bear the most fruit, more psychiatrists must become knowledgeable about the TM program and its theoretical aspect, the Science of Creative Intelligence, and more TM instructors must receive training in working with psychiatric patients. Progress in both these areas is already taking place. For example, the standard psychiatric textbook by Friedman, Kaplan, and Sadok now has a chapter that includes a section on the benefits of the TM program. This chapter was written by Dr. Louis Jolyon West, Chairman of the UCLA technique hold promise for advancing the theory and program, Dr. West recognizes that the Science of Creative Intelligence and its practical aspect, the TM program, hold promise for advancing the theory and practice of psychiatry. From the side of the TM organization, the Institute for Social Rehabilitation (ISR) has been established in affiliation with Maharishi International University to train TM instructors to work in rehabilitative settings. ISR also assists public and private rehabilitative institutions in designing, implementing, and evaluating the TM programs.

A revolutionary breakthrough in our understanding of the mind and its development is at hand. Mental health professionals are just beginning to appreciate the unique contribution of the TM program to psychiatry. With further theoretical and clinical understanding of the interface between the TM program and therapy, they will, I expect, recognize that the Science of Creative Intelligence offers a major new paradigm that illuminates and expands other theories of the mind such as psychoanalysis and behaviorism. Toward this end, our forthcoming book explains how SCI offers a unitive understanding of the mind and brings fulfillment to diverse psychotherapeutic schools such as psychoanalysis, behavior therapy, Transactional Analysis, Gestalt therapy, Reality therapy, and others. Through the TM program, expanding happiness and ultimately enlightenment can become realities in the lives of millions.

8

TM and the Life Cycle

"Is life a tortuous maze with traps and pitfalls at every turn?" I began wondering toward the end of my psychiatric training. Having treated patients of all ages in varying degrees of misery, I started to think so. I saw sad-faced children from broken homes, alienated teenagers with a seething discontent, quareling couples on the verge of divorce, adults anxiously preoccupied with difficulties in their relationships, and elderly people broken by despair and depression — all reflecting emotional turmoil specific to their particular life stages. Looking at these patients, one would think that each life stage was inherently fraught with difficulties and deserved to be approached with caution and trepidation; however, the TM program introduces a new dimension to change this picture.

To discover a means of infusing the entire life cycle with harmony and happiness has remained among humanity's primary goals. Over the past several decades, psychologists have written "how-to" manuals for almost every stage of life (i.e., enriching marriage, raising children, growing older gracefully, and so on), yet the tide of neurosis rises yearly. It can be helpful to understand the tasks and potential difficulties of each life phase, but "how-to" formulas alone usually fall short of helping people get the most out of living. I do not say this to be critical of "how-to" manuals but simply to point out that something more than a behavioral prescription is necessary to achieve the ancient goal of infusing happiness throughout the life cycle.

Great men of science and philosophy have identified this "something more" which assures a fully satisfying life as wisdom. Few terms can equal *wisdom* for the cloak of mystery that seems to surround its definition. I like to define wisdom in terms of the wise person. In any situation, he shows an intuitive ability to choose the course of action that brings the most happiness to himself and others. To put it simply, he has a knack for doing the right thing at the right time and enjoying himself in the process. He seems to be always in tune with nature, the needs of others, and his own greatest possibilities for growth.

The means for acquiring wisdom may appear elusive. It is clear that education per se is not the key. Many well-educated people with lots of information about child development, group processes, the human sexual response, and behavioral ideals have high rates of personal and family turmoil. On the other hand, many people with little formal education seem admirable for the quality of happiness which they enjoy and the high human ideals which their lives reflect. I am not trying to suggest that ignorance is bliss, but I do believe that the ability to lead a fully satisfying life—wisdom—bespeaks not a person's level of education but his attunement with the natural, his overall degree of ease and orderliness — technically his degree of psychophysiological integration or level of consciousness.

One way to understand the value of the TM program is in terms of the infusion of wisdom. In hundreds of my patients embroiled in the conflicts at each stage of the life cycle, the TM program has sparked an intuitive ability to resolve conflicts and increase joy and harmony. It has helped them to become more natural, freely in touch with their desires and capacities. The following cases illustrate how the TM program allows each stage of the life cycle to blossom with vitality, joy, and happiness.

Childhood

"When a child is born," Maharishi writes, "his means of expression are limited and his powers undeveloped; but as he grows up and engages in the field of activity there is no limit to the development of his powers, his strength, intelligence and creativity, nor to the degree of happiness which he can experience and radiate."[1]

This year, two-and-one-half million Americans will become parents for the first time, while another three-and-one-half million will be increasing their families. Though every child, as Maharishi points out, offers a beautiful and magnificent promise, never before in U.S. history (and perhaps the history of the world) have parents felt so overwhelmed and inadequate. Faced with a myriad of choices and a lack of consensus on parenting values, parental anxiety is at an all-time high. Caught up in the anxious decision making between raising children strictly or permissively, emphasizing competition or cooperation, more parents are seeking professional help in rearing their children than ever before. Americans have lost confidence in their intuitive ability to raise children and this wisdom is what the TM program can help restore. Now that having children is a matter of choice and not chance, thanks to birth control technology, the expansion of happiness must become the central basis for rearing a family.

A child enters the world helpless, and in all probability, two decades will pass before he becomes fully capable of taking responsibility for his own growth and well-being. During the first five years of life, a child depends almost entirely on his parents or other adults to keep him warm, well-fed, and sufficiently stimulated to assure the flowering of his physical, intellectual, and emotional capacities. If his needs are seriously neglected or if he is abused, either emotionally or physically, stress and trauma register in his physical, intellectual, and emotional make-up. The joy of discovery, the pleasures of touching and feeling, and the delight of play come easily to the child, but the child's vulnerability to stress is remarkably high. Psychoanalysts have delineated the many ways parents inadvertently foster stress in their children. Insufficient affection, premature weaning, introducing shame into toilet training, overindulgence, poor limit-setting, or even an enraged look can mean emotional trauma for the child during the early years.

What is sometimes most tragic about the parent-child relationship is that none but the most highly disturbed parents really want to cause their children distress. Even seemingly cruel parents will weep in a psychiatrist's office when they honestly stop and look at how they are mistreating their children, perhaps in the same way they themselves were mistreated by their parents. Freud was the first to note that neurosis can spread like a contagious disease from one generation to the next. The classic example of this process is child abuse, which, quite shockingly, is reaching epidemic proportions. Every day in the U.S. one or two children under five years old are killed by their parents, and in addition, every hour five infants are injured by their parents or guardians. Parents most likely to beat their children were themselves beaten as children. This infectious quality of distress is in no way restricted to families with highly disturbed individuals. On the contrary, mild middle-class neurosis — the feelings of self-doubt and mistrust, anxiety, repressed anger and the tendency toward depression, psychosomatic complaints, and so on — passes from parents to children with probably as much consistency as the more severe disturbances.

The reason distress passes so easily from parent to child is very simple. Reflection and deliberation alone are rarely sufficient for parents to act wisely, for the parent-child relationship is so intimate that feelings will frequently dominate the best of parental intentions. Despite their desires to act patiently and intelligently, parents almost inevitably respond to their children with the spontaneity and force of their deepest feelings. They can only stop passing on their own emotional troubles to their children by first gaining an inner ease and happiness for themselves, which spontaneously nourishes all their family interactions.

By gaining inner ease and happiness for herself, a mother who practices the TM program can affect her child's development even before he is born. The effect of the TM program on a child's development may begin right in the uterus. Because mother and child share the same circulation, what happens to the psychophysiology of the pregnant mother affects the fetus developing in her womb. If a mother has a high level of stress hormones circulating in her blood, this chronic stress is bound to make an imprint upon the nervous system of the fetus. On the other hand, if the mother is relaxed and happy, her well-being may optimize physiological conditions for fetal maturation. Because the TM technique fosters a physiological state in the mother ideal for the fetus's growth, it is recommended that a pregnant mother practice the TM technique as much as is comfortable during her pregnancy. For example, under the direction of her TM instructor, a woman may meditate for fifteen minutes every two hours during the last trimester of her pregnancy. The additional rest helps the mother cope with the high metabolic demands of pregnancy. After the child is born, the mother goes back to the standard routine of TM sessions twice daily. Anecdotal reports from meditating mothers suggest that the TM program makes for easier deliveries and healthier babies. A formal research project is very much in order.

Especially during the first few weeks of life, the mother is her baby's entire world. Though the infant cannot process verbal information, he is highly sensitive to his mother's emotional tone. If the mother is tense, then the child will perhaps pick up that tension as the underlying tone of his world. If the mother is paranoid or suspicious, the infant may internalize this fearful quality and retain a basic attitude of mistrust. If the mother is depressed, then the child cannot help but feel the world is an unhappy place. The child's early non-verbal interaction with his mother lays the foundation for all future interactions with the world. Psychoanalyst Erik Erikson described the first year of life as that time when the child internalizes a basic attitude of trust or mistrust, safety or danger in relation to the world.

Inadequate mothering during the first years of life is among the most common contributors to the personality problems and emotional distress that bring people to the psychiatrist's office. The psychiatrist tries to provide corrective emotional experiences to heal this deep-seated mistrust, but few tasks are more difficult. It would be easier and far wiser to provide an optimum maternal environment from the outset. By directly increasing her own ease, order, and baseline happiness, the mother practicing the TM program helps ensure that her child will internalize a basic trust of the world and get the best psychological start in life.

How the TM program helped Marianne, a 24 year-old wife of a young executive, with the birth of her second child illustrates what the TM program can add to a mother's relationship to her child. Marianne came to see me because she was experiencing some "tension" and mild insomnia in the second month of her second pregnancy and wanted to know if it was safe for her to get a prescription for tranquilizers. Though she was somewhat unsure of herself, psychiatric evaluation did not reveal any serious emotional disturbance or any obvious psychological causes for her current discomfort. Because she was relatively healthy emotionally, I suggested that, instead of taking tranquilizers, she begin the TM program. Within a few weeks after starting the program, her anxiety began to disappear, her insomnia cleared up, and she was feeling much better. I saw her for a total of three visits, after which we agreed that no more visits seemed necessary, but that I would be available to her as needed. A year later, Marianne was contacted to see whether she still practiced the TM program and what changes might have occurred in her life. She noted:

> I do TM twice daily. It really seems to be opening me up to myself, my husband, and my children. My children are much more of a joy to me since I've been meditating. I remember sometimes feeling that my first baby was a burden and doubting my abilities as a mother, probably because I was tired and tense a lot. My husband is meditating now, too, and helps a lot more with the children. We enjoy our time with them and TM has had a lot to do with that.

The change in Marianne's underlying emotional tone from tense and uncertain to one of ease and confidence cannot help but enrich her children's lives.

Children may learn a children's TM technique as early as age five if at least one but preferably both parents are TM practitioners. Between the ages of five and ten, the child practices this technique for a few minutes a day while playing or getting dressed. It is generally not until a child reaches the age of ten that he is physiologically mature enough to learn the adult technique, in which he sits down for ten minutes twice a day to meditate with eyes closed.

The seven year-old daughter of a friend of mine started the TM program. Three months later, her mother mentioned to me in passing, "She's become so much livelier. She was becoming a bit shy, I'm afraid, but all that has passed now. Her teacher tells me that she's doing much better in school, paying attention more, and getting along better with the other children. I know she's happier, because she's more expressive. She's even taken an interest in drawing. I couldn't get her interested in it at all before she started the children's TM technique, but within days of learning I found her one afternoon sitting in her room with crayons and paper drawing the most wonderful abstract pictures, filling the paper with beautiful color. I was truly amazed." Such glowing reports about the benefits of the children's technique are typical.

Because each life stage becomes the foundation for the next, unhappiness during the early phases can lay the groundwork for a lifetime of distress and turmoil. When a child begins the TM program, he establishes a secure foundation from which to enjoy all subsequent life stages.

Adolescence

Adolescence is the most stormy stage of life, especially in contemporary American society. Adolescent drug abuse and alcoholism are rising at a frightening rate. I have already treated a number of children under age 15 for severe alcoholism. Juvenile delinquency is also increasing at an alarming rate. One-half of all crimes are now committed by juveniles; one child in nine can be expected to appear in juvenile court before the age of 18. Another sure sign of rising adolescent distress is the rising rate of illegitimate births among teenagers. Despite the widespread availability of birth control and abortion services, one out of every ten teenage girls, married and unmarried, is a mother by age 18. Why? One reason may be an attempt to alleviate adolescent turmoil by plunging headlong into adulthood. Teenage motherhood usually does not work and perpetuates a continuing cycle of family disruption, divorce, and the rearing of children under highly stressful circumstances.

Caught in the middle ground between childhood and adulthood, the teenager is neither completely dependent upon nor yet fully independent of his parents. Adolescence is a period of struggle, not necessarily with the parents, though often so, but with the conflicting fears and drives that accompany the adolescent's search for independence and identity. Ushering in the teenager's struggle for independence are bodily changes of enormous magnitude. The onset of menses in the girl and spermatogenesis in the boy unleashes powerful new drives with which the young person must cope. On the one hand, the teenager wants to stand up for himself, make his own rules and his own mistakes. "Don't ask me when I'm coming in tonight; I can take care of myself now," the teenager will say. On the other hand, the teenager wants support, he needs approval, and he wants to avoid taking too much responsibility all at once.

Erik Erikson popularized the concept of "identity crisis" to describe the constellation of psychological issues that the adolescent must master. According to Erikson: "Identity is where we realize that in some ways we are like all other people, in other ways like some other people, and in some ways we are unique, like no other people." Identity crisis refers to the great difficulty that many teenagers have in discovering who they are and what they want to do with their lives. Identity formation requires a synthesis of all past experiences (dependence) and the creation of an individual psyche capable of autonomous growth (independence). Unwilling to turn to his parents and unable as yet to rely on a stable sense of self, the confused or troubled adolescent will turn to his peer group for support. Needing to feel different from his parents, yet relishing the security of peer-group conformity, the adolescent often becomes dependent upon cultural fads in his modes of self-exploration, rebellion, and limit-testing. Drugs, promiscuity, and tastes in music become sterotyped expressions of the adolescent mind seeking directions for the surge of energy and self-discovery beginning at puberty.

Adolescence is a period marked by very high stimulation requiring much integration. The teenager has the task of synthesizing tremendous amounts of input on physiological, psychological, and sociological levels. If he is simply at the mercy of all of these divergent needs and forces, the teenager may find growing up to be very painful. But if he or she can develop a secure inner platform for dealing with and integrating all this change, then the process of identity formation can become a joyous one.

The energy, self-confidence, and general feeling of well-being that follow 15 minutes (not 20 minutes as adults do) of the TM technique twice daily seem particularly appealing to teenagers. They find a respite from turmoil and an opportunity for natural integration to take place. "When I do TM regularly," said one 16 year-old girl, "I'm not worried about what other people think. I just feel good inside." A 14 year-old boy noted, "I'm a lot less nervous since I started the TM program. Even my acne has cleared up." A 17 year-old young man stated, "I relate more honestly to my girl friend because I'm in touch with myself a lot more since starting the TM program." These comments just begin to touch upon the far-reaching impact of the TM program in making adolescence easier and healthier.

The TM technique permits the adolescent to satisfy a longing for profound inner experience upon which new experiences can be firmly anchored and wisdom unfold. Erikson noted that the process of identity formation can lead beyond a synthesis of old roles, experiences, and self-images to the most primordial experience of consciousness and a universal identification with life. One very sincere and intelligent young man shared with me what the experience of pure consciousness deep in TM meditation meant to his personal search for identity.

> For the last few months I've been having a very beautiful experience during my TM sessions. Completely naturally, without trying or imagining, my mind has been

settling down to a state in which there are no thoughts, no inner conversations with myself, no images, no fantasies, yet I remain conscious, fully awake. I've never experienced a greater peace in my entire life. This must be infinity. If God lives anywhere, he lives here. The TM teachers call this experience pure consciousness, but I think it should be called pure life. I know in my heart that this pure life is the most basic thing that I am.

By gradually opening a person to the universal element in his identity, the TM program provides a natural basis for identity formation and the growth of wisdom. This experience creates a foundation for recognizing how people can be identical at their core and yet uniquely different in their activities and personalities. As I will be describing in more detail later, the budding of this experience of pure consciousness is the budding of enlightenment.

Psychiatrists are seeing more adolescent patients now than ever before. Twenty years ago, less than one patient in ten might have been under 21; today at least one in five is a teenager. A whole new sub-specialty of adolescent psychiatry has emerged. Many of these young patients find themselves in psychiatrists' offices at the insistence of courts or parents. Drug abuse, delinquency, and promiscuity are among the chief behavioral problems for which teenagers are obliged to get psychiatric help. Some of these young patients suffer from a major psychiatric disorder or characterological disturbance, but many show a benign adjustment reaction of adolescence.

Most frightening is the evidence indicating that adolescent suicide is on the rise. It has become the second leading cause of death among young Americans between the ages of 15 and 24. For ages 14–19 alone, the suicide rate from 1960 – 1970 went up an astounding 200 times. Not only are suicides among young people on the increase, but also estimates of attempted suicide by adolescents run as high as 400,000 per year. Psychologists have postulated that the rise in adolescent suicide may be a dangerous sign of family and social disintegration, a symptom of a "sick" society. The increased availability and abuse of drugs along with a profound mistrust and lack of faith in what America has to offer certainly contribute to adolescent suicide.

The TM program has much to add to the life of any teenager, but the following case illustrates how the TM program can make a critical difference in the growth of a troubled and suicidal young man.

Tom was a 17 year-old high school student when he was admitted to our general hospital's psychiatric unit with the chief complaint, "I tried to murder myself off." For a week prior to his hospital admission, he had become increasingly depressed; he took an overdose of pills on the night of his admission. His history revealed two previous suicidal gestures. An abrupt rejection by a girl friend of three months apparently precipitated his most recent suicidal despair. Apparently the end of this relationship triggered a crisis in Tom's masculine self-image and his feelings of self-depreciation. Adding to his despondency were his inability to find a job and a very unhappy home life. Though he did not suffer from a serious sleep disorder, he had lost quite a bit of weight in the three-week period prior to his hospital admission.

Tom described his childhood as very unhappy. Both his mother and father drank heavily. He remembers them "constantly fighting," until they finally got a divorce when Tom was 13. He apparently received inadequate support and attention throughout much of his childhood. With the onset of adolescence, his early feelings of rejection surfaced to cause strong feelings of self-doubt. He was highly self-critical and turned his anger with his parents against himself. Underneath a veneer of lightheartedness, he felt chronically depressed and "generally useless." Psychological tests confirmed my clinical impression that he was hypersensitive to criticism, quick to blame others for his difficulties, and had a strong tendency to see rejection in the benign actions of others. On the positive side, Tom was industrious, intelligent, idealistic, and did well in school. He was not psychotic but suffered from a reactive depression and a severe personality dis-order.

Patients such as Tom are highly vulnerable to the vicissitudes of life. Because they lack feelings of inner well-being, they become dependent on others for maintaining their self-esteem. The termination of a relationship can send them reeling in despair. Especially with a family history of alcoholism, they frequently start abusing alcohol as a way of coping. Left feeling chronically empty and alone, they live out lives of quiet depression or finally succeed in killing themselves.

Tom's prognosis was guarded because the psychological damage resulting from poor mothering during his earlier years had been so great. During his two weeks in the hospital, he began individual and group psychotherapy to help him improve his interpersonal skills. I also recommended that he begin the TM program, which he did just prior to discharge. He also started an occupational therapy program to learn some job skills.

In terms of Tom's long-range development, beginning the TM program was a critical element in his treatment. Psychotherapy primarily deals with verbal interchanges, whereas Tom needed profound non-verbal corrective experiences. Although long-term intensive psychotherapy can sometimes provide corrective emotional experiences, it cannot resolve the deeply internalized negative feeling "mother is not at home," the world is uncaring and unsafe. When Tom practices the TM technique for 20 minutes twice a day, he gets in touch with that nurturing force of life, "mother" in the most universal sense, which sustains his life and all creation. This natural wisdom of creative intelligence can transform the deepest feelings of terror and insecurity into a profound sense that all is well, the world is safe, and everything will be all right.

Tom liked the TM program from the start because he found the experience of the technique "simple and very soothing." Upon discharge from the psychiatric unit, he was placed for an additional two months in an adolescent residence facility where he actively participated in the treatment program and regularly practiced the TM technique.

It is now a year since Tom began the TM program, and he has made much progress. He is making good use of outpatient psychotherapy and is on a steady course of improvement. He is no longer troubled by active suicidal ideation, his depression has lifted, and he seems to be losing his great dependence upon others for his self-esteem. Having grown in confidence, he is once again dating and has a lovely girl friend. Though he still occasionally has the thought, "I wish I were dead," after a particularly painful experience, he no longer feels compelled by that thought and sees it as an expression of sadness that does not need to be acted upon. In general, his baseline feeling of happiness has become strong enough that, even in the face of rejection or an interpersonal problem, he feels an underlying safety, a feeling that "mother is at home," and that everything will work out. This growth of inner stability is perhaps the most important sign that Tom is making steady and lasting progress.

What may be somewhat tragic about cases such as Tom's is that if he had begun the TM program at age 12 or 13, he very likely would have avoided such severe suicidal depressions. Though he would still have had developmental difficulties, his problems would probably not have grown severe enough to precipitate suicide attempts, hospitalization, and the need for psychiatric attention. I base this hypothesis on the remarkeable way in which Tom began to take hold of his life after he started the TM program.

All forms of medical treatment are more effective when used early in the development of a disorder, but the TM program is particularly helpful when begun early in life for two reasons. First, by healing old emotional wounds before they cause severe psychiatric symptoms, the TM program safeguards mental health. Second, by expanding a person's access to his inner resources of stability, adaptability, and integration, the TM program enhances an individual's opportunities for joy and success in life.

If larger numbers of young people started the TM program during their school years and meditated regularly, it would not be unreasonable to expect a dramatic reduction in the mental health problems of the society as a whole. Certainly adolescent drug abuse, suicide, psychosomatic disease, illegitimate births, and crime would diminish because the young people would grow up free from the tension and stress at the root of these mental health problems. At the same time, they would grow in wisdom, the basis for a life of maximum achievement and happiness.

Marriage and Family Life

It's no secret that marriage and family life in our society are suffering. The U.S. divorce rate, already the highest in the world, continues to rise. It has been estimated that 40 per cent of all marriages end in divorce; in 1975 the number of divorces exceeded one million, double the figure of ten years ago. Especially troublesome is the rising divorce rate among families with children. The parents of over one million children were divorced in 1974; single parents are now raising nearly 20 per cent of the nation's children. While custody battles are on the increase, frequently neither parent really wants the children.

Many reasons have been hypothesized to explain the rising divorce rate and the general breakdown of family life over the past two decades, but stress is almost certainly an important contributing factor. Because family life is so intimate, the growth of stress in one family member cannot but influence everyone else in the family. The dis-ease of stress is highly communicable, especially in a family, where emotions rule more powerfully than in any other relationship.

The TM program is proving very helpful in marriage and family therapy for three reasons. First, it gives a person a chance to release accumulated stress in the privacy of his own mind rather than passing the stress on to other family members. Second, it strengthens the baseline happiness of each family member, thereby enhancing each person's ability to enjoy the sharing of family life. Finally, it allows natural feelings of love to blossom by dissolving negative feelings which keep family members cut off from one another.

How the TM program helped save Mr. and Mrs. D's marriage illustrates what the TM program can add to marriage and family life. Mr. and Mrs. D sought my help when their marriage problems had grown so intense that they had begun actively contemplating divorce. They had been married for 15 years and had two children, ages seven and four. In taking their history, I could see clearly how their relationship had deteriorated. Certain landmark emotional events marked stages in the breakdown of their marriage, but the series of events taken together traced a steady decline over the last five years. Despite the emotional distance that had developed between Mr. and Mrs. D, and their deep despair over the state of their married life, the fact that they were seeking help together suggested that a strong bond of love still existed between them, and they appeared motivated for therapy.

Their marriage problems began when Mr. D, who was an automobile salesman, received a series of rapid promotions at work. Rising from the position of salesman to sales manager, Mr. D found increasing stress and strain in his work with each new responsibility and developed a success neurosis. Gradually, his distress became so intense and chronic that he came home every night exhausted and would need a couple of martinis to relieve his tension. Increasingly unable to leave the emotional frustrations of work behind him, he became more and more edgy in his home life and frequently found reasons to yell at his wife. At the same time, Mr. D started feeling that his wife had stopped showing him the compassion and emotional support which he needed. He felt under-appreciated for the efforts he was making to provide the family with a higher economic standard of living.

Contrary to Mr. D's fantasy, Mrs. D was not spending a nice quiet day at home playing with the children and enjoying her free time. After making breakfast for everyone, she had to take the oldest child to school, and then return home to dishes, laundry and the four year-old child. Shopping, gardening, church work, house cleaning, ironing, cooking, and taking care of her children and husband kept her very busy, and she wanted some attention and appreciation for her efforts. When Mr. D came home from the office Mrs. D wanted not only to hear his problems but also to share her experiences.

Instead of showing one another mutual appreciation, what Mr. and Mrs. D began sharing with each other every night was their stress and frustration. Conditions worsened so much that they often would not talk to one another at the dinner table. When they sought psychiatric help, they really thought their marriage might be finished.

I spent the first two psychotherapy sessions helping them see why their relationship had taken a downhill course, and restoring confidence that their marriage could possibly be saved. When Mr. and Mrs. D began to see what they had been doing to one another, they became very remorseful. Once they recognized the role of stress in the deterioration of their marriage they were ready to hear about the TM program.

I explained that the TM program was a well-researched, reliable, and safe means of reducing accumulated stress which could help each of them enjoy life more whether or not they decided to stay together. Mr. D was somewhat skeptical, but they both agreed to enroll in the TM program that week. I followed them in therapy weekly for the first three months, bi-weekly for another two months, and monthly for a few more months until it became clear to us that the TM program alone was sufficient to sustain continued improvement in their lives.

The TM program reversed the downhill trend of the D's marriage by providing each of them with a very efficient, twice daily psychological housecleaning which enabled them to stop unloading all their accumulated stress on one another. Mr. D still came home tired, though less so because of the energy boost from his morning TM session, but instead of having a few martinis and starting to get irritated with Mrs. D, he would sit down to do his TM practice for 20 minutes. In his brief period, the frustrations of the day would dissolve, his exhaustion would dissipate, and afterwards he would find himself feeling cheerful and refreshed. Similarly, Mrs. D also began finding that she had more energy, patience, and understanding in the evenings because she too would dissolve the daily stresses and strains in her afternoon TM sessions. Within just a few weeks, Mr. and Mrs. D discovered they were no longer becoming irritated with one another in the evenings and began to enjoy once again those qualities in one another which had once made their marriage very rewarding.

Three months later, Mr. and Mrs. D both commented that the whole atmosphere in their home life had changed. The tension that "used to be so thick you could cut it with a knife" had given way to a general feeling of happiness and ease. They had become much more attentive to one another and discovered a renewed interest in each other. "It's really wonderful," said Mrs. D, "to feel close to one another again." Though they had thought their two children were relatively oblivious to their marital strife, both Mr. and Mrs. D noted that the children seemed happier now. The seven year-old was "more caring and respectful, no longer such a discipline problem." Mr. and Mrs. D also noted that they were enjoying their children a lot more since starting the TM program. They had not noticed how much their mental strife had been interfering with the family's capacity to love and enjoy each other.

Six months after Mr. and Mrs. D had begun the TM program, it was clear that their marriage had taken a strong uphill turn. This improvement occurred fairly quickly, considering the magnitude of their problems, but did not happen without some rough spots. During Mr. and Mrs. D's second month in the TM program, the encrusted feelings of frustration and bitterness surfaced. My support and leverage as their therapist was important in seeing them through this rocky period.

It should not be concluded from this one case history that all couples who start the TM program to solve their marital difficulties will find themselves staying together. Sometimes a couple will establish an unconscious emotional contract that says, "Look how much I suffer for you. You should be willing to suffer a lot for me, too." Through the TM program, they may begin to see this established negative emotional contract and decide they would be better off living apart. In these cases, the TM program seems to give each partner sufficient inner strength to get out of a destructive or limiting relationship. The emotional cost of continuing a relationship can sometimes be far greater than the emotional turmoil of ending one, yet the end of a marriage is a difficult and stressful emotional experience. Research psychiatrist Dr. Thomas Holmes ranks divorce as the second most stressful experience a person can have. The TM program has proved to be very helpful to both marriage partners in sustaining their inner sense of well-being and self-worth and maintaining an open optimistic attitude toward the future.

The TM program is also proving to be a useful adjunct to family therapy. Many therapists, when appropriate, have begun to abandon the one-on-one, isolated relationship of traditional psychiatry and work with a patient's whole family. Their aim is to identify and change family patterns that create individual emotional disorders. Freud was the first to describe the dynamics of how the emotional stress in a family can precipitate psychiatric symptoms in its weakest member. Severe psychiatric problems arise out of the interplay between a highly stressful environment and an individual who is constitutionally or genetically predisposed to developing a particular stress disorder. Family therapists are finding that the disturbed emotional system of a family can help produce physical ailments, including asthma and heart attacks, neurosis and psychosis (some are convinced even cancer). This process is well illustrated by the development of manic-depressive illness in people who have a genetic predisposition but only show psychotic decompensation when family tension peaks.

Little can be done to alter a person's genetic or constitutional predisposition toward disease, but clinical observation clearly indicates that the TM program can sharply reduce the general distress level in a family. Whereas distress brings out the potential of an individual and his family for dis-ease and dis-order, the TM program helps to protect this and to bring fulfillment to family life. Learning the TM technique provides a very concrete first step to help all members of a family recognize and fulfill their responsibility for the happiness and well-being of the whole family.

Aging

Socrates:	I enjoy talking with the very aged. For...we have to learn of them as it were from wayfarers who have preceded us on a road on which we too...must sometime fare — what it is like? Is it rough and hard-going or easy and pleasant to travel?
Cephalus:	Some...elders...repine in the belief that the greatest things have been taken from them and that then they lived well and now it is no life at all. And some of them complain of the indignities that friends and kinsmen put upon old age and thereto recite a doleful litany of all the miseries for which they blame old age. But in my opinion, Socrates, they do not put the blame on the real cause. For if it were the cause I too should have had the same experience so far as old age is concerned, and so would all others who have come to this time of life....These complaints [have] just one cause, Socrates — not old age, but the character of the man.[3]

Old age in itself is not a disease. Research on the role of stress in aging has demonstrated, however, that stress may be the single most important factor in the aging process. A sufficient dose of stress hormone injected into young mice can transform them into debilitated, senile old mice in a matter of weeks. Stress contributes to the loss of mental and physical flexibility and increased susceptibility to disease, especially those diseases of aging such as arthritis, cardiovascular disease, and senility. Because the TM program so effectively reduces stress, it has been suggested that it might retard the physiological deterioration which usually accompanies aging. Use of the TM program with the aged indicates that it can help relieve the emotional distress that troubles many older people.

With the rise of modern technological society, attitudes toward aging have drastically changed. Whereas the aged were once regarded with respect for their vast accumulation of knowledge and experience, technological development has placed a greater premium on youth's ability to generate and quickly adapt to new ideas. Traditional ways of doing things, and even the aged themselves, have become "obsolete" in today's technocratic world. Almost every aspect of society changes so rapidly that the aged tend to be faulted or just disregarded because of their inability to keep up with the pace. In many businesses and professions, retirement is encouraged at earlier and earlier ages in order to sustain maximum dynamism in the organization. Aging is equated with loss of function, narrow and rigid thinking, emotional inflexibility, slowness, and illness. In our youth-worshipping culture, aging is more and more seen as an incurable disease which is an inevitable and tragic part of living. Ironically, the more aging has become distasteful, the longer science has enabled people to live and the more aged people there are. Instead of being able to enjoy their "golden years," however, the aged all too frequently become warehoused with the mentally ill and the rest of society's rejects.

Erik Erikson identified the last stage of life as a time of reflection, when feelings of integrity or despair may become a predominant emotional theme. While many people do find old age to be a golden time of life when they can look back on their work, their families, and their friends with profound feelings of fulfillment, many more older people find their last years shrouded by despair. Almost made to feel that they are a burden to their families, many aged people develop serious problems with depression. Early misdiagnosed as the onset of senility, severe depression can lead the older person to stop taking care of himself, to become withdrawn and uncommunicative, or to develop child-like mentality. Mild depressions contribute to feelings of uselessness, lack of energy, irritability, as well as memory, sleep, and appetite disturbances.

The possibility of depression or social isolation must be considered when ever the label *senile* is contemplated. Contrary to the popular stereotype, psychogeriatric patients are mainly afflicted (70 per cent) with depressive and schizophrenic illnesses that are suscepti-ble to modern treatment. Instead of indiscriminate institutionalization of the "senile," precise diagnosis and skilled use of psychotherapeutic drugs can lead to rehabilitation for the 70 per cent who have treatable disorders.

The TM program can be useful for the individual geriatric patient, as well as for older people in general, because it helps relieve depression and restore energy. More than a treatment for depression, however, the TM program helps older people begin to experience the eternal value of life, pure creative intelligence, deep within themselves. Though subtle and simple, this experience characteristically widens older people's constricted horizons and helps them discover deep meaning and wisdom in their lives. What the TM program can add to an older person's life is well illustrated by Arlene.

A 74 year-old widow, Arlene had been slipping into a deep depression ever since her husband died one year ago. She had stopped eating and taking care of herself properly, and she was unresponsive to encouragement from her social worker, who thought she might be a serious suicide risk and asked me to evaluate Arlene for possible psychiatric hospitalization. During her initial evaluation visit with me, Arlene described a lifetime of frustration and complained of numerous bodily aches and pains for which she was receiving symptomatic treatment from her internist. Though her marriage had been an unhappy one because of her husband's weekend drinking, she felt, "At least when he was alive I had someone." She felt abandoned by her family and had become hopeless. When I asked her to mention just one interest she might still have, she acknowledged a long-standing curiosity about Eastern philosophy and a desire to do more gardening, but she complained about not having enough energy to pursue either.

When I told Arlene about the TM program, she expressed a willingness to try it. In addition, I started her on anti-depressant medication. The first activities for which Arlene had gotten out of the house in several weeks were the introductory lectures about the TM program. She began the TM course immediately and by the time of her second psychiatric visit, she was already improved. When she came for her third visit, which was only two weeks after I first saw her, she showed a marked decrease in ruminations about the past and had a much more hopeful attitude. In addition, her chronic neck and back pain had begun to become less troublesome. Her fourth visit showed her depression to be clearly lifting, and I began to taper down her medications, which were producing bothersome side effects such as dry mouth and dizziness. Within six weeks after beginning the TM program, Arlene was completely off medication and no longer depressed. She was eating properly once again, keeping herself and her home clean, and had begun to look into gardening clubs that she might join. Weekly visits to my office were no longer necessary, and I asked her to come in on a monthly basis for about six months just to be sure that she remained free from depression. She continued to improve over that period and became involved in both gardening and social activities. She also enjoyed attending advanced lectures on the Science of Creative Intelligence at the TM center in San Diego. No longer did she spend our sessions talking about her loneliness or unhappy past; she could not wait to tell me about what she was doing, the insights she was getting from advanced lectures, and the plans she had for the future.

Loneliness is often a very troublesome problem for older people, though it afflicts most people at some time in their life. Loneliness is a close relative of depression, where the person becomes so caught up in his problems and unhappiness that he becomes isolated from emotional contact with other people. Simply placing the lonely person in a crowd of friendly people is no sure cure for loneliness. Lonely people often keep themselves trapped in their loneliness because they are too afraid to make friends and secretly hope that somehow, someone will insist on becoming their friend and love them. Looking for warmth and friendliness from someone else rarely helps solve the problem of loneliness. Once a person discovers warmth within himself, he will find that warmth overflowing toward others, and he will make friends more easily. The TM program appears helpful to this process by increasing baseline happiness. In addition, loneliness need not accompany being alone. If a person feels a strong unity with life and a natural intimacy with nature, he can be completely alone but not feel lonely. By opening individual awareness to the universal value of life at the depth of the mind, the TM program helps people discover their natural intimacy with all of life, which protects them from loneliness whether they are in their apartment or visiting a foreign country.

Widespread practice of the TM program seems to promise a fundamental change in social attitudes toward aging. Because TM practitioners experience a steady growth of wisdom in their lives, they tend to look forward to, rather than regret, the process of getting older. Experience of growth through the TM program provides direct evidence that living is an evolutionary process in which growth continues throughout life in steps of rest and activity. Because people who practice the TM program tend to experience increasing happiness year after year, they naturally begin to look forward to the future just as much as a child looks forward to Christmas. While many people find the daily benefits of the TM program are enough to sustain their optimism about the future, other people find the prospect of achieving the state of enlightenment through the TM program a profoundly meaningful and practical goal. How powerful the TM program can be in changing attitudes toward aging became very apparent when Arlene commented:

> TM is a delight. This may sound strange for an oldster like myself, but it's opening up new vistas in my life. I'm starting to have the energy for gardening and I'm going out and meeting people. I'm no longer watching the clock tick away my years or just thinking about my aches and pains, running from one doctor to the next. I'm ready to enjoy as much time as nature is willing to give me.

I'm Happy, Do I Need the TM Program?

Occasionally when I lecture on the benefits of the TM program, someone in the audience will say, "Doctor, the TM program sounds good, but I don't think that I really need it." Often implicit in this statement is the belief that the TM program is primarily a therapy for sick people. Perhaps the greatest danger inherent in a psychiatrist writing a book on his experience with the TM program is that this belief may be reinforced. I cannot help but be concerned about this possible misunderstanding because it might lead some people to miss out on a great opportunity for expanding happiness in life. Maharishi has passed on the TM program from an ancient tradition of enlightened teachers not just as a means of reducing anxiety and relieving insomnia, but as the technology of fulfillment, the surest and fastest path to enlightenment. Far from a therapy for the sick, the TM program is a systematic means for almost everyone to develop his or her full mental, physical, and spiritual potential.

Two kinds of people generally make an issue of the fact that they do not "need" the TM program. One type of person may be showing denial, a fairly common psychological defense against feeling emotional distress. The person denies the existence of his personal problems and insists that everything is just peachy. In answer to the question, "Why are you unhappy today?" this person will answer abruptly, "What are you talking about? Unhappy, I'm not unhappy. Everything's fine. Leave me alone!" This kind of person generally winds up, not in the psychiatrist's office requesting help with his emotional difficulties, but in the cardiologist's office suffering from hypertension and coronary disease. What generally motivates a person to deny any underlying emotional tension is fear of being overwhelmed by negative emotions. Because the TM program is perhaps the most gentle means available for relieving stress and anxiety, it is among the most helpful things that the person caught up in denial can do to start feeling "Everything really is fine."

The second type of individual who might say, "I don't need the TM program; I'm already happy," is the person who genuinely feels content and may be what Maslow called the "self-actualized individual." It would be absurd to think that there are not some people in the world who have accumulated very little stress, who were born with healthy and resilient nervous sustems, and who are already well integrated, dynamic, and happy. Maslow estimated that less than one tenth of one per cent of the population are such self-actualizing individuals. What is interesting to note, however, is that even the self-actualizing individual can accelerate his growth through the TM program. Because the self-actualizing person is already relaxed and relatively free from stress, he may not especially notice the relaxation which the TM technique provides. Instead, what such a person begins to appreciate is a greater than usual flow of creative ideas, even more energy for dynamic activity, enhanced ability for fulfilling desires, and more of what Maslow called "peak and plateau experiences." What the self-actualizing person will appreciate most from the TM program is the joy of enlightenment dawning in his own consciousness.

Many top athletes have started the TM program because it increases energy, mental clarity, and ability for peak performance. Joe Namath claims that the TM program "has done a great deal for me....I am helping my mind and body live life in the right way. I've enjoyed it and I'm going to keep on enjoying it." Philadelphia Phillies shortstop Larry Bowa began practicing the TM program after the 1974 baseball season, when his batting average was .211. In 1975 he batted .305 and was the National League all-star shortstop. He feels that the TM program contributed to this improvement because "it takes away tensions and anxieties. I don't let little things bother me anymore. Last year every game I played carried over. I let things build up and before I knew it I was 0 for 28; I was buried. Now, If I go 0 for 4, I start all over again the next day just like a new season for me. The same thing with my home life. I used to take things out on my wife, but TM helps me leave my baseball problems at the ball park." Another TM enthusiast, Craig Lincoln, Olympic medal winner and diving coach at the University of Minnesota, said, "The best dives I have ever done have been natural and spontaneous — and that's just how I have found the practice of TM to be. My diving has definitely benefitted from the practice of TM; my whole experience of the Olympic Games and what was going on there was more real to me because I had been meditating."

The TM program has also won many endorsements from senators, congressmen, astronauts, leading corporation presidents, Pentagon generals, Wall Street brokers, Broadway playwrights, Nobel Prize-winning scientists, artists, professors, and everyday people from all walks of life. Major General Franklin M. Davis, Jr., former assistant chief of staff and commandant of the War College, found that "my blood pressure went down ten points, my wife said my disposition improved, and minor stresses and strains of life around Washington didn't bother me anymore." The TM program is taught at West Point and the Air Force Academy and has been introduced at several military posts. Entertainers such as Merv Griffin, Clint Eastwood, and Mary Tyler Moore described on national television the benefits that they have received from the TM program. Among the many large firms where executives practice the TM program are General Motors, Blue Cross/Blue Shield, Exxon, Connecticut General Corporation, Warner Communications, Ampex, Monsanto and many more. The Honorable Arlen Gregorio, member of the State Senate of California, reports, "It's changed my life. I'm more stable emotionally. I don't get depressed after high-pitched tension. I think I'm able to be more effective."

One further indication that the TM program is not primarily a therapy for the sick deserves mention. School systems all over the country are beginning to include courses in the Science of Creative Intelligence and the TM program. The New Jersey Department of Education is in the process of validating this course as a means of helping students to become better able to learn — more intelligent, more creative, more interested in learning, and more able to define personal goals. Jerry Jarvis, the President of the World Plan Executive Council, taught the first college course in the Science of Creative Intelligence at Stanford in 1970. The course attracted the largest enrollment of any course ever offered there. Since then, Yale, Harvard, Columbia, the University of California, and dozens of other colleges and universities have offered courses in SCI.

Sometimes the question is raised whether there are special sociological factors that cause people to take up the TM technique and experience the benefits. Stek and Bass reported in *Psychological Reports*[4] that no significant differences in personality and mental health scales were found among four groups of Indiana University students: (1) those who took up the TM technique on their own, (2) those who went to introductory lectures on TM but did not start the practice, (3) those who knew that TM was offered but did not go to lectures, and (4) those who had never heard of TM before. The researchers concluded that college students who are interested in or who pursue the program are neither more nor less neurotic nor self-actualized than their non-interested counterparts. In a Standord Research Institute study, Dr. Demetri Kanellakos reported that the TM course could be taught very effectively to people non-predisposed to the TM program. The physiological and behavioral changes that take place within from three to six months of TM practice cannot be explained on sociological grounds. Among the many hundreds of thousands of TM practitioners in the U.S. are representatives from all socio-economic groups, professions, races, nationalities, and religions.

Research indicates that people with low anxiety as well as those with high anxiety show significantly reduced anxiety after four to 12 weeks of the TM program. Evidently, all people, regardless of their anxiety level, can become less anxious and therefore more productive and fulfilled. Through the TM program almost anyone can achieve a level of contentment and smooth functioning previously thought possible for only a few highly gifted individuals.

Those people who show the greatest improvement in their energy, intelligence, creativity, and performance after starting the TM program are often those who are the most healthy to begin with. This finding suggests two things. First, few of even the most emotionally and physically healthy people in the world are actually making use of their full potential and enjoying life as much as it could be enjoyed. Second, those people who are already using more of their potential than the average will find that the TM program works most quickly in unfolding their untapped potential. If one takes the perspective that the vast majority of people in American today are suffering from varying degrees of what I have called mild middle-class neurosis, then almost everyone can benefit from the psychotherapeutic value of the TM program, which provides psychological house cleaning of the highest order.

In evaluating whether to begin the TM program, an individual faces the difficult task of estimating how much happier he might become and how well the TM program might work in expanding his happiness. Unfortunately, no one can really know how much more happiness he might find in his life until he actually experiences that expanded state of happiness. People practicing the TM program over a period of years regularly report amazement when they look back each year and notice how much their happiness has grown. This development unfolds automatically and accompanies a parallel growth of love and wisdom.

The TM program appears capable of increasing almost anyone's happiness no matter where he may be in the life cycle. As one grows toward enlightenment, the life cycle gains a special quality of enrichment and fulfillment. For many people, enlightenment may yet seem a fanciful idea, but the world's scientific community is gradually giving it increasing attention.

9

Dawn of the Age of Enlightenment

During America's celebration of its one hundredth birthday, a New England newspaper ran the following:

> A man was arrested yesterday, charged with attempting to obtain money under false pretenses. He claimed he was promoting a device whereby one person could talk to another several miles away, by means of a small apparatus and some wire. Without doubt this man is a fraud and an unscrupulous trickster and must be taught that the American public is too smart to be the victim of this and other similar schemes. Even if this insane idea worked, it would have no practical value other than for circus sideshows.

A short time later, Alexander Graham Bell took out a patent on the telephone.

Many scientific discoveries that have transformed human life seemed no less than preposterous when first proposed. The airplane, the electric bulb, the internal combustion engine — all now taken for granted — were considered the dreams of lunatics during their early development. Even when a few people started using the light bulb, the telephone, or the automobile, the great majority doubted whether these new "contraptions" had any practical future. New discoveries often invite skepticism because most people develop world views into which new ideas simply don't fit. The rapid pace of progress over the last several decades has changed this situation to some degree, but some discoveries that promise world transformation still inspire disbelief.

After sitting down nightly to watch the six o'clock news, most people have difficulty with the statement, "The dawn of the Age of Enlightenment is at hand." An Age of Enlightenment suggests a world where happiness, harmony, and unrestricted progress prevail. Who could believe that such a world might be on the horizon? In the face of rising crime rates, worldwide terrorism, inflation, and the ever-present fear of global war and nuclear holocaust, most people find predictions of continued social distress the most rational way to view humanity's future. The sociologist or psychologist who foresees disruption and the growth of social tension rarely meets a skeptical reaction. Let someone foresee the rise of happiness and harmony, however, and he is seen as a naive utopian or just plain crazy.

On January 12, 1975, aboard the flagship Gotthard on Lake Lucerne in Switzerland, Maharishi Mahesh Yogi inaugurated the dawn of the Age of Enlightenment for the entire world at an all-day ceremony attended by eminent scientists, Nobel Laureates, world leaders of the TM movement, and over one thousand teachers of the TM program. Two months later, he traveled around the world to speak at similar inaugural ceremonies for each of the five major continents — Europe, Asia, North America, South America, and Africa. Maharishi's theme at each inaugural ceremony was the same: *Through the window of science we see the dawn of the Age of Enlightenment.* Pointing out that an inauguration of the dawn must always occur amidst darkness, he insisted that scientific research on the TM program provides a window for seeing through the darkness of present worldwide problems to the dawning of a better world.

Many men before Maharishi have predicted the coming of a new age of peace and harmony, yet the new age has yet to arrive. It follows that, to some people, Maharishi's vision may sound preposterous, while to others it may seem hopeful but overly optimistic. A

careful look at the process of gaining enlightenment
through the TM program and the collective effects of
single individuals initiating this process is necessary to
appreciate fully the social significance of the TM
program and Maharishi's vision of a new age.

Unfolding Human Potential

The process of becoming enlightened is one of
systematically and naturally unfolding the full potential
of the human biomachinery. Far from a state of self-
delusion or self-denial, enlightenment represents the
ultimate development of what are ordinarily considered
the most valuable qualities of human life — intelligence,
creativity, compassion, freedom, and the capacity for
spontaneous, life-supporting responses under any
circumstances. Enlightenment results from the continuous and progressive neurophysiological refinement
or purification of the nervous system until a state of
perfect psychophysiological integration is achieved. This
physiological state of maximum ease and order supports
the state of enlightenment.

Maharishi has said that the average person is "like a
millionaire who has forgotten his wealth and position
and goes begging in the street."[1] This analogy implies
that everyone has the natural capacity to gain access to
his or her full creative intelligence in the state of
enlightenment, but as long as a person fails to do so,
suffering is inevitable.

This theme is not new and has become central to much
current psychological thinking. Fritz Perls, the founder
of Gestalt Therapy, frequently pointed out that most
people use no more than five or ten per cent of their full
potential. At the turn of the century, the father of
American psychology, William James, wrote:

> I have no doubt whatever that most people live whether
> physically, intellectually or morally, in a very restricted
> circle of their potential being. They make use of a very

small portion of their possible consciousness and of their soul's resources in general. Much like the man who, out of his whole organism, should get into the habit of using and moving only his little finger....[2]

This image graphically illustrates the link between the long history of human unhappiness and the failure of most people to actualize their full potential. People use so little of their natural capacity that they are for all practical purposes unprepared for the challenges of living. How could a person who had only learned to move his little finger not run into problems at every step of his efforts to fulfill his desires? Similarly, if such a person began using his whole hand, arm, or body, what had appeared as insurmountable problems and causes of intense suffering would disappear.

Almost always, my patients either blame their unhappiness on others or criticize themselves as wholly inadequate and destined to be miserable. What they don't realize is that problems have their roots in the weakness of the individual. An essential therapeutic insight for all my patients is recognizing that what may be a problem for a weak person can turn out to be an opportunity for a strong person. The implication of this insight is obvious. To start solving problems and enjoying the expansion of happiness, a person must increase his inner strength, he must get in touch with his full measure of creative intelligence.

I am amazed at how willingly most people accept using but a small fraction of their innate creative intelligence. If these people learned from an expert that their cars were running at only five per cent efficiency, they would be outraged. Yet, when they hear from medical experts that they use only five per cent of their mental, physical, and emotional potential, they respond with little more than a shrug of the shoulders and a nod of acceptance. It seems ironic that people want the very best of all the outer material aspects of living but they are willing to settle for so little when it comes to development of the inner dimension, their own creative intelligence. What makes this situation especially ironic is that outer achievement depends upon inner development.

When Maharishi discusses the unfoldment of full human potential in the state of enlightenment, he speaks of living 200 per cent value of life. Neither inner spiritual development nor outer material achievement alone is sufficient to define a fully developed human being. In the process of becoming enlightened, inner and outer development complement one another to unfold 100 per cent of a person's inner creative intelligence and 100 per cent of his potential for achievement and fulfillment. When people ask me whether happiness is solely an internal state or primarily a result of satisfying desires in the world, I answer by explaining that a person cannot know his full measure of happiness until he or she lives 200 per cent of life in the state of enlightenment.

In my discussions of enlightenment, I find that people frequently have misconceptions about it. Perhaps the most common is that gaining enlightenment requires withdrawal from the world to sit meditating in a cave for many years. This kind of misunderstanding has led naturally to the belief that enlightenment may be a state of "eternal bliss," but it is most impractical for a dynamic person and tantamount to renunciation of the material world. In fact, enlightenment requires neither spending years in a cave nor denial of the world. Maharishi has made enlightenment a practical and accessible goal for the active Westerner, while scientific research on the TM program illuminates the mechanics by which an individual systematically attains this state.

If enlightenment is a natural capability of the human biomachinery, what prevents most people from living that state right now? What obstructs a person's immediate access to his full creative intelligence? Scientific research on the TM program suggests that what restricts a person from living life fully is lack of complete ease and order in the functioning of his nervous system. Deep-rooted stresses appear to play the major role in keeping the human biomachinery in a state of dis-ease and dis-order. Because the TM technique permits almost anyone to gain a state of maximum ease and order, its regular practice leads steadily and systematically to enlightenment. When the backlog of deep-rooted stresses has been completely dissolved, the nervous system regains its natural state of perfect functioning and enlightenment dawns automatically. This understanding of the mechanics of unfolding full human potential has dispelled the belief that gaining enlightenment requires giving up material possessions and then withdrawing to a monastery or cave.

Maharishi uses an excellent anaolgy to illustrate how this process of purification transforms the experience of self as enlightenment dawns. He compares the nervous system to a muddy pond reflecting the sun. When the mud is stirred up in the pond, the reflection of the sun may be very poor. On the other hand, when the mud settles and the water becomes pure, the reflection can become so perfect that it shines with nearly all the brilliance of the sun itself. Similarly, the nervous system may be thought of as a reflector of creative intelligence, and deep-rooted stresses may be compared to mud obstructing the nervous system's reflecting capacity. As long as the nervous system remains cluttered with stresses, the individual poorly reflects the highest values of creative intelligence. He experiences himself primarily in terms of the boundaries of daily living — his body, job, interests, family, friends, thoughts, feelings, and so on. Maharishi notes that the word self, written with a lower case s, usually refers to this quality of self-consciousness. On the other hand, when the nervous system becomes a perfect reflector of pure creative intelligence, in the state of enlightenment, a person experiences the universal and unchanging values of the self in all his activities. Maharishi adds that in describing this state of self-consciousness, the S of Self deserves to be written in the upper case. The process of becoming enlightened, then, may be described in terms of raising a person's level of self-consciousness to an individual state which reflects universal values. The basis of this growth is purification, dissolving the backlog of deep-rooted stresses.

Albert Einstein described the need for expanding individual awareness when he wrote:

> A human being is part of the whole, called by us "universe," a part limited in time and space. He experiences his thoughts and feelings as something separate from the rest — a kind of optical delusion of his consciousness. This delusion is a kind of prison for us, restricting us to our personal decisions and to affection for a few persons nearest to us. Our task must be to free ourselves from this prison by widening our circle of compassion to embrace all living creatures and the whole nature in its beauty.[3]

William Blake succinctly describes the whole matter in his verse: "If the doors of perception were cleansed, everything would appear to man as it is — infinite." His poetic vision further portrays how, once enlightened, the individual is able "to see a world in a grain of sand, and heaven in a wild flower, hold infinity in the palm of [his] hand, and eternity in an hour."

Another common misconception of the process of gaining enlightenment is that achieving a universal Self-consciousness will result in a loss of individuality. People are not the same when their backlogs of deep-rooted stresses dissolve. On the contrary, stresses tend to foster stereotyped behavior and to inhibit creativity and self-expression. When stresses dissolve, only then can a person truly discover his unique talents and capacity to contribute to the world. In putting a person in touch with his maximum energy, intelligence, and creativity, enlightenment does not obscure but rather enhances individual differences. At the same time, enlightenment assures harmony among differences and unity amidst diversity by structuring a universal awareness in each person's consciousness.

History records the dream of an ideal society — creative, peaceful, productive, and just — in every generation. On what basis could such a society ever become a living reality? A remarkable agreement on this issue exists among philosophers and scientists throughout the ages. If an ideal society is possible, it can arise only from the minds, hearts, and behavior of fully developed, happy individuals. Bertrand Russell, the great twentieth-century philosopher, expressed this consensus well when he wrote:

> When I allow myself to hope that the world will emerge from its present troubles...I see before me a shining vision: a world where work is pleasant and not excessive, where kindly feelings are common, and where minds released from fear create delight for eye, ear and heart. Do not say this is impossible. It is not impossible...if men would bend their minds to the achievement of the kind of happiness that should be distinctive of man.[4]

Russell went on to add that "true happiness for human beings is possible only to those who develop their godlike potentialities to the utmost."

An Age of Enlightenment is no longer an impossible dream. The prospect of millions of people unfolding their full potential through the TM program heralds the dawn of such an age. Of course, this vision is still hard to appreciate for most people. But who would have believed in 1955 that an American would walk on the moon in 1969? The prospect of a moon walk would have sounded like science fiction to most people in 1955, yet a few bold scientists knew that the technology for such a feat was at hand and needed only systematic application. Today, a growing number of scientists recognize that the technology of enlightenment is at hand and can give rise to a new age through its systematic application.

The Enlightened Individual

What are the characteristics of the enlightened individual? Is it possible to pick an enlightened person out of a crowd? People often ask these questions with the expectation that I will give some dazzling description of the enlightened person walking on water or performing other remarkable feats. This expectation stems from the belief that enlightenment is a super-normal state, far removed from the realities of everyday living. In fact, the enlightened person does show some remarkable characteristics but at the same time appears more normal and natural than the so-called "normal" person. A backlog of deep-rooted stresses causing dis-ease and dis-order may be common to most people today, but this situation hardly deserves to be called normal. Maharishi points out that enlightenment is the most normal state of human life. What could be more normal than a person functioning at his full potential? Abnormal or subnormal would be the failure to use one's full creative intelligence due to the accumulation of stress. These stresses can be systematically eliminated by the TM program so that normal functioning is assured. Because enlightenment is the most normal, natural state of living, its special characteristics are not extraordinary, but, rather, fully developed qualities already present to some degree in the unenlightened state. I believe that enlightenment will provide the criterion which modern psychology has been looking for to define the fully healthy individual.

The enlightened person enjoys an unshakeable baseline happiness and an optimum mental temperature. Underlying all shifts in mood or emotion is an inner contentment that assures maximum enjoyment of whatever is at hand. The enlightened person doesn't walk around thinking how happy he is or how much he is enjoying himself. On the contrary, a natural innocence, almost childlike in quality, characterizes his interactions with others. Just as a child enjoys the spontaneous bubbling up of happiness, the enlightened person radiates an inner happiness that wells up from within the most basic element of his being. Childhood is often regarded as an enviable time of life because the child is not self-conscious about his feelings; he just expresses them. The strong baseline happiness of the enlightened person permits a re-emergence of that childlike spontaneity against a background of mature emotional and intellectual development.

The optimum mental temperature of enlightenment means that a person wastes no energy on worries or anxieties. Perfect balance in the autonomic nervous system allows for a smooth and unruffled flow of energy. Feelings of fatigue, dullness, or loss of alertness are foreign to the enlightened individual. At the same time, the pleasures of enjoyments and excitements are infinitely available. Indeed, the enlightened person discovers ripples of pleasure in everything he does. In no way should enlightenment be thought of as a state of dry serenity. On the contrary, the enlightened person enjoys such an inner fullness of happiness that he cannot help but overflow in laughter and in expression of warmth and friendship.

Another important characteristic of enlightenment is freedom. In the process of becoming enlightened, the TM program dissolves all of a person's deepest fears and inhibitions. When enlightenment finally dawns, these limitations are nowhere to be found. As a result, the barrier that most people feel between their inner and outer lives melts away and a harmonious integration is spontaneously achieved. No longer do unspoken wishes or pent-up feelings keep a person cut off from himself and others. Game playing disappears and intimacy becomes the natural way of relating to others. At the same time, the unshakeable quality of the enlightened person's inner contentment keeps him from losing his equanimity and becoming overly caught up in other people's problems or even his own pleasures. Because the enlightened person is free from deep-rooted stresses, he is also free from unconscious cravings or unfulfilled desires which distort his thinking or behavior. He is free to perceive his own feelings, the feelings of others, and the world around him as they *are* instead of as they *appear* to be through the screen of his own stress, which inevitably clouds accurate perception. Finally, the enlightened person's sense of Self is so strong that he experiences an independence of his innermost being from all the changing aspects of living.

The enlightened person's experience of Self is so enriched that it can best be called unbounded. When a person transcends the thinking process during TM meditation, his mind settles into the least excited state of consciousness, the ground state of consciousness, in which localized boundaries of thought and perception are not present. Maharishi points out that in the process of becoming enlightened, a person gradually begins to identify more and more with this state as his own Self. The small self opens up to its own deepest reality, the large Self. In growing to enlightenment, a person is said to become "established" in unbounded awareness. His mind becomes capable of sustaining contact with this universal value of consciousness while engaging in the activities of perceptions, thinking, speech, and behavior.

An important result of becoming established in unbounded awareness is gaining the ability to sustain wide comprehension along with the capacity to focus the mind sharply. Maharishi uses the analogy of a wide-angle lens to describe the consciousness of an enlightened person. The lens covers a broad territory yet focuses precisely on individual details. Narrow vision frequently causes problems where none need exist. A classic example is the businessman who focuses on immediate profit making to the detriment of long-range planning. In the process of gaining enlightenment, consciousness expands until a person naturally entertains all possibilities in any given situation. For this reason people on the way to enlightenment through the TM program frequently find situations that had appeared as obstacles now turning into opportunities. I saw this clearly in one of my patients who felt very isolated raising three small children but after taking the TM program successfully organized a community day care center. She mobilized her creativity and dynamism for improving her life circumstances while also serving an important need in her community.

Another characteristic of enlightenment is ease of activity. Straining to achieve is a classic feature of the average middle-class neurotic, but nature does not work according to the principle of strain. Physicist Lawrence Domash points out that nature is always maximally economical in its expenditure of energy; the law of least action operates everywhere in nature. For example, when a beam of light passes from air to water it bends because in doing so it travels from one point to another in the least possible amount of time. Nature automatically computes the path that gets the light from the one point in air to the other in water with the greatest economy. In getting back in tune with the natural, the enlightened person acts more in accordance with the law of least action. For this reason, TM meditators typically report that they are doing less but accomplishing more. As a result, work becomes more pleasurable. Strain for achievement can yield some success but it loses all the joy of the process. William Blake made this point well when he wrote:

> He who bends to himself a joy
> Does the winged life destroy;
> But he who kisses the joy as it flies
> Lives in eternity's sunrise.

Perfectly attuned to the law of least action, the enlightened person enjoys the process of achievement as well as the goal itself.

In growing to enlightenment, TM meditators also find a progressive increase in the speed and spontaneity of the fulfillment of their desires. When a person's consciousness begins to vibrate on the unbounded level of least excitation, his thinking gains the power of all the laws of nature which promote growth everywhere in creation. A flower does not have to think in order to blossom nor must a tree compute how to bear fruit. Laws of nature automatically compute and direct these processes. The human biomachinery apparently has the capacity to function spontaneously with great precision and in accordance with all the laws of nature. In doing so, the thoughts and desires that arise meet support rather than resistance from the environment. Maharishi states that in growing to enlightenment, a person gains "the support of nature." What this means very practically is that the enlightened person finds even the smallest details of his life working out easily and comfortably. For example, he may need to get in touch with a friend or colleague and will succeed in doing so with one phone call, not three or four. If he needs some obscure information, someone nearby will just happen to have it or it may be in a magazine that he happens to pick up. He may need to meet a group of four or five other people but have only one day free for it; everyone else will also happen to have that same day available.

People have gotten so accustomed to things not working out and struggling to fulfill their needs that these ideas of spontaneous fulfillment of desire and support from nature sound quite mysterious. Yet, these principles are everyday experiences in the lives of hundreds of thousands of TM meditators and appear as laws of nature to the enlightened. Because people have lived out of tune with nature for centuries, all too many have gotten the idea that nature has stacked the "deck of life" against them. Once a person starts making real progress on the path to enlightenement, he sees that nothing could be further from the truth. If anything, nature has stacked the deck of natural laws in his favor. Just by getting back in tune with nature, almost anyone will start finding steadily growing support in the environment for the fulfillment of his or her desires. I cannot help but recall the myth, which appears in almost every culture, of humanity being thrown out of paradise. By regaining attunement with the natural, the enlightened person rediscovers the lost paradise, not in some nether world or mystical state, but right here on earth for all to enjoy.

Spontaneity is another quality of the enlightened person. The stressed person is not spontaneous, in part because he cannot afford to be. When a person is spontaneous, he displays his innermost feelings to everyone around him. Anxiety and tension play such a large role in the stressed person's emotional make-up that spontaneous expression of feelings would not be rewarding. But once he begins developing a strong baseline happiness, the inner controls that keep a lock on spontaneity start to wither away because they are no longer necessary. The enlightened person can enjoy maximum spontaneity because his actions are always natural and appropriate.

Maharishi emphasizes that enlightenment is not an abstract, intangible state, but one which brings many concrete benefits including "skill in action":

> What is skill in action? It is the technique of performing an action so that the whole process becomes easy. The action is completed with the least effort, leaving the doer fresh enough to enjoy the full fruits of his action while at the same time remaining untouched by its binding influence. And not only this; the action is performed quickly so that the doer begins to enjoy the results immediately. Skill in action does not allow any negative influence from outside to hinder the performance of action nor does it produce any negative influence either upon the doer or upon anyone anywhere; on the contrary, the influence it creates is wholly positive.[5]

The enlightened person does not make mistakes; his every action brings joy to himself and others. The basis of this skill in action is attunement with all the laws of nature through establishment of individual awareness at the least excited state of consciousness — optimum mental temperature and maximum baseline happiness. The ancients included "skill in action" among the chief characteristics of the enlightened person.

One further dimension of enlightment deserves mention — the ability to perform spontaneous right action. Wise men of every generation have sought ultimate criteria for right and wrong behavior. Laws have evolved to fill the need for a system of right and wrong, but laws paint a picture of right and wrong only with broad strokes. How can a person always know what is the right course of action in his daily life? This question is especially troublesome to the mild middle-class neurotic. One woman came to me after discovering that her husband was having an affair. She was paralyzed with indecision about what was the right course of action. Should she ignore the situation? Should she confront her husband? Should she leave him? Should she talk to the other woman? A couple consulted me when they found out that their teenage daughter, with whom they had a poor relationship, had begun abusing drugs and engaging in promiscuous behavior. They wanted help in deciding whether to discipline her harshly, try to have a rational discussion, or send her to a psychiatrist. "I just don't know what's the right thing to do," the father told me with a look of desperation. One young man expressed great distress when he learned that his best friend was stealing from their mutual employer. The radical changes that have occurred in cultural values over the past several decades have contributed to confusion about right and wrong.

In the face of a breakdown in cultural values, Maharishi points out that one absolute criterion of right and wrong is accordance with all the laws of nature. If a person acts naturally to bring the best effect to himself and others, his actions are right. Intellectual efforts to determine whether or not an action will be in accordance with nature can yield few certain conclusions. Who can possibly know, much less intellectually consider, all the natural laws involved in even the simplest of actions? Because the process of gaining enlightenment "offers an absolute basis for right action...by natural inclination, by natural taste, wrong thoughts and wrong actions are not considered."[6] I have noted in my friends and patients who practice the TM program that issues of right and wrong become less troublesome because they begin automatically feeling or intuiting what's right in any given situation. When following these intuitions turns out to produce positive effects for all, a TM practitioner grows in confidence about his ability to intuit what is right.

This brief catalogue of the characteristics of enlightenment can hardly do justice to the value of becoming enlightened. "This state," says Maharishi, "has been the object of humanity's great quest from time immemorial because it glorifies all aspects of life."[7] With scientific research on the TM program, this great quest has come to fruition. Enlightenment is now subject to careful scientific investigation and can be systematically gained by almost anyone who chooses to do so.

The Neurophysiology of Enlightenment

The world scientific community has been investigating so-called "higher" states of consciousness for well over a century. A search for physiological correlates of these higher states began in the 1930s when several researchers took EEG equipment to India in order to study supposedly enlightened individuals. Since then, interest in studying the neurophysiology of enlightenment has steadily grown and has now blossomed with worldwide scientific investigation of the TM program.

At the Twenty-Sixth International Congress of the Physiological Sciences, physiologist R. Keith Wallace addressed scientists from all over the world on the neurophysiology of enlightenment. "Recent and rapidly growing investigation into the reality of enlightenment," he noted, "is certainly the most important event in the history of physiology, for it connects the known values of physiology with the ultimate possibilities for human development.... Neurophysiological research has taken the process of gaining enlightenment out of the realm of abstruse mystical phenomena and made it understandable in modern scientific terms."[8]

Every state of consciousness depends upon a corresponding and unique physiological state. Prior to Aserinsky and Kleitman's ground-breaking sleep research in 1953, scientists knew of only two physiological distinct states of consciousness — waking and sleeping. Aserinsky and Kleitman showed dreaming to be a third distinct state. Physiological research on the fourth state of consciousness dates back to 1935, but not until Wallace published his landmark study on the physiological effects of the TM program did any substantial scientific evidence of a fourth state exist. Restful alertness, technically a wakeful hypometabolic state, is now recognized as a fourth major state of consciousness in addition to the three previously defined states of waking, sleeping, and dreaming. It is interesting to note that the Vedas contain explicit references to a fourth state of consciousness called *turiya*, distinct from the three ordinary states of consciousness.

If restful alertness is a fourth major state of consciousness, then enlightenment is in all probability a fifth state. Maharishi describes the process of gaining enlightenment in terms of the regular alternation of restful alertness with the other three major states of consciousness. In this way, deep-rooted stresses dissolve, and the degree of ease and order in the functioning of the nervous system increases. When this process of neurophysiological refinement reaches completion, the fifth state of consciousness results. A distinct feature of the fifth state, enlightenment, is the permanence of unbounded awareness. The enlightened person continues to experience the cycle of waking, sleeping, and dreaming, but his physiology is so refined and orderly that he naturally maintains Self-consciousness throughout the cycle of these other states. In one sense, the physiology of enlightenment spills over and underlies the other states of consciousness. For this reason, Maharishi calls enlightenment an all-inclusive state of cosmic consciousness. This infusion of the fourth state into waking, sleeping, and dreaming suggests that the process of gaining enlightenment involves distinct physiological changes during dreaming and sleeping as well as the normal waking state.

Maharishi uses a simple analogy which I find very helpful in explaining growth to enlightenment. He compares the process of becoming enlightened to that of dying a piece of cloth. First dipped into the dye, the cloth is taken out and bleached until all but a trace of color remains. That remaining color is colorfast. By repeating the process, the cloth eventually becomes colorfast with the rich color of pure dye. Similarly, the TM practitioner gains a state of maximum ease and order in the state of restful alertness and then comes out into the pressure of his daily activity. After a few hours, the ease and order gained from a TM session wear off but a trace remains. Each TM session followed by normal daily activity makes permanent a certain degree of neurophysiological refinement. Eventually, the person unfolds his ability to sustain maximum ease and order even amidst dynamic activity. He gains enlightenment.

From the standpoint of physics, enlightenment involves raising life to its highest value. A basic law of physics states that non-living systems tend to increase in disorder, entropy. However, a living system maintains maximum order, minimum entropy, in the face of a disorderly environment. Scientific research on the effects of the TM technique shows that it increases order in the functioning of the mind and body. If enlightenment represents a state in which ease and order are maximum at all times, then it is also a state of minimum entropy. In a physical sense, as well as on an experiential level, it is a state of being maximally alive.

It is important to recognize that enlightenment does not require development of any new faculties of the nervous system. The process of becoming enlightened is not comparable to a muscle-building program in which new tissue is added to the body. On the contrary, the process of becoming enlightened does not involve adding anything to the nervous system but rather removing the deep stresses that inhibit normal functioning. Through systematic neurophysiological refinement, a person on the path to enlightenment unfolds the natural capacity of his mind and body to function perfectly and coherently. When this innate capacity unfolds fully, enlightenment dawns. Because almost everyone has the natural capacity to become enlightened, Maharishi has said, "There is no reason today, in our scientific age, for anyone to remain unenlightened."

Exciting research on the neurophysiology of enlightenment is under way at Maharishi European Research University (MERU) in Switzerland. The focus of current research is upon coherence of brain wave activity appearing in advanced TM practitioners. Dr. Paul Levine, director of the MERU neurophysiology laboratory, which is among the most sophisticated in the world, recently reported very provocative findings on the brain wave activity of a 26 year-old woman who has been meditating for 15 years. Levine noted that of all the subjects he has studied, she showed the highest levels of brain wave coherence, which, as mentioned earlier, is an indication of integrated brain functioning. Whether she was producing alpha, theta, or beta waves alone or in combinations, all were coherent. The coherent fast wave activity (beta) seemed to be harmonically related to the slow wave (theta and alpha) activity. Particularly striking was the abrupt appearance of theta band coherence as soon as she started her TM practice. High levels of alpha and beta coherence showed up both inside and outside the TM sessions. In addition, brief periods in which she described experiencing pure consciousness, were correlated with a suspension of respiration, a dramatic drop in heart rate, cessation of phasic skin resistance activity, and a high level of basal skin resistance. These periods were also marked by especially high levels of brain wave coherence, particularly in the theta frequency. These physiological correlates were consistently found during six TM sessions in this experienced TM practitioner with frequent clear experience of pure consciousness. Also noteworthy is the fact that this woman, though young, holds a position of great responsibility and displays a remarkable degree of happiness and psychological integration.

With the neurophysiology of enlightenment becoming better defined, Maharishi has designed courses to speed the process of gaining enlightenment. Residence courses, one-month SCI courses, and TM teacher training courses all accelerate growth to enlightenment. Additionally, Maharishi has recently developed a six-month advanced program for TM instructors in order to maximize the pace of growth to enlightenment. Maharishi specifically defines the purposes of the six-month program as enabling people to begin enjoying the spontaneous fulfillment of their desires and to unflod all the latent potentialities of consciousness. The preliminary psychophysiological research on six-month course participants indicates that the program is remarkably effective in accelerating growth to enlightenment.

Research on the physiological effects of the TM program and the neurophysiology of enlightenment indicate clearly that TM is far more than a technique of deep relaxation. In promoting rapid growth to enlightenment, the TM program promises the unfoldment of full human potential for millions upon millions of people and the dawn of a new age. "This has always been the characteristic of great scientific discoveries," noted Dr. Wallace at the conclusion of his address, "to produce unforeseen technological breakthroughs of, immense benefit to human life."[9]

Total Health

What will be the social effects of large numbers of people stepping onto a rapid path to enlightenment through the TM program? When people ask this question, I usually start trying to answer it in terms of the TM program's potential impact on health care, because I am most familiar with this field. To put it simply, I foresee the widespread practice of the TM program as a public health benefit of the first order.

Over the past couple of decades, new medical technologies such as kidney dialysis and heart transplants have captured headlines. Yet the greatest achievements in medicine remain advances in public health measures, because prevention is the number one goal of medicine. For example, in the long history of the fight against polio, the development of the iron lung in the early part of this century will not be remembered as a monumental medical achievement, while the names of Salk and Sabine will go down in history as the men who conquered polio because they developed the means of preventing this dreaded childhood illness.

The achievements of preventive medicine over the past several decades have been numerous. Highly dangerous infectious diseases such as smallpox, diphtheria, and tetanus have been largely eliminated through immunization programs. Rheumatic fever and bacterial endocarditis, not so many years ago considered the major heart diseases, have become rare through the widespread use of antibiotics to control streptococcal infections. Pasteurization of milk has ended epidemics of tuberculosis. The annihilation of the Anopheles mosquito has ended the ravages of malaria. Uterine and cervical cancers were once the leading fatal cancers in women, but Pap tests and early treatment have reduced the mortality rate from these cancers by half. These few examples (many more could be cited) give some feeling for the critical role prevention has played and continues to play in improving world health. Many more lives have been saved and much more suffering has been avoided through preventive public health measures than through the combined efforts of all health care professionals in the treatment of disease.

Several shocking statistics indicate, however, that progress in health maintenance has begun creeping to a halt. For example, American life expectancy has not increased since 1961 even though Americans now spend over one hundred billion dollars annually on private and public health care. Twenty billion dollars is spent each year on the care of people with circulatory diseases alone, but high blood pressure and heart attacks continue in epidemic proportions. Especially troublesome concerning the spread of circulatory disorders is their increasingly frequent appearance in young people. One man in five will have a heart attack before age 60, and this rate is constantly increasing. The over-the-counter sale of billions of dollars worth of non-prescriptive pain relievers and other remedies suggests that Americans are feeling less and less healthy. Everywhere in the media appear images of people needing a pill to relieve tension, headache, sinus trouble, back pain, indigestion, heartburn, constipation, or insomnia.

At the root of this deterioration in health is what can be called the modern epidemic of stress. Chronic distress obstructs the body's ability to function normally and opens the door to psychosomatic and organic diseases of all kinds. Modern medical science has not come up with an effective means of helping people get out of the stress cycle and thereby halting the stress epidemic. Here is where I believe the TM program can make an immense contribution. Widespread practice of the TM program appears to be an effective and economical way to wipe out this modern plague.

All the research on the TM program suggests that it is both an "antibiotic" and "vaccine" against distress. TM meditation produces effects exactly opposite to those of the stress response, thereby directly *reducing* accumulated stresses. In this way, the TM program serves as an "antibiotic" against distress. It helps the body's regenerative processes throw off daily and deep-rooted stresses in almost the same way in which antibiotics aid the body's immune system. At the same time, the TM program strengthens the person by increasing ease and order in the functioning of the nervous system, thereby *preventing* the further accumulation of stresses. In this way, the TM program acts as a "vaccine" and immunizes a person against the stress cycle. Widespread practice of the TM program could foreseeably put an end to the stress epidemic, just as the Salk vaccine has all but eliminated polio.

Chronic distress plays a critical role in all the major diseases of our time — heart disease, high blood pressure, gastrointestinal ailments, emotional disorders — and contributes to behaviors such as cigarette smoking and drug abuse, which are major health hazards. If the TM program could reduce hypertension, cigarette smoking, and drug abuse alone, it would add immeasurably to health maintenance by reducing the risk of such killers and cripplers as heart attack, stroke, lung cancer, and emphysema. Were children to begin the TM program around age ten, I would anticipate sufficient equilibration of their emotional development and strengthening of their baseline happiness to prevent in most cases the appearance of emotional disorders such as anxiety neurosis, depressive illness, and even schizophrenia.

Perhaps a less dramatic but even greater contribution of widespread TM practice to health would occur in terms of helping people begin feeling healthier. By increasing resistance to disease, the TM program could be expected to reduce the incidence of colds and minor infections. The additional rest provided by the TM program would increase feelings of vitality and reduce minor aches and pains due to chronic fatigue. People would stop running from doctor to doctor or from psychotherapist to psychotherapist trying to find out why they "just don't feel good." A strong baseline happiness and respect for the body's natural capacity to stay healthy would enable people to stop exaggerating a minor ache or pain. The disappearance of irregularities in sleep and gastrointestinal activity would also add greatly to a person's feeling of health. All this would mean much less time and money spent trying to artifically recover a state of well-being natural to a person not caught up in the stress cycle.

An additional contribution of the TM program to health deserves mention. Modern medicine presently looks upon health merely as the absence of disease. This criterion may be appropriate for the average person today who uses only five, ten, or 15 per cent of his physical, mental, and emotional potential. What are the standards of health for a person who uses 100 hundred per cent of his potential in the state of enlightenment? The answer to this question promises to be one of the most exciting contributions of the TM program to health maintenance. The TM program can introduce a new dimension into health standards by including among the basic critera of good health the capacity to enjoy life fully.

In light of what the TM program can contribute to world health, I sometimes think that present efforts to fight the diseases of stress are much like a struggle to treat end-stage poliomyelitis with bigger and better iron lungs while the polio vaccine awaits widespread distribution. Maharishi emphasizes this point:

> To build more hospitals to alleviate sickness and suffering for people who have already fallen ill is a laudable act of charity. But it is infinitely more important to find ways and means of preventing people from falling sick and ensuring that they will always enjoy good health.[10]

The TM program appears to be such a means. Through its widespread practice, the nation will be able to reduce its health bills substantially but at the same time significantly increase general levels of health and well-being.

The health care institutions can play an important role in making the TM program universally available. I am one of a group of physicians petitioning Medi-Cal, the California state health insurance system, to pay for the cost of TM instruction. I believe that the TM program adds so much to human well-being that it should be considered a person's basic right to have TM instruction just as it is a child's right to receive public education. Because TM teacher training is highly systematic, it would be a relatively simple matter for public health agencies, schools, hospitals, and other government agencies to send some of their personnel to become TM instructors. These instructors could then return to their local communities and make the TM program available to the whole population. The cost of instructing 20 million people in the TM program would probably be around two billion dollars. Such an expenditure may sound enormous, but compared with the hundreds of billions of dollars it could save in reducing drug abuse, crime, illness, accidents, welfare costs, and inefficiency, and compared to what it would add to the quality of life in general, such an expenditure would be small indeed.

Imagine!

At my lectures people inevitably ask about the larger social implications of widespread TM practice. Can the TM program contribute to solving such long-standing social problems as interracial strife, poverty, and crime? Won't a happy person tend to withdraw from social problems and the distress of others? How can the TM program really bring about an age of harmony and happiness, an Age of Enlightenment? These questions will receive definitive answers as ever larger numbers of people begin the TM program. In the meantime, I like to have my audiences picture themselves participating in an imaginary experiment that illustrates how the TM program can precipitate a new age.

The experiment begins with one thousand people in a large room: men, women, and children of different races and backgrounds, all relatively healthy and representing a good cross section of America. Adequate food, water, sanitary and recreational facilities are available, and the people are relatively happy at the outset of the experiment. Now, the experimental variable is the stress level of the individuals in this group. This room is set up in such a way that we can look in on these people and have complete control of how stressful their living conditions will be at any particular time. We can increase the stress level through physical or psychological means. For example, we could introduce a viral infection, raise or lower the room temperature, or reduce the food supply. These would be physical stresses. We might simply start a rumor that the food supply will be cut off or put an extremely agitated stranger in the room to serve as psychological stressors.

Let's imagine that the group has become accustomed to the room and is living comfortably when we decide to start increasing stress levels. Let's say we begin causing drastic temperature changes and start a rumor that food is growing scarce. Very shortly after we start turning up the stress dial, the behavior of the group would start to change. At first, group members might just become more irritable and edgy with one another. If we kept gradually raising the stress level, we would begin seeing people frowning frequently and expressing a good deal of concern and agitation. At times the pace of activity would become frenetic, with everybody rushing around trying to figure out "what's wrong." At other times people would become very sluggish out of depression and despair. They would show signs of helplessness and hopelessness, such as walking around with shrugged shoulders and palms held outward as if to say, "What can I do?" If the stress level continued to increase, interpersonal strife would seize the group. Some people would begin hoarding supplies even though ample food might be available. Family members would start fighting with one another. A movement might appear among the majority of the group to blame one sub-group for everyone's suffering. By this time, we would not have to do anything from the outside to continue raising the group's stress levels. The group would be thoroughly caught up in the individual and social stress cycles where irritability, conflict, despair, and frantic behavior kept further reinforcing stress levels. Eventually physical conflict might break out, with people venting their anger and frustration upon one another.

Illness would also plague the groups and add to the stress cycle. Depending on genetic and constitutional factors, different people would come down with different health problems. Perhaps two or three hundred people in the group with a predisposition to circulatory disorders would develop high blood pressure. Roughly 100 people would develop peptic ulcer disease and another 50 – 100 people would start becoming alcoholics. Those people with a predisposition to emotional disorders would also start showing symptoms. These would be the screamers who, instead of turning their anxieties inward on their internal organs, would start taking out their frustrations by yelling at other group members. There would also be the depressives who would become hopeless, withdrawn, and so full of despair that they would stop taking care of themselves. Another group, perhaps as many as 100, would start showing psychotic symptoms — hallucinations, delusions, paranoia — and might eventually suffer a schizophrenic break.

By simply increasing the stress level of this group, we would have transformed their relatively peaceful life into a miserable existence. This room of 1,000 people would have become a place where not only happiness but survival itself was difficult. Perhaps the most frightening result of our experiment would be the self-sustaining nature of the chaos we created. Without our further intervention in the group, confusion and discord would continue to grow on its own until someone in the group discovered a means of breaking the stress cycle or we intervened to lessen the stress level.

Does the above sound all too familiar, a lot like the six o'clock news? Now let's imagine that we decide to turn the stress dial in the opposite direction, towards increasing ease and order. Our first effort to do so might involve restoring normal temperature and providing abundant food and other supplies to make everyone in the room as physically comfortable as possible. We might distribute antibiotics to bring infections under control and tranquilizers to ease emotional distress. These factors would ease stress levels to some degree but would not by themselves reduce the internal distress of each person because the memories and pent-up feelings from the period of high stress would remain.

The high stress period would have left a psy-chophysiological imprint which would keep each member of the group in a state of chronic alarm. Even though supplies might become adequate once again, bickering would continue because people would continue to feel anxious and edgy. The health problems which each group member had developed would also continue to linger.

To decrease the internal distress of the group members, we would now introduce a TM teacher. He might start introductory lectures on the TM program. Most people in the group would be too caught up in their own internal distress to listen. They would continue to believe that other people were to blame for their frustrations and anxieties, and that happiness depended on an aggressive "grab it while you can" attitude. A few individuals, however, might recognize that the problems within the group were arising in large measure from the discontent inside each group member. As a result, these few would take the TM course and start reducing their distress and strengthening their baseline happiness. Soon, others would notice the benefits that these few were deriving from the TM program and also start. In this way, TM practice would spread among the group members.

The results of individual group members increasing the ease and order in their own nervous systems would begin to show up immediately. Frowns would start giving way to smiles. We would start seeing group members laughing a little more often, not taking life quite so seriously, not feeling quite so overwhelmed by problems. Expressions of affection would increase. Family members and friends might start hugging one another again instead of fighting and bickering. Consumption of alcohol and cigarettes would decrease as each person's baseline happiness grew. The screamers in the group would quiet down, and the depressives would start engaging in activity again. Psychosomatic symptoms would abate. Insomnia, indigestion, headaches, constipation, and bodily aches and pains would lessen. Those people who had developed high blood pressure and peptic ulcer disease would soon be able to bring these conditions under control. Individuals would once again be able to engage in specialized tasks — distribution of food, cooking, cleaning, child care, health care, etc. — necessary for the well-being of the whole group without fear of malice or dishonesty on the part of other group members. Cooperation would replace antagonism. Individuals and the group as a whole would step out of the stress cycle and into a growth cycle where internal harmony and happiness reinforce external harmony and achievement, and vice versa.

With the steadily increasing feelings of well-being in the group, individuals would start showing more interest in the arts, philosophy, religion, and the expansion of knowledge in general. Awakening to the incredible glory and miracle of life, they would want to express their feelings in dance, music, poetry, and drama. A desire to understand the mysteries of nature would lead some members of the group to science and others to theology. Everyone in the group would begin to value the pursuit of knowledge as being among the most fulfilling and worthwhile of endeavors. Continuing to practice the TM program not just to reduce stress but also to tap their deepest reserves of creative intelligence, individuals in the group would soon be reflecting the highest ideals of wisdom. Group members might be saying that a new age, an age of enlightenment, had dawned among them.

This imaginary experiment is meant to illustrate how the TM program can have comprehensive social effects. Obviously, the TM program does not magically do away with the hardships of economic deprivation, malnutrition, poor housing, inadequate education, years of racial and religious prejudice, or the many other real problems that cripple human growth. If we had continued to deny the 1,000 people in our experiment adequate food, the TM program would not have saved them from starvation. Nevertheless, the TM program does appear capable of making possible solutions to intractable social problems by reducing people's internal discord, which fuels these problems, and by unfolding people's full creative intelligence so necessary to find solutions where none have existed in the past.

Maharishi very succinctly summarized the social significance of the TM program when he wrote:

> Homes are made by individuals. Shops, ships, farms, and factories are manned by individuals. Professions, firms, industries, and public services are operated by individuals. Government departments are run by individuals — the whole day-to-day and future destiny of every nation is in the hands of individuals. The external harmony and progress of the entire human race is founded on the internal harmony and progress of every individual.[11]

In promoting the fastest possible growth to enlightenment, the TM program is the most effective means available for unfolding inner harmony and progress.

A Global Transformation

After audience members envision their participation in the above imaginary experiment, the next questions are: How long will it take for the TM program to produce social changes everyone can see and feel? If an age of enlightenment is dawning, when will the confusion and negativity in the world start to measurably diminish? Scientists at MIU have recently been studying the social effects of the TM program. Their findings suggest that the Age of Enlightenment may be dawning right now.

Great epochs in knowledge and social evolution are visible throughout history, but few people in the past have been privileged to recognize these great transformations while they were occurring. One hundred and fifty years ago few people foresaw the social impact of textile mills and rising urban populations at the dawn of what historians now call the Industrial Revolution. Even fewer appreciated the importance of Copernicus' new methods in astronomy or Gutenberg's revolutionary means of printing at the dawn of the Renaissance. It is doubtful that many Romans recognized the end of their civilization in the dawning of Christianity; and it is certain that no one recognized the significance of discovering how to extract iron from ore at the close of the stone age. Yet, today's acceleration of progress is allowing people to witness immense social transformations in their own lifetime. For example, humanity jumped from earthboundedness to space travel in little more than a decade. The technology is now at hand for humanity to master not only outer space, but, perhaps more importantly, inner space as well. With rapid and widespread implementation of the TM program, there is every reason to believe that we could just as quickly achieve the dawning of a new age of happiness, peace, and prosperity.

Great historical shifts have happened not gradually, in a smooth and progressive fashion, but through discrete leaps which marked the beginning of a new age or period. Dr. Lawrence Domash, Professor of Physics at MIU, points out that such recognizable shifts are very common throughout nature. For example, water does not freeze gradually as the temperature drops from 70 to 20 degrees Fahrenheit but, rather, quite suddenly when the temperature reaches 32 degrees. Physicists use the term *phase transition* to refer to this principle of abrupt transformations in a system from a disorderly to an orderly state or vice versa. Only a small fraction, as little as one per cent, of the elements in a system must become orderly for the whole system to start showing increased orderliness. Because nature often works in parallel ways from one level of creation to another, Professor Domash suggests that the mechanics of phase transitions may offer insight in to the mechanics of great historical transformations.

The study of phase transitions suggests that only a very small percentage of the people in a city, state or nation need begin the TM program before one sees definite signs of positive social change. An example will illustrate why. When a bar of iron becomes magnetic, it undergoes a phase transition. Magnetism in the iron bar results from its electrons moving in harmony with one another. When 99 per cent or more of the iron bar's electrons are not moving in harmony with one another, it shows no magnetic properties. However, when only one per cent of the electrons start spinning in harmony with one another, the bar starts becoming magnetic. All phase transitions in nature work in a similar way. Only a small fraction, as little as one per cent, of the elements in a system must become orderly for the whole system to start showing increased orderliness.

For the past 15 years, Maharishi has been predicting that only one per cent of a city or country need practice the TM program for definite signs of increasing social harmony to appear. This one per cent figure appears to be the necessary number of people practicing the TM program in a country for that nation to undergo a phase transition from an age of distress and disharmony to an Age of Enlightenment.

Does this mean that all social problems in a country will disappear when one per cent of its population begins the TM program? No. A phase transition marks the beginning of increasing order in a system. There will be a big difference between the social effect of one per cent and five or ten per cent of a population starting the TM program. Maharishi points out that when one per cent of the people in a country begins the TM program, the light of the dawn of the Age of Enlightenment will become evident, but the bright light of midday will require that five or ten per cent meditate. It is also worth noting that phase transitions do not always occur perfectly smoothly. Some signs of social discord may accompany the sign of increasing harmony as the number of people practicing the TM program approaches one per cent.

Is there any scientific evidence that this one per cent prediciton is true? Several studies indicate that crime rate is a good index of social tension because it fluctuates with levels of unemployment, density of population, and other social stressors. In a recent study, Dr. Candace Borland and Garland Landrith, social scientists at MIU, found that when the number of people practicing the TM program nears one per cent, an abrupt drop in crime rate occurs. They report:

> A comparison of the 12 cities with .97 per cent or more of their population meditating in 1972 (one per cent cities) to matched control cities showed that the mean change in crime rate from 1972 to 1973 among the control cities (7.7 per cent increase) was significantly different from that observed among the one per cent cities (8.8 per cent decrease). Further analysis indicated that factors other than reaching about one per cent of the population meditating were unlikely to account for the subsequent change in crime rate in the one per cent cities.[12]

Though only preliminary evidence, this study foreshadows measurable changes in social trends toward greater harmony when one per cent or more of a city population are practicing the TM program. Borland and Landrith are now conducting a second study to determine whether other indices of quality of life (such as accident rates, unemployment, and psychiatric hospital admissions) also improve when one per cent of a city populaiton starts the TM program.

Because this crime rate study bears out Maharishi's one per cent prediction, the phenomenon of increasing social harmony occurring when one per cent of a population begins the TM program has been called the *Maharishi Effect.* Maharishi summarized the basis of the Maharishi Effect when he wrote: "An individual influences the entire cosmos by every thought, word,

and action. Therefore, someone with peace in his heart
naturally radiates peace and harmony and influences the
whole universe."[13] When a few individuals increase their
own ease, order, and baseline happiness, they radiate
harmony and neutralize tension in all their interactions.
It may seem surprising that such a small percentage of a
population need practice the TM technique for the
Maharishi Effect to become apparent, but happiness,
love, and good will can be very contagious.

Sociologists have already documented how global
communications and intercontinental travel are rapidly
diluting cultural values. As a result social
anthropologists have voiced concern that a homogenizing of cultures and loss of cultural integrity will be the
inevitable result. When some people hear about the
Maharishi Effect, they express concern that the
widespread practice of the TM program will destroy
cultural traditions by diminishing and homogenizing
cultural differences. In fact, the opposite is true.
Maharishi suggests that by strengthening each nation's
adaptability, stability, integration, purification, and
growth, the TM program can preserve cultural integrity
while enhancing cultural exchange. Maharishi states:

> The individual members of every society, growing in
> these qualities, (adaptability, stability, integration,
> purification and growth) will naturally become stabilized
> in their own cultural values and at the same time,
> remaining adaptable, will be able to welcome any outside
> influence, purify it, and integrate the best of it into their
> own culture....[14]

The TM program will strengthen the integrity and
harmony of each individual, social institution, and
culture just as it enhances the unique capacities and
harmonious functioning of each cell, tissue, and bodily
organ in the individual.

Among the most inspiring potentialities of the
dawning age of enlightenment is a world of peace.
Psychiatrist R. D. Laing points out that human beings
have slaughtered over one hundred million of their

fellow men and women in this century alone. The problem of war has proven so intractable that some theorists such as anthropologist Conrad Lorenz have suggested that destructive aggression may be an innate human characteristic. Buckminster Fuller told me prior to a symposium in which we were both participating that the developed nations spend nearly 80 per cent of their resources on defending themselves. When I heard this figure, I couldn't help but think that nations of stressed individuals tie up their energies in defense in the same way that so many of my patients pour the vast majority of their energies into psychological defense mechanisms. Nations are, after all, collections of individuals, and the collective consciousness of the nation will reflect the consciousness of its individuals.

In this light, Maharishi points out that the solution to the problem of world peace lies in solving the problem of individual peace. He is not the first to assert that it is suffering of single individuals which ultimately gives rise to the collective cry of "War!" However, until the TM program became widely available, the prospect of solving the problem of individual peace remained dim. The phase transition to the Age of Enlightenment will be sufficient, Maharishi estimates, to end the likelihood of another world war. He adds that "the family of nations will be completely without fears with five per cent of the world population practicing the TM program." Throughout history, statesmen have tried to end the problem of war with armies and treaties but as the UNESCO charter states, "Wars start in the minds of men."

The formula for world peace lies in bringing peace to individuals. "Any generation whose leaders sincerely try to apply this principle widely," Maharishi writes, "will succeed in creating lasting world peace. If present statesmen and public leaders do this, the credit will be theirs and they will have the satisfaction of leaving a better world for coming generations."[15]

To hasten the Age of Enlightenment, Maharishi has established a World Plan and a worldwide TM organization. The World Plan calls for the establishment of one TM center for every one million people, or 3,600 centers spread all over the world. There are presently 8,000 TM instructors active in centers throughout the world. Teacher training is another important component of the World Plan. Ideally, each World Plan center will train 1,000 teachers of the Science of Creative Intelligence. This will assure the availability of the TM program to anyone who might wish to learn it. Additional elements of the World Plan include "forest" academies near every metropolitan area for residence courses and other advanced residential programs, and TV stations to broadcast the knowledge of the Science of Creative Intelligence into every home. In the United States, several forest academies are already operating and the first TV station (KSCI, channel 18 in the Los Angeles area) is already on the air.

Maharishi has formulated seven goals for the World Plan. These are:

1. *To develop the full potential of the individual.*
2. *To improve governmental achievements.*
3. *To realize the highest ideals of education.*
4. *To solve the problems of crime and all behavior that brings unhappiness to the family of man.*
5. *To maximize the intelligent use of the environment.*
6. *To bring fulfillment to the economic aspirations of the individual and society.*
7. *To achieve the spiritual goals of mankind in this generation.*

Under the umbrella of the World Plan Executive Council, the parent organization of the TM movement, Maharishi has established five educational service divisions to achieve these seven goals. The International Meditation Society (IMS) offers TM and SCI courses to the general public while the Students International Meditation Society (SIMS) is active on college campuses and in secondary schools everywhere. The Foundation for the Science of Creative Intelligence (FSCI) serves business, industry, and government. To enrich all academic disciplines with the light of SCI and to achieve the highest ideals of education, Maharishi International University (MIU) has been established and accredited with its main campus in Fairfield, Iowa. Finally, Maharishi formed the Spiritual Regeneration Movement (SRM) for those interested in a spiritual emphasis on developing wholeness of life.

The goals of the World Plan are certainly ambitious, and inaugurating the dawn of the Age of Enlightenment at this time might appear optimistic. I am confident, however, that the full significance of Maharishi's contribution to the world will become more steadily apparent in the coming years. For those people who see Maharishi on videotape in the future or read this book five, ten, fifty, or one hundred years from now, the great transformation begun in this decade will be obvious. Hundreds of thousands of people are beginning the TM program all over the world. In many countries, the number of TM practitioners is rapidly approaching one per cent. Phase transitions are already occurring in some communities and are imminent in several large nations. For centuries, the world has been plodding through an age of distress, in which almost everyone assumed that struggle and suffering were inherent in life. Over a remarkably few years, single individuals reducing their stress and unfolding their full potential, have brought humanity to the dawn of a new age in which happiness is the norm. In fact, an epidemic of happiness appears to be on the horizon and it may prove to be incurable!

MAJOR WORLD PLAN CENTERS IN USA

There are over 400 TM teaching centers in the United States. For the one nearest you, ask directory assistance for "Transcendental Meditation Program," or contact one of the centers listed below.

Ann Arbor
1207 Packard
Ann Arbor, Mich. 48104
Phone: (313) 761-8255

Atlanta
3615 N. Stratford Road N.E.
Atlanta, Ga. 30342
Phone: (404) 231-1093

Baltimore
809 St. Paul Street
Baltimore, Md. 21202
Phone: (301) 837-6114

Berkeley
2716 Derby Street
Berkeley, Calif. 94705
Phone: (415) 548-1144

Boston
73 Newbury Street
Boston, Mass. 02116
Phone: (617) 266-3770

Cambridge
33 Garden Street
Cambridge, Mass. 02138
Phone: (617) 876-4581

Charlotte
1532 E. Morehead Street
Charlotte, N.C. 28207
Phone: (704) 332-6694

Chicago
145 E. Ohio
Chicago, Ill. 60611
Phone: (312) 467-5570

Cincinnati
3047 Madison Road
Cincinnati, Ohio 45209
Phone: (513) 631-6800

Columbus
1818 W. Lane Avenue
Columbus, Ohio 43221
Phone: (614) 481-8877

Dallas
3603 N. Hall
Suite 204
Dallas, Tex. 75219
Phone: (214) 528-3600

Denver
240 St. Paul Street
Suite 102
Denver, Colo. 80206
Phone: (303) 320-4007

Des Moines
1311 34th Street
Des Moines, Iowa 50311
Phone: (515) 255-1547

Detroit
17108 Mack at Cadieux
Grosse Pointe, Mich. 48230
Phone: (313) 885-5566

Greensboro
211 S. Edgeworth
Greensboro, N.C. 27401
Phone: (919) 275-2772

Hartford
61 S. Main Street
West Hartford Ctr., Conn. 06107
Phone: (203) 233-4493

Honolulu
227 S. King Street
Honolulu, Hawaii 96813
Phone: (808) 537-3339

Houston
2518 Drexel
Houston, Tex. 77027
Phone: (713) 627-7500

Kansas City
6301 Main Street
Kansas City, Mo. 64113
Phone: (816) 523-5777

Los Angeles
1015 Gayley Avenue
Los Angeles, Calif. 90024
Phone: (213) 478-1569

Memphis
1639 Madison Avenue
Memphis, Tenn. 38104
Phone: (901) 726-6691

Miami
3251 Ponce de Leon Boulevard
Suite 210
Coral Gables, Fla. 33134
Phone: (305) 444-6172

Milwaukee
400 E. Silver Spring
Whitefish Bay, Wis. 53217
Phone: (414) 962-7560

Minneapolis
6534 Walker Street
Suite 212
Saint Louis Park, Minn. 55426
Phone: (612) 929-0071

New Haven
1974 Yale Station
New Haven, Conn. 06520
Phone: (203) 776-5784

New Orleans
2324 Napoleon Avenue
New Orleans, La. 70115
Phone: (504) 899-6380

New York
133 E. 58th Street
New York, N.Y. 10022
Phone: (212) 826-6620

Omaha
14961 Drexel
Omaha, Nebr. 68137
Phone: (402) 895-1755

Philadelphia
315 S. 17th Street
Philadelphia, Pa. 19103
Phone: (215) 732-9220

Phoenix
2234 N. Seventh Street
Suite 2
Phoenix, Ariz. 85006
Phone: (602) 257-8611

Pittsburgh
5883 Forbes Avenue
Pittsburgh, Pa. 15217
Phone: (412) 521-6000

Portland
7743 S.W. Capitol Highway
Portland, Oreg. 97219
Phone: (503) 245-3361

Richmond
1810 Monument Avenue
Richmond, Va. 23220
Phone: (804) 359-2772

Sacramento
2015 J Street
Suite 32
Sacramento, Calif. 95814
Phone: (916) 443-4895

San Diego
4020 30th Street
San Diego, Calif. 92104
Phone: (714) 280-1840

San Francisco
256 Laguna Honda Boulevard
San Francisco, Calif. 94116
Phone: (415) 661-7050

Seattle
912 15th Avenue E.
Seattle, Wash. 98105
Phone: (206) 322-1800

St. Louis
7438 Forsyth
Suite 205
St. Louis, Mo. 63105
Phone: (314) 726-0200

Tampa
10921 56th Street
Suite 203
Tampa, Fla. 33617
Phone: (813) 988-5294

Washington, D.C.
2127 Leroy Place N.W.
Washington, D.C. 20008
Phone: (202) 387-5050

MAJOR WORLD PLAN CENTERS IN CANADA

There are over 80 TM teaching centers in Canada. For the one nearest you, call or write one of the following major centers.

Calgary
218-11th Avenue, S.W.
Calgary
Alberta T2R 0C3
Phone: (403) 262-1030

Edmonton
Le Marchand Mansions
101 - 11523 100th Avenue
Edmonton
Alberta T5K 0J8
Phone: (403) 482-1371

Halifax
2045 Poplar Street
Halifax
N.S. B3L 2Y6
Phone: (902) 422-5905

Hamilton
1960 Main Street W.
Hamilton
Ontario L9G 2V9
Phone: (416) 527-0444

Moncton
256 Cameron Street
Moncton
N.B. E1C 5Z3
Phone: (506) 855-0225

Montreal West
3666 Lorne Crescent
Montreal
P.Q. H2X 2B3
Phone: (514) 285-1298

Ottawa
65 Bank Street
Ottawa
Ontario K1P 5N2
Phone: (616) 236-0648

Quebec
1085 Avenue des Erables
Quebec
P.Q. G1R 2N3
Phone: (418) 529-2149

Regina
2326 Albert Street
Regina
Saskatchewan S4P 2V7
Phone: (306) 586-4012

Saskatoon
707 University Drive
Saskatoon
Saskatchewan S7W 0J3
Phone: (306) 242-6317

St. John's
16 Shea Street
St. John's
Newfoundland A1B 1Y1
Phone: (709) 726-9410

Sudbury
262 Edmond Street
Sudbury
Ontario P3E 1M2
Phone: (705) 675-8405

Toronto
4844A Yonge Street
Toronto
Ontario M2N 5M8
Phone: (416) 226-0116

Vancouver
1170 Hornby Street #202
Vancouver
B.C. V6Z 1V8
Phone: (604) 688-4528

Victoria
1270 Pandora Avenue
Victoria
B.C. V8V 3R4
Phone: (604) 383-9822

Winnepeg
51 Horace Street
Winnipeg
Manitoba R2H 0V8
Phone: (204) 247-5565

INTERNATIONAL WORLD PLAN CENTERS

The TM program is taught in over 90 countries throughout the world. For the address of the center nearest you write to one of the centers listed below:

World Plan Executive Council
Seelisberg
Switzerland

Academy of Meditation
Shankaracharya Nagar
Rishikesh
U.P.
India

World Plan Executive Council
17310 Sunset Boulevard
Pacific Palisades, California 90272
United States

NOTES

Chapter 1. Why Not Happiness?

1. Sigmund Freud, *Civilization and Its Discontents*, trans. J. Strachey (New York: W. W. Norton Co., 1962) p. 23.

2. Abraham H. Maslow, "Cognition of Being in the Peak Experiences," *Monograph* (Waltham, Mass.: Psychology Department, Brandeis University, 1956) p. 1.

3. Maharishi Mahesh Yogi, transcription of a lecture.

4. Maharishi Mahesh Yogi, quoted in *International Symposium on the Science of Creative Intelligence* (Seelisberg, Switzerland: MIU Press, 1972) p. 48.

5. Abraham H. Maslow, *Motivation and Personality* (New York: Harper, 1954) p. 352.

6. Maharishi Mahesh Yogi, *The Science of Being and the Art of Living* (London: SRM Publications, 1966) p. 264.

7. Allen E. Bergin, "Evaluation of Therapeutic Outcomes," *Handbook of Psychotherapy and Behavior Change*, ed. A. E. Bergin and S. L. Garfield (New York: John Wiley and Sons, 1971) pp. 217–270.

8. Arthur Janov, *Primal Scream* (New York: Dell Publishing Co., 1970) p. 21.

9. Marcel Proust, *Remembrance of Things Past, Swann's Way*, trans. C. K. Scott Moncrieff (New York: Random House, 1934).

Chapter 2. TM and the Mind

1. Harold H. Bloomfield *et al.*, *TM: Discovering Inner Energy and Overcoming Stress* (New York: Delacourt Press, 1975) pp. 13–23.

2. Eugene Aserinsky and Nathaniel Kleitman, "Regularly Occurring Periods of Eye Motility and Concomitant Phenomena during Sleep," *Science*, vol. 118, 1953, pp. 273–274.

Chapter 3. TM and Other Techniques Compared

1. Bernard C. Glueck and Charles F. Stroebel, "Biofeedback and Meditation in the Treatment of Psychiatric Illness," *Comprehensive Psychiatry*, vol. 16, no. 4. July/August, 1975, p. 314.

2. *Ibid.*, pp. 315–316.

3. *Ibid.*, p. 314.

4. Mark Brewer, "We're Gonna Tear You Down and Put You Back Together," *Psychology Today*, August, 1975.

Chapter 4. The Psychophysiology of Happiness

1. Charles M. Schulz, *The World According to Lucy*, Hallmark Cards, Inc.

2. Elmer E. Greene, Alice M. Greene, and Edward D. Walters, "Voluntary Control of Internal States: Psychological and Physiological," *Journal of Transpersonal Psychology*, vo. 2. no. 1., 1970. p. 3.

3. Maharishi Mahesh Yogi, *On the Bhagavad-Gita: A New Translation and Commentary, Chapters 1–6* (Baltimore: Penguin Books, Inc., 1969) p. 314.

4. W. Ross Adey and Thomas Tokizane, eds., *Structure and Function of the Limbic System, Progress in Brain Research*, vol. 27 (Amsterdam: Elsevier, 1967).

5. William Shakespeare, *King Lear*, act 2, scene 4, lines 108–109.

6. Ivor Mills, "Can the Human Brain Cope?," *The New Scientist*, October 16, 1975, p. 139.

7. Charles Dickens, *Oliver Twist*, Library of Classics (London: Collins Clear-Type Press, 1957) p. 277.

8. Robert L. Maulsby, "An Illustration of Emotionally Evoked Theta Rhythm in Infancy: Hedonic Synchrony," *Electroencephalography and Clinical Neurophysiology*, vol. 31, 1971. pp. 157-165.

9. Fritz Perls, *Gestalt Therapy Verbatim* (Lafayette, Calif.: Real People Press, 1969) pp. 30, 37.

10. Maharishi Mahesh Yogi, *On the Bhagavad-Gita*, p. 159.

11. Maharishi Mahesh Yogi, *The Science of Being*, p. 82.

12. Arthur J. Deikman, "Experimental Meditation," *Altered States of Consciousness*, ed. Charles Tart (New York: John Wiley & Sons, Inc., 1969) p. 217.

13. Henry A. Murray, "Vicissitudes of Creativity," *Creativity and Its Cultivation*, ed. H. A. Anderson (New York: Harper and Row, 1959) p. 107.

14. Walt Whitman, "Passage to India," *Leaves of Grass*.

15. Maharishi Mahesh Yogi, *Love and God* (Norway: SRM Publications, 1965) p. 21.

16. *Ibid.*

17. *Ibid.*

18. Maharishi Mahesh Yogi, *The Science of Being*, p. 251.

19. *Ibid.*

Chapter 5. How a Shrink Became a Stretch

1. Carl G. Jung, *Modern Man in Search of a Soul* (New York: Harcourt Brace, 1933).

2. Karen Horney, *Our Inner Conflicts* (New York: W. W. Norton Co., 1945.

3. Robert Assagioli, *Psychosynthesis* (New York: Hobbs, Corman, 1965).

4. Abraham H. Maslow, *Toward a Psychology of Being* (New York: Van Nostrand, 1968).

5. Andrew M. Greeley and William C. McCready, "Are We a Nation of Mystics?," *New York Times Magazine*, January 26, 1975.

6. Assagioloi, *Psychosynthesis*, p. 47.

7. Jung, *In Search of a Soul*, p. 55.

8. Albert Ellis, *Reason and Emotion in Psychotherapy* (New York: Lyle Stuart, 1962) p. 377.

9. Patricia Carrington and Harmon Ephron, "Clinical Use of Meditation," *Current Psychiatric Therapies*, vol 15, ed. J. Wasserman (New York: Grunne and Stratton, 1975) pp. 106-107.

10. Francis J. Braceland, "Psychiatry and the Science of Man," *Psychiatry and Mysticism*, ed. S. R. Dean (Chicago: Nelson-Hall, 1975) p. 22.

Chapter 6. Rx for Dis-ease and Dis-order

1. Arnold A. Lazarus, "Notes on Behavior Therapy: The Problem of Relapse and Some Tentative Solutions," *Psychotherapy: Theory, Research and Practice*, vol. 8 (Washington, D.C.: Division of Psychotherapy, American Psychological Association, 1971) pp. 192-194.

2. William Osler, *Lectures on Angina Pectoris and Allied States* (New York: D. Appleton & Co., 1897).

3. Donald Miskiman, "The Treatment of Insomnia with the TM Program," *Scientific Research on the Transcendental Meditation Program: Collected Papers*, vol. 1., ed. D. W. Orme-Johnson and J. T. Farrow (New York: MIU Press, 1976).

4. Maharishi Mahesh Yogi, *The Science of Being*, p. 322.

Chapter 7. TM and Therapy: Facts and Fantasies

1. Mills, "Human Brain," p. 140.

2. Alfred P. French, Albert C. Schmid, and Elizabeth Ingalls, "Transcendental Meditation, Altered Reality Testing and Behavior Change: A Case Report," *The Journal of Nervous and Mental Disease*, vol. 161, no. 1, July, 1975, pp. 54-58.

3. Bernard C. Glueck and Charles F. Stroebel, "Biofeedback and Meditation in the Treatment of Psychiatric Illness," *Comprehensive Psychiatry*, vol. 16, no. 4. July/August, 1975, p. 309.

4. Bernard C. Glueck and Charles F. Stroebel. "Biofeedback and Meditation in the Treatment of Psychiatric Illnesses," *Current Psychiatric Therapies*, vol. 15., ed. J. Wasserman (New York: Grunne and Stratton, 1975) p. 111.

5. *Ibid.*

Chapter 8. TM and the Life Cycle

1. Maharishi Mahesh Yogi, *The Science of Being*, p. 81.

2. Ray E. Helfer and C. Henry Kempe, eds., *The Battered Child* (Chicago: University of Chicago Press, 1974).

3. Plato, *The Collected Dialogues of Plato*, ed. E. Hamilton and H. Cairns, Bollingen Series LXXI (Princeton: Princeton University Press, 1961) p. 578.

4. Robert J. Steck and Barry A. Bass, "Personal Adjustment and Perceived Locus of Control Among Students Interested in Meditation," *Psychological Reports* 32, 1973, pp. 1010-1022.

Chapter 9. Dawn of the Age of Enlightenment

1. Maharishi Mahesh Yogi, *The Science of Being*, p. 81.

2. William James, *William James in Psychical Research*, ed. G. Murphy and R. V. Ballon (New York: Viking Press, 1963) pp. 275-276.

3. Albert Einstein, quoted in the *New York Times*, March 29, 1972.

4. Bertrand Russell, *Human Society in Ethics and Politics* (New York: Simon and Schuster, 1955) p. 225.

5. Maharishi Mahesh Yogi, *On the Bhagavad-Gita*, pp. 142-143.

6. Maharishi Mahesh Yogi, *The Science of Being*, p. 173.

7. *Ibid.*, p. 240.

8. Robert Keith Wallace, *Neurophysiology of Enlightenment*, (New York: MIU Press, 1974) pp. 3-6.

9. *Ibid.*

10. Maharishi Mahesh Yogi, *The Science of Being*, p. 190.

11. Maharishi Mahesh Yogi, *Alliance for Knowledge* (Seelisberg, Switzerland: MIU Press, 1973) p. 25.

12. Candace Borland and Garland Landrith, "Influence of the Transcendental Meditation Program on Crime Rate in Cities," *Scientific Research on the Transcendental Meditation Program: Collected Papers*, vol. 1., ed. D. W. Orme-Johnson and J. T. Farrow (New York: MIU Press, 1976).

13. Maharishi Mahesh Yogi, *The Science of Being*, p. 244.

14. Maharishi Mahesh Yogi, quoted in the *Neurophysiology of Enlightenment* (New York: MIU Press, 1974) p. 5.

15. Maharishi Mahesh Yogi, *The Science of Being*, pp. 245-246.

INDEX